To The Sch

Many thanks for facilitating my visit to TRU and providing exceptional hospitality.

Best wishes,

Alisha

Information and Communication Technologies for Sustainable Tourism

Sustainable development is a highly topical issue and is of critical importance to tourism as the environment is of utmost significance for the continued development and prosperity of the industry. There have been numerous texts written on sustainable tourism and the measures which can be used to mitigate and manage this, but none have acknowledged Information and Communication Technologies (ICT) as a mechanism of doing so, despite it being an emerging area of research. ICT in this context refers to innovative tools which form an integrated system of software and networked equipment that facilitates data processing, information sharing, communication and the ability to search and select from an existing range of products and services for an organisation's benefits. Despite the symbiotic relationship that exists between ICT and sustainable tourism, there has been little research into how the use of such technology can be used to make sustainable tourism development a more workable reality.

This opportune book is the first to provide a focus on the interrelationship of these two important topics, demonstrating their synergies and providing insight into a new and innovative approach to managing sustainable tourism development. It considers the use of technology to reduce the negative impacts of tourism from both the demand and supply perspectives. The book also provides a critical review of a range of cutting-edge technologies used by tourists and businesses to assess their usefulness in managing sustainable tourism development from the macro to the micro level. It further integrates examples and practical applications to show how ICT can be an invaluable mechanism in the management of sustainable tourism development.

This cutting-edge volume provides a wealth of information on an important yet neglected subject. The book will be invaluable reading for students, researchers, academics and members of the tourism industry looking for new and innovative ways of fostering a more sustainable tourism industry.

Alisha Ali is a Senior Lecturer in Hospitality Business Management at Sheffield Hallam University, UK.

Andrew J. Frew holds the Chair of IT and Tourism and is a Research Professor in the School of Arts, Social Sciences and Management at Queen Margaret University, UK.

Routledge Advances in Tourism

Edited by Stephen Page
School for Tourism, Bournemouth University

1. **The Sociology of Tourism**
   Theoretical and empirical investigations
   Edited by Yiorgos Apostolopoulos, Stella Leivadi and Andrew Yiannakis

2. **Creating Island Resorts**
   Brian King

3. **Destinations**
   Cultural landscapes of tourism
   Edited by Greg Ringer

4. **Mediterranean Tourism**
   Facets of socioeconomic development and cultural change
   Edited by Yiorgos Apostolopoulos, Lila Leontidou, Philippos Loukissas

5. **Outdoor Recreation Management**
   John Pigram and John Jenkins

6. **Tourism Development**
   Edited by Douglas G. Pearce and Richard W. Butler

7. **Tourism and Sustainable Community Development**
   Edited by Greg Richards and Derek Hall

8. **Tourism and Political Boundaries**
   Dallen J. Timothy

9. **Leisure and Tourism Landscapes**
   Social and cultural geographies
   Cara Aitchison, Nicola E. MacLeod and Stephen J. Shaw

10. **Tourism in the Age of Globalisation**
    Edited by Salah Wahab and Chris Cooper

11. **Tourism and Gastronomy**
    Edited by Anne-Mette Hjalager and Greg Richards

12. **New Perspectives in Caribbean Tourism**
    Edited by Marcella Daye, Donna Chambers and Sherma Roberts

13. **The Advanced Econometrics of Tourism Demand**
    Haiyan Song, Stephen F. Witt and Gang Li

14. **Tourism in China**
Destination, cultures and communities
Edited by Chris Ryan and Gu Huimin

15. **Sustainable Tourism Futures**
Perspectives on systems, restructuring and innovations
Edited by Stefan Gössling, C. Michael Hall and David B. Weaver

16. **Advances in Tourism Destination Marketing**
Managing networks
Edited by Metin Kozak, Juergen Gnoth and Luisa Andreu

17. **Drive Tourism**
Trends and emerging markets
Edited by Bruce Prideaux and Dean Carson

18. **Tourist Customer Service Satisfaction**
An encounter approach
Francis P. Noe, Muzzafer Uysal and Vincent P. Magnini

19. **Mining Heritage Tourism**
A global synthesis
Edited by Michael Conlin and Lee Jolliffe

20. **Tourist Experience**
Contemporary perspectives
Edited by Richard Sharpley and Phillip Stone

21. **Sustainable Tourism in Rural Europe**
Edited by Donald Macleod and Steven Gillespie

22. **The Critical Turn in Tourism Studies**
Creating an academy of hope
Edited by Nigel Morgan, Irena Atelkevic and Annette Pritchard

23. **Tourism Supply Chain Management**
Haiyan Song

24. **Tourism and Retail**
Edited by Charles McIntyre

25. **International Sports Events**
Impacts, experience and identities
Edited by Richard Shipway and Alan Fyall

26. **Cultural Moment in Tourism**
Edited by Laurajane Smith, Emma Waterton and Steve Watson

27. **Contemporary Tourist Experience**
Richard Sharpley and Philip Stone

28. **Future Tourism**
Political, social and economic challenges
James Leigh, Craig Webster for Stanislav Ivanov

29. **Information and Communication Technologies for Sustainable Tourism**
Alisha Ali and Andrew J. Frew

Forthcoming:

Responsible Tourist Behaviour
Clare Weeden

Human Rights and Global Events
Rebecca Finkel

Tourist Experience and Fulfilment
Insights from positive psychology
Sebastian Filep and Philip Pearce

Information and Communication Technologies for Sustainable Tourism

Alisha Ali and Andrew J. Frew

LONDON AND NEW YORK

First published 2013
by Routledge
2 Park Square, Milton Park, Abingdon, Oxon OX14 4RN

Simultaneously published in the USA and Canada
by Routledge
711 Third Avenue, New York, NY 10017

Routledge is an imprint of the Taylor & Francis Group, an informa business

British Library Cataloguing in Publication Data
A catalogue record for this book is available from the British Library

Library of Congress Cataloging in Publication Data
Ali, Alisha, 1970-Information and communication technologies for sustainable tourism/
Alisha Ali and Andrew J. Frew.
p. cm.
Includes bibliographical references and index.
1. Sustainable tourism. 2. Tourism–Computer network resources.
3. Tourism–Environmental aspects.
I. Frew, Andrew J. II. Title.
G156.5.S87A43 2012
910.285–dc23 2012027616

ISBN: 978-0-415-67317-4 (hbk)
ISBN: 978-0-203-07259-2 (ebk)

Typeset in Times New Roman
by Sunrise Setting Ltd

Printed and bound by CPI Group (UK) Ltd, Croydon, CR0 4YY

Contents

Figures

Tables

Preface

The impetus to produce this text stemmed from our observation that despite the considerable body of research in the tourism literature focusing on sustainable tourism development, very little offered pragmatic solutions to how sustainable tourism can indeed become a workable reality. We contemplated that this might be accomplished through the use of technology and, indeed, the doctoral research completed by Alisha Ali was founded on this premise.

The research established that there was little published work on the uses, applications, values and benefits of using technology for sustainable tourism development. Despite an acute understanding of the relationship between tourism and the environment and tourism and technology, there was limited consideration of how technology can be used to alleviate the challenges faced in sustainable tourism development. This led to our decision to write this volume, which offers a starting point in exploring this emerging topic not only for researchers and students, but also for industry practitioners and policy makers.

The core intention of this text is to provide a heightened understanding of how technology can be used for sustainable tourism development. Given the organic nature of the tourism industry, its numerous stakeholders and the rapid developments in technology, we have attempted to adopt a multi-disciplinary approach. We tried to paint a representative landscape of technology use in tourism by first developing an understanding of sustainable tourism, and then drilling down into the differing applications of technology. Research in this area thus far has been disparate, and we have drawn on this and other sources of literature to offer a cohesive picture of how we can implement such technology for sustainable development in the tourism industry. Alongside this backdrop, we have used illustrative examples and case studies where appropriate, provided a glossary for the technical terms and have raised questions related to each chapter to help the reader in his/her understanding.

Sustainability and technology are by no means new topics, but in a world where resources are finite and tourism faces new trials on a daily basis, a new ethos needs to be adopted for us to think about creative ways to propel the industry forward ahead of these challenges. The topic of technology use for sustainable tourism can undoubtedly be idealised; however, research and understanding is integral for its successful implementation. We hope this text has provided useful insights for those who would like to engage with this subject.

Acknowledgements

We are deeply indebted to many people who have helped us throughout the process of producing this text. Alisha would like to thank her family and friends for their unwavering support and encouragement, and her colleagues at Sheffield Hallam University. Andy would also like to thank his family for their patience and support; Nicole Chmura and Mareba Scott, PhD candidates, for their challenging and pertinent questions; and last but not least his co-author for her calm encouragement! Finally, both authors would like to express their deepest thanks to Carol Barber from Routledge for her unwavering support throughout the course of getting this manuscript to production.

Acronyms and abbreviations

1G	First-generation mobile phone network
2G	Second-generation mobile phone network
3G	Third-generation mobile phone network
4G	Fourth-generation mobile phone network
ADSL	Asymmetric digital subscriber link
API	Application programming interface
AR	Augmented reality
B2C	Business-to-consumer
BRIC	Brazil, Russia, India, China
C2C	Consumer-to-consumer
CC	Carbon calculator
CEA	Cumulative effects assessment
CI	Community informatics
CIS	Community-based information system
COC	Code of conduct
CS	Computer simulation
DMO	Destination management organisation
DMS	Destination management systems
DSS	Decision support system
EIAS	Economic impact analysis software
EIA	Environmental impact assessment
EMIS	Environment management information system
EMS	Environment management system
eWOM	Electronic word of mouth
G2C	Government-to-consumer
GDP	Gross domestic product
GIS	Geographical information systems
GPS	Global positioning systems
GSM	Global system for mobile communications
GSTC	Global Sustainable Tourism Council
GTBS	Green Travel Business Scheme
GUI	Graphical user interface

HCI	Human computer interface
IATA	International Air Transport Association
ICT	Information and communication technology
IoT	Internet of Things
IP	Internet protocol
IPCC	International Panel on Climate Change
ISO	International Standards Organisation
ITS	Intelligent transport systems
LAC	Limits of acceptable change
LBS	Location-based services
LTE	Long-term evolution
M2M	Machine-to-machine
MMORPG	Massive multiplayer online role-playing games
MUD	Multi-user dungeons/dimensions
NFC	Near field communication
NUI	Natural user interface
OECD	Organisation for Economic Co-operation and Development
OFCOM	The Office of Communications
PAGIS	Participatory approaches and geographical information systems
PDA	Personal digital assistant
RDF	Resource description framework
RFID	Radio frequency identification
RSS	Really simple syndication
SMS	Short message service
TAM	Technology acceptance model
TIS	Tourism information system
UGC	User-generated content
UMTS	Universal mobile telecommunication system
UNCTAD	United Nations Conference on Trade and Development
UNWTO	United Nations World Tourism Organisation
VERP	Visitor experience and resource protection
VIM	Visitor impact management
VoIP	Voice over internet protocol
WCOCFS	Weather, climate and ocean change forecasting software
Wi-Fi	The Wi-Fi Alliance label for a WLAN
WiMax	Worldwide Interoperability for Microwave Access
W3C	World Wide Web Consortium
WLAN	Wireless local area network
WMAN	Wireless metropolitan area networks
WPAN	Wireless personal area network
WTTC	World Travel and Tourism Council
WWAN	Wireless wide area networks

1 Introduction to technology and sustainable tourism

Learning outcomes

This chapter provides an overview of the relationship between technology and sustainable tourism. After reading this chapter you should be able to understand:

- the importance of technology for sustainable tourism;
- why there has been little uptake of technology for sustainable tourism; and
- who would benefit from using technology for sustainable tourism.

Background

Tourism continues to develop as a major economic activity. Forecasts currently predict that international arrivals should reach one billion in 2012, representing a contribution of 5 per cent to world GDP and 6 per cent of total exports, and employing one in twelve people (United Nations World Tourism Organisation (UNWTO) 2012). These economic gains related to tourism development have led to debate on its development as an industry (McCool and Lime 2001; Holloway 2002; Croes 2006; Page and Connell 2006) – tourism has been and continues to be regarded as a cure for the fiscal challenges of many countries (Saveriades 2000; Pforr 2001; Andereck *et al.* 2005). Today it is still promoted by numerous developing and developed countries as a lucrative means of diversifying their economies, especially in these times of recession. This dominant focus on the economic aspects of tourism, however, has prevented the subject from being developed with the environmental concerns which should be considered from the outset (Barrow 2006).

Like any economic activity, tourism has produced detrimental environmental and socio-economic effects (Becken and Patterson 2006) which are destroying tourism's chief product: the environment (Poon 1993; Murphy 1985). Furthermore, irresponsible tourism management has led to degradation of environments, with many destinations having experienced damage as a result of *ad hoc* and unplanned tourism development (Choi and Sirakaya 2006; Ruhanen 2008). Often these effects are irreversible and this may leave many destinations with a legacy of economic, environmental and social problems, which harm both the local community and the tourists (Hall and Lew 1998). In the literature there is no shortage of examples of the negative impacts of tourism – they have been well documented (see for example Inskeep 1991; Coccossis 1996; Swarbrooke 1999; Mason 2003; Andereck *et al.* 2005; Archer *et al.* 2005; Cooper *et al.* 2005; Wall and Mathieson 2006). The tourism industry is therefore increasingly confronted with the problem of finding the right balance between the level of economic growth and maintenance of the environment (Edgell 2006).

Tourism's continued success depends on all environments being maintained, protected and preserved for the future. The continued growth of the economies of Brazil, Russia, India and China (BRIC) will contribute to the environmental problems that the industry already faces, with more people now travelling from these countries, as will the new growth markets, such as Nigeria, Vietnam, Turkey and Mexico.

Another burgeoning concern for the industry is climate change (Gössling 2009). On 20 March 2009, Prince Charles of the UK warned there could be as little as 100 months left to save the world from the irreversible damage of climate change. The clock is ticking. Tourism's contribution to climate change is attributed mainly to greenhouse gas emissions from the aviation industry (Gössling and Hall 2006) and this will no doubt intensify with the growth of the emerging markets, low-cost airlines and cheap holidays. The main concerns for tourism in relation to climate are the threat to low-lying coastal destinations caused by rising sea levels and increasing desertification and damage to sports and sightseeing activities in polar and mountainous areas as snow and ice-covered areas ebb. Destinations' levels of preparedness for these environmental threats will be a critical factor for the continued prosperity of the industry. Tourists are also continuously changing their tastes and values and are now insisting on a higher quality environment, more exotic forms of activities and better value for money. This places greater demands on resources, leading to worsening impacts on the environment.

Taken collectively, the tourism industry has responded to these challenges by applying the concept of sustainable development to tourism policy and planning – i.e. sustainable tourism (Butler 1991; Hardy and Beeton 2001; Choi and Sirakaya 2006). This is reflected in the growth of sustainable tourism policy statements, guidelines, strategies and initiatives being developed by local communities and at all levels of institutions at the destination (Hardy and Beeton 2001). Sustainable tourism has been regarded as a mechanism for achieving economic development whilst protecting, preserving and enhancing the environment (Swarbrooke 1999; UNWTO 2004a).

Enormous efforts have been made since the Earth Summit in 1992 (United Nations Conference on Environment and Development 1992) to apply the principles of sustainable development to tourism, with the hope of ensuring the industry's continued viability and its contribution to sustainable development (de Sausmarez 2007). A plethora of ideas, techniques and philosophies have been developed due to growing concern about how destinations can develop in a sustainable manner (Swarbrooke 1999; Hasse 2003). However, most of the work on sustainable tourism has focused on theorising and policy formulation. Theorising is a useful method of putting issues into context, but there needs to be some way to implement the theory of sustainable tourism (Bramwell and Lane 1993; Liu 2003; Ruhanen 2008). The challenge lies in finding practical tools for tourism professionals to transform theory into action (Coccossis 1996; Wright 1998). An article by Pigram (1990: 8) stated that sustainable tourism 'runs the risk of remaining irrelevant and inert as a feasible policy option for the real world of tourism development without the development of effective means of translating the ideal into action'. This statement still applies to the industry today. Ruhanen (2008) undertook a study which examined the transfer of academic knowledge in sustainable tourism to the public sector in Queensland, Australia. This research found that despite the vast body of knowledge on sustainable tourism, there has been little diffusion of this knowledge to the people who need to use it to plan and manage tourism at the destination level.

The research work on sustainable tourism development has not progressed beyond formulation and discussion of the principles and assumptions of sustainable tourism, and the alternative forms of tourism provide no more than a minimal solution to a larger issue (Liu 2003). Attempts have been made to apply the concept of sustainable tourism by developing indicators, monitoring, eco-labelling, codes of conduct, educating the tourist and other best practices. Most of these attempts, however, have been identified with 'lack of quality, technical content, reliability, maturity, equity and effectiveness' (van der Duim and van Marwijk 2006: 449). Buckley (2012) observed that measures such as self-regulation and eco-certification have been fruitless. Moreover, many stakeholders have tended to adopt a narrow view of sustainability by only considering the environmental sphere, and this has led to the development of models which lack practicality in destination management (Ko 2005; Choi and Sirakaya 2006). In reality there appears to be a widening gap between the principles of sustainable tourism and what is actually being achieved (Trousdale 1999), and no real progress is seeming to be made towards solving the problems of tourism development (Hall 2000).

Future trends therefore indicate that stakeholders need to find a solution to ensure that tourism is developed along the principles of sustainable tourism development and that theorising and policy making are translated into practical applications. In view of the above, this book develops the proposition that sustainable tourism can become an effective concept in tourism planning and development through the use and application of technology. In this text, when we refer to technology, we are specifically making reference to Information and Communication Technology (ICT). ICT is the technology required for information processing and flow: innovative tools that form an integrated system of software and networked equipment that facilitates data processing, information sharing, communication and the ability to search and select from an existing range of products and services for an organisation's benefits. It is an umbrella term that refers to any product that stores, retrieves, manipulates, transmits and receives digital data, and to how these differing applications work with each other (Buhalis 2003).

Many developmental problems can be alleviated through the use of ICT (United Nations Conference on Trade and Development 2004). The use of ICT in tourism is not a new idea; rather, the tourism industry has been influenced by ICT for the past thirty years (European Commission 2006), and it continues to be one of its greatest influences, fuelling dramatic changes within the industry (Werthner and Klein 1999; Frew 2000). The strength of ICT for sustainable tourism will revolve around the way in which it is used by tourism stakeholders rather than in technical functions. Tourism impacts can be 'managed, mitigated and controlled', but this depends on the effort that participants in the tourism process are willing to expend (McCool and Lime 2001: 381).

ICT and sustainable tourism – a symbiotic relationship

It is agreed that sustainable tourism is a valuable concept, but its implementation has resulted in difficulties (Ahn *et al.* 2002; Wall and Mathieson 2006). There has been a lack of common sense, with over-emphasis on strategy formulation and limited emphasis on strategy implementation (Swarbrooke 1999; Page 2005). The most radical solution that can be proposed is to reduce the future growth of tourism by decreasing the amount of travel (air, rail, bus, coach) that occurs. This solution, however, is neither feasible nor beneficial to anyone. Tourism is a fact of life and the associated problems need to be corrected as soon as possible (Theobald 2005). The difficulties associated with sustainable tourism should not lead us to be critical and complacent; rather, we should develop realistic, and practical solutions to progress (Bramwell and Lane 1993).

For tourism to be sustainable in the long run, significant changes are required (Gössling 2000). Management action is needed before destinations deteriorate beyond repair (Wall and Mathieson 2006). It is time for new and innovative methods for tackling the problems of sustainable tourism development to be introduced. Re-evaluation of tourism and current sustainable tourism practices is necessary and new approaches and management techniques are required (Gezici 2005; Saarinen 2006).

Moreover, tourism managers are faced, on a daily basis, with numerous challenges and decisions with respect to the proper planning and developing of their destinations. Many of these decisions and challenges are related to sustainability concerns. Managers need to be equipped with practical tools and mechanisms to ensure they make the most accurate and reliable decisions with respect to the sustainable tourism development of their destinations and businesses. The application of ICT to sustainable tourism development can be the kind of useful mechanism that tourism professionals require. Evidence exists which demonstrates that ICT can play an invaluable role in an organisation's efficiency and productivity (Buhalis 1998) and in dealing with environmental sustainability (Erdmann and Goodman 2004). ICT has also been deemed as essential to the success or failure of the impacts of tourism at a destination (Buhalis and Spada 2000).

The intention of this book is to demonstrate that technology can be used for sustainable tourism, the ways in which this can be done, and who can use such technology. New technologies offer considerable promise for dealing with environmental degradation whilst simultaneously promoting economic growth (Organisation for Economic Co-operation and Development [OECD]

2002). There is no doubt of the value of ICT for tourism. Numerous noteworthy publications have been written on this (see for example Poon 1993; Sheldon 1997; Buhalis 2003). This publication does not seek to repeat what has been written in these previous texts, but rather to expand knowledge on an area of the ICT-sustainable tourism research domain which has been relatively under-researched.

There is indeed an interaction between technology and sustainable tourism development. In the academic and professional tourism community there has been much discussion of the challenges and benefits of using ICT for sustainable tourism, but there has been limited concrete work done in this avenue. Mention must, however, be made of the United Nations Conference on Trade and Development's (UNCTAD) efforts to promote the use of ICT in sustainable tourism development as part of their eTourism initiative. The work of the ENTER conference must also be credited, as in recent years they have devoted a research stream and workshops to understanding this topic. This conference is held yearly by the International Federation for Information Technologies in Travel and Tourism (IFITT) and it focuses on state-of-the-art and topical issues in eTourism.

As it is a heavily discussed topic, one may wonder why there has been little application or practical use. A variety of reasons can be offered for this. Despite the immense growth in tourism research, there has been poor dissemination and usage of this research by tourism businesses (Cooper *et al.* 2004). This may be attributed to inadequate linkages between industry and academia (Stamboulis and Skayannis 2003), with tourism businesses viewing this research as difficult to access and irrelevant to their needs (Ruhanen 2008). Tourism stakeholders such as destination management organisations (DMOs) view such research as quite complex and highly advanced, when they are instead searching for uncomplicated techniques and easily applied solutions (Ritchie and Ritchie 2002; Xiao 2006).

There is also an apparently prevalent inherent fear of the use of technology, and tourism professionals are often unaware of how technology can assist them in different aspects of their business operations. Many destinations and tourism businesses are still grappling with setting up a good web presence and Internet marketing effort and have not even begun to seriously consider more sophisticated uses of technology. Moreover, they are also struggling with the age-old debates regarding sustainable tourism – what it means, who is responsible for managing it and how to go about making it an effective, implementable concept. If the fundamental premise of sustainable tourism is not clearly understood then engaging with technology solutions will not be feasible. All of these factors have resulted in the low implementation of technology for sustainable tourism.

The main purpose of this text is to demonstrate how technology, particularly ICT, can lead the tourism industry to become more sustainable. A synergistic relationship exists between ICT and the core components of sustainable tourism, which are the economic, environmental and socio-cultural environments. Economic sustainability can be achieved by using ICT for the better management and provision of information and this technology can be used to map and monitor economic impacts. ICT can be a force for environmental sustainability through its use in managing and controlling development, identifying sensitive areas, spreading the distribution of tourism and providing fast, accurate and up-to-date information for decision-making. The socio-cultural environment can be protected and enhanced by using ICT to allow the local community to have a voice in the tourism development process; it also provides them with a means of protecting and preserving their culture and heritage for future generations.

The beneficiaries

This volume is designed to benefit any tourism stakeholder who has an interest in seeing the industry developed in a sustainable fashion. The research presented here recognises the immense potential of the use of technology as a new and innovative approach to lessening some of tourism's negative impacts. It presents a wide-ranging collection of technology-based tools that can be used to manage different aspects of sustainable tourism. Decision makers – who may be destination managers, tourism business owners or tourists – can add technology to the list of options available to them in selecting the best management approach as they attempt to alleviate tourism's negative impacts. The use of technology facilitates better decision-making in dealing with various aspects of sustainable tourism development, and also enhances communication between the different tourism stakeholders by bringing together different views and perspectives, all with the aim of making tourism more sustainable.

The approach of this book

This volume approaches technology for sustainable tourism from a wide-ranging perspective. Technology and sustainable development, the root concepts of sustainable tourism, are indeed well recognised research disciplines, and our approach not only draws on the tourism literature but also explores a wider array of publications in these fields.

In Chapter 1, we begin by cogitating on the relationship between technology and sustainable tourism and demonstrating that this technology can indeed be useful in helping the tourism industry mitigate and manage negative impacts. As the tourism industry continues to grow, so do its impacts on the environment. With the current approaches to managing sustainable tourism not as successful as expected, this chapter develops the proposition that technology can be a mechanism used to mediate the relationship with sustainable tourism. The reasons why this has been a heavily debated topic, but with little application and practical use, are discussed. The chapter also examines the linkages between technology and its application to sustainable tourism by demonstrating the synergistic relationship that exists and how technology contributes to the three main areas of sustainability: economic, environmental and socio-cultural.

This leads us into Chapter 2, where we provide a short yet concise analysis of the relationship between technology and tourism. Technology is heavily embedded in many aspects of tourism and has transformed the ways in which the industry processes information and distributes its products, as well as fundamentally changing consumer behaviour. Despite the exploitation of technology in these areas and the advancing literature stream, there is still limited insight into how technology can support sustainable tourism development. This chapter provides the reader with more in-depth knowledge of the relationship between technology and tourism and investigates some of the indicative technologies that can be used for sustainable tourism development. This list is by no means exhaustive, but serves as a pivotal introduction in identifying how technology can indeed be used for sustainable tourism development.

We then begin to drill down into the main components of tourism. First, we look at tourism destinations in Chapter 3. It is the destination that attracts the tourist; this is also the place where the impacts of tourism are most heavily felt. Operating a sustainable destination is a weighty task, as managers are continuously being challenged to make the most optimal resource allocation. We look at the relationship between sustainable development and sustainable tourism and the current approaches being used by destinations in managing tourism's negative impacts. This is highly important in setting the stage for how technology can be used to support destination development. We then focus on the areas in destination management where such technologies can be used, after which we provide a list of indicative technologies and identify how they can support sustainable tourism development, linking this back to the economic, environmental and socio-cultural perspectives.

Chapter 4 allows us to switch our perspective to a different entity, the tourism business. These businesses take various forms and provide different services. Tourism businesses continuously face increasing pressure to be innovative and to reinvent how they conduct their trade in order to satisfy customer demands, whilst also keeping abreast of changes to the operating environment, such as economic, social, demographic and technological changes, which threaten their competitiveness and survival. It is therefore imperative that such businesses (namely visitor attractions, transport, accommodation and food and beverage businesses) understand how technology can be of value to help them become more sustainable. We discuss the motivations for these businesses to adopt and use technologies for sustainable tourism and focus specifically on visitor attractions, transport, accommodation and food and beverages.

Building on the business perspective, in Chapter 5 we move to supply chains, which are an integral component of any tourist business and the destination as a whole. Tourism supply chains are under increasing pressure from both government and tourists to become more sustainable. Businesses are also increasingly aware of the necessity of engaging in a sustainable supply chain, as this can improve their strategic performance and long-term competitive advantage. Technology can indeed be a critical component in this process, and this chapter investigates the relationship between technology and sustainable supply chain management. We define sustainable tourism supply chain management, address what is required for it to be achieved and demonstrate how technology can support this by allowing firms to network, co-ordinate and communicate.

Having considered destinations, tourism businesses and supply chains, in Chapter 6 we focus on an integral player in the tourism industry: the tourist. The relationship between technology, sustainability and tourism is a constant and complex interplay of drivers influencing the paths tourists ultimately take. It is important to conceptualise the perceived place of sustainability in the mind of the tourist. This chapter provides an overview of the motivations for and barriers to technology's adoption and use by the tourist. It emphasises the importance of awareness, education and motivation in broad sustainability issues. We examine how and why tourists would be inspired to engage in sustainable tourism and consequently take up the use of technology in doing so. A typical tourist journey is depicted, demonstrating how technology can be engaged with for sustainable tourism development at each stage of their journey: namely pre-trip, transit, in-trip and post-trip.

No discussion of technology can be complete without considering the power and value of social media. This takes us to Chapter 7, where we develop our understanding of how social networks can enhance sustainability at both a macro and micro level in tourism, and how destinations, businesses and the tourist can become engaged. Social media is a powerful agent of change for sustainable tourism and we stand at an interesting and important crossroads, where criticality is possible. Here we explore the possibilities of this latent potential fusing and argue that sustainability could be progressed through the use of Web 2.0 tools such as wikis, blogs and podcasts. An appreciation of Web 2.0 and its applications and examples will be gained, along with an understanding of social media and networks, their uses and how they can support sustainable tourism development.

As we have established a knowledge base on how technology can be used for sustainable tourism, our voyage now takes us to Chapter 8, where we address the critical issues which will influence the uptake of technology for sustainable tourism development. For technology use to become an effective concept, stakeholders must have knowledge and understanding of the factors that can have a bearing on the successful implementation of these technologies. Awareness of these factors is vital to ensuring that these limitations form part of tourism stakeholders' strategic planning.

We conclude in Chapter 9 by deliberating on the immediate, mid-term and long-term steps the industry should take in applying technology for sustainable tourism. We consider some potential futures through taking three main perspectives: the technological environment in which future tourism may take place, the way in which this environment is accessed and examples of activities in which tourists might engage. Here we consider the prospective shape and capability of future networks, study an environment replete with cyber objects and gain insight into how a future web comprising content accessible by humans and machines may significantly change business and tourist behaviours. We hope to stimulate the reader to consider, in the light of the aforementioned chapters, how the anticipated step-change in these future technologies may offer very different possibilities for sustainable tourism development.

Chapter 1 questions

1 Give some examples of developmental problems which may arise in tourism and which might be positively addressed through the use of ICT.
2 What are the arguments for and against reducing the variety and volume of traffic as a solution to the growth problems facing tourism?
3 Demonstrate ways in which you think it may be possible for ICT to facilitate better decision-making in relation to sustainable tourism development.

2 Sustainable technologies

Learning outcomes

This chapter focuses on the technologies that can be used for sustainable tourism development. After reading this chapter you should be able to:

- understand the relationship between tourism and technology; and
- discuss some of the technologies which can be used for sustainable tourism development.

Introduction

Tourism as a technology-based industry has now a well-established body of literature, as there is no doubt that this technology has brought about a metamorphosis of tourism. Technology is not only a critical factor for destination competitiveness (Poon 1993; Sheldon 1997; Buhalis 2003) but is also transforming the tourism system worldwide with regard to structure and operations (Buhalis and O'Connor 2006). This chapter begins by discussing the technology–tourism relationship, then focuses on some indicative technologies that can be used in the management of sustainable tourism development.

Technology and tourism

Technology use in tourism has not only defined methods of making existing processes more efficient but has also provided new ways of performing these existing functions (Cronin 1996). In tourism, this technology has unlimited uses, such as marketing, managing customer relationships, managing daily operations and site selection, site development and monitoring site usage.

ICT, in essence, is the technology required for information processing. ICT-based tools/applications can be grouped into three sectors: ICT equipment, software products and ICT services and carriers. These can be further sub-divided into microelectronics, new functions, networks, ICT devices and interfaces, software, knowledge management services and applications (Erdmann and Behrendt 2003). Today, ICT applications include mobile phone applications, Internet, wireless voice over information processing, geographical information systems, global positioning systems, location-based services, convergence (data, voice, media), digital radio and applications on demand. These ICT applications depend on a variety of products such as personal computers, Internet servers, mobile phones, cables, satellites and peripheral devices (screens, printers, scanners). These technologies are used by consumers, businesses, tourism marketing organisations, regulatory agencies, natural resource managers, local government transport system managers, students and researchers, rendering their influence pervasive throughout the tourism system.

The growing significance of ICT in tourism has led to the coining of the phrase eTourism with regard to its use and applications. eTourism is defined as 'reflecting the digitalisation of all processes and value chains in the tourism, travel, hospitality and catering industries' (Buhalis 2003: 76). It involves all the ICT-based tools/applications that can be used by the tourism industry for business management, planning, development, marketing and distribution (Werthner and Klein 1999; Buhalis 2003). The literature in the eTourism domain has focused on how ICT has impacted and transformed tourism structure and performance. Milne and Ateljevic (2001) identified six areas as the main focuses of eTourism research – knowledge management, changing consumer tastes, new product development, empowering small businesses, labour market impacts and disintermediation – whilst Buhalis and Law (2008) identified three: consumer and demand dimensions, technological innovations and industry functions. This demonstrates that eTourism research has continued to focus on the same areas over the years. 'Consumer and demand dimensions' encompass research in changing consumer tastes and knowledge management; 'technological innovation' includes new product development; and 'industry functions' refers to empowering small businesses, labour market impacts and disintermediation. Despite the main research areas remaining the same, the focus in these areas has shifted over the years. Discussions no longer revolve around tourism organisations investing in technology. It is an accepted fact that once you are in the marketplace the use of technology is a given; it is no longer considered to be a new strategic weapon for organisations. Rather, the research in these areas now evolves around how organisations engage with and use this technology to interact with consumers, businesses and stakeholders to increase their business performance, efficiency and effectiveness. Some of the main areas relating to this are discussed below: namely, information processing, changing consumer requirements, suppliers and virtual communities.

Information processing

Tourism has been very well documented as an information-intensive area of business (Poon 1993; Sheldon 1997; Werthner and Klein 1999; Buhalis 2003). Baggio (2006) rightly commented that any ICT which can be used to manage the information needs of the tourism industry will undoubtedly be useful. Tourism is a confidence good and therefore the choice of destination depends on the information available, not the actual destination itself (Staab *et al.* 2002). The characteristics of the tourism product make it high-risk, requiring timely and accurate information relevant to customers' needs (Zehrer and Hobbhahn 2007). Effective information utilisation is therefore central to business success, since information has now become as valuable as capital and labour (Werthner and Klein 1999).

The use of ICT – and, especially, the Internet – has changed the way in which information is collected, stored, distributed, processed and managed in tourism. It acts as a mechanism for reducing the information gap (Zehrer and Hobbhahn 2007). Tourists are also demanding better, quicker and more reliable information (Gratzer *et al.* 2002), and using ICT fulfils this through the provision of timely, appropriate and accurate information. The tourism industry has benefited tremendously from ICT by using it to communicate, market and promote to potential tourists. It also serves as a mechanism for new distribution channels (Wöber 2003; Flouri and Buhalis 2004) and increases communication and interaction with and between stakeholders (Buhalis and O'Connor 2006). Table 2.1 displays the some of the technological tools which can be used to manage the information requirements of the tourism industry.

Changing consumer requirements

The use of technology in tourism has definitely led to a paradigm shift, since it has empowered the consumer and now assists in shaping how they make their decisions. InternetWorldStats.com (2011) estimated that in December 2011 there were over 2.2 billion Internet users. Customers are now in a better position to compare prices and product offerings and expect destinations, and tourism businesses at the destinations, to have an online presence and the technology they require when they are there. These savvy Internet customers want packages which are flexible to their requirements. They want more personalised products and services, and they want these to be available online. Travellers now have access to a vast amount of

Table 2.1 Information sources and tools within phases

Phase	*Task*	*Tools*
Information gathering and modelling	Information gathering	Electronic search tools i.e. scanning, browsing, retrieving
	Performance monitoring	Statistical tools
Analysis and forecasting	Market analysis and segmentation	Market portfolio, data mining
	Forecasting and extrapolation	Econometrical models, simulation
Planning and decision	Product planning and creation	Optimisation models, simulation
	Distribution channel selection	Optimisation models, simulation
Implementation and operation	Information distribution	Statistical tools
	Negotiation and sales	Decision models, game theory

Adapted from Werthner and Klein 1999.

information provided not only by suppliers but also by tourist organisations, businesses and the travellers themselves. Information search is an important part of the purchase decision-making process; through the use of ICT, uncertainty and risks can be reduced and the quality of the experience enhanced. According to Buhalis and Law (2008), more research leads to more information; a more informed customer can identify the products and services that best cater to their needs and better interpret and interact with the local culture and resources.

The Internet has not only allowed organisations to engage more with the customer, but has also decreased the time between communications, leading to faster response rates. With the advanced development of the Internet and Web 2.0, customers are now able to network with each other and interact with businesses and local people at the destination. O'Reilly (2006) defined Web 2.0 as 'the business revolution in the computer industry caused by the move to the Internet as platform and an attempt to understand the rules for success on that new platform'. In recent years Web 2.0 applications have taken on a life of their own, causing fundamental changes in how travellers use the Internet and their online experiences and expectations. Prior to Web 2.0 consumers were only able to engage in information search and possibly make purchases. Now customers are able to identify, customise, comment on and purchase tailor-made products. Web 2.0 has placed the tourist at the centre of functionality and product delivery (Buhalis and Law 2008). The Web today is characterised by information pull rather than push, with a second generation of web-based services such as wikis, folksonomies, social networks, user-generated content, openness, sharing and collaboration (Tapscott and Williams 2006). The content generated on these sites is shaping tourists' tastes and choices of destination products and services. Organisations should use the power of these new technologies to quickly identify the needs of these tourists and provide them with comprehensive, personalised and updated products and services. They should have dedicated staff to scan through blogs and online communities to view what tourists are posting about their experiences, and should use this information to better cater to their needs.

However the Internet is still changing, with the third round of evolution being referred to as Web 3.0 or the Semantic Web. The creator of the World Wide Web, Tim Berners-Lee, proposed this idea, which he views as 'a web of data that can be processed directly and indirectly by machines'. Computers currently present data on the Internet without interpretation, as they are unable to understand this data in order to present the user with meaningful information based on a query. In the case of the Semantic Web, meaning is added to data as computers can identify, analyse and process content on the Internet for easier transactions, filtering of information and production of more appropriate data, with the end result of greater user satisfaction. Mistilis and Buhalis (2012) observed that tourists are now engaged in more complex relationships on the Internet, through the assembling of travel itineraries, online search and engagement with social media; this has led to a growth in online tourist traffic, personalised and detailed tourist schedules and an increasing demand for online suppliers. The Semantic Web will be invaluable for tourism businesses' development and delivery of their products to tourists as their engagement over the Internet increases, changing the way they behave.

Suppliers

The areas in tourism perhaps most affected by the use of ICT have been distribution and marketing (O'Connor 2000; O'Connor and Frew 2002). The Internet's revolutionising of tourism with regards to distribution channels and booking systems has been well documented (Sheldon 1997; Werthner and Klein 1999). Disintermediation refers to how the role and functions of intermediaries are being reduced, or in some cases disappearing, in the tourism value chain through the use of ICT (Werthner and Klein 1999). The Internet has re-engineered the production and delivery of tourism products (Belbaly *et al.* 2004; Gratzer *et al.* 2004; Buhalis and O'Connor 2006; Ndou and Petti 2007) and has dramatically altered both operational and strategic practices (Buhalis and Zoge 2007), since it has allowed tourism suppliers to be flexible and creative in their strategies by providing them with enhanced features to attract and sell to the consumer.

Before the Internet, tourism suppliers had no alternative but to use intermediaries for product distribution (Buhalis and Law 2008). The widespread use and adoption of the Internet presented suppliers with the opportunity to distribute their product directly to end-consumers without the involvement of a third party. The Internet has therefore added an element of transparency in the marketplace (Buhalis and Law 2008). This significantly altered the role of tour operators and travel agents, since online bookings changed their sales channels (Werthner and Klein 1999; Buhalis 2003; Werthner and Ricci 2003). ICT has also empowered small and medium-sized enterprises by facilitating competition with larger organisations through using the Internet strategically. They can distribute, market and promote their products online just as large enterprises do, hence allowing them to be more competitive; this results in cost savings for the businesses.

Moreover, web marketing is now considered the norm in tourism, as the Internet is now seen as a multi-promotion tool and distribution channel for the industry (Gretzel *et al.* 2000; O'Connor and Frew 2004). Suppliers can now have one-to-one conversations with consumers dispersed over a wide geographical sphere in a cost-efficient manner, using a variety of online promotional activities. ICT has provided an avenue for new product development in tourism. It offers great possibilities for price differentiation and greater networking for dispersed elements, and fosters a wider array of product choices (Milne and Ateljevic 2001). Buhalis and Law (2008) describe this as 'fitness to purpose', in which ICT is used to package the tourism product to cater to the individual needs of the traveller and thereby offers huge opportunities for both the consumer and the supplier, resulting in an enhanced final product. The Internet has also enabled the profiling of consumers, which allows organisations to become more customer-centric. Tourist portals collect and organise information which can then be used to match a product to tourists' requirements (La Micela *et al.* 2002). Recommender systems have also been developed. These are applications which can provide suggestions to customers based on their needs and constraints regarding products and services and influence the decision-making process (Ricci 2002).

The adoption of ICT by organisations is also having important consequences in relation to the demand for and use of labour (Milne *et al.* 2005). This has resulted in increasing demand for high-quality IT staff, new skills and managerial requirements, as well as organisations needing to train their staff in use of the technology (Koutsoutos and Westerholt 2005). According to Milne and Ateljevic (2001), researchers have started to focus on the consequences of an eBusiness strategy on the use of labour training and delivering quality service.

ICT usage is critical to tourism suppliers since it allows them to develop, manage and distribute their offerings worldwide (Buhalis 1998). To remain competitive in the future, tour operators and travel agencies need to re-examine their product offerings and incorporate ICT into their business practices. They now have to focus on consulting and offering more complex and diversified products (Werthner and Ricci 2003).

Virtual communities

Virtual communities are becoming a powerful force in the tourism world, since they serve as a forum for customer-to-customer or customer-to-local resident communication rather than a form of marketing. Rheingold (1993: 58) defined a virtual community as ‘a group of people who may or may not meet one another face-to-face and who exchange words and ideas through the mediation of computer bulletin boards and networks’. Virtual communities are now commonplace, with the development of sites such as Facebook, Twitter, Foursquare and Pinterest, and these groups are growing daily. The communities are used for information sharing amongst members with a common interest (Chalkti and Sigala 2008) and allow them to post and share comments, opinions and personal experiences with others (Xaing and Gretzel 2009). The attraction of using these communities is that they provide seemingly unbiased comments/opinions/reviews from people who have experienced what one is about to experience and offer key insights, tips and tricks which one could not have received before. This process is influenced by trust amongst the community members (Usoro *et al.* 2007).

Virtual communities also build relationships amongst people and provide an easy source of information. According to Wang *et al.* (2002), online holidaymakers are keen to meet with other travellers who share their attitudes, interests and ways of life. The sharing of knowledge, advice and experiences in these online communities is replacing old customs of hoarding and accumulation. Given the many questions about the quality and credibility of information on the Internet, virtual communities offer a sense of security, since consumers seek the opinions of others who have shared or are about to engage in similar experiences in order to manage perceived risks. Organisations need to pay attention to these rapidly growing virtual communities in order to better understand consumers’ behaviour and motivations. This will allow organisations to better position their products, offer tailor-made services, deal with customer complaints and determine what customers like and dislike. Brand awareness and brand association can also be strengthened through the assistance of virtual travel communities (Buhalis and Law 2008).

Technology is becoming more advanced and complex, but it is also getting cheaper and more user-friendly, thereby allowing wider access to more users. ICT convergence is eliminating the boundaries between equipment and software (Werthner and Klein 1999) and this is facilitating a holistic integrated and networked system of hardware and software for more effective data processing and communication (Buhalis and Law 2008). The future ICT–tourism relationship will be one focused on user involvement and interactivity, using these new ICT-based tools/applications to communicate, interact and fulfil customers' needs.

Despite the exploitation of the areas described above, there are still other areas in tourism where ICT can be better used, with sustainable tourism development being one such avenue. The application of ICT to sustainable tourism will not only expand the eTourism research domain beyond web-based marketing and distribution (Frew 2000), but will also stimulate innovation in the tourism industry. The next section reviews a number of technologies that can be used for sustainable tourism. This list is by no means exhaustive, but it is hoped that it serves as a comprehensive guide to understanding how technology can begin to assist in sustainable tourism development. As we continue through the chapters we will encounter other technologies which can assist in managing sustainable tourism development; the list presented here is just a starting point.

Overview of the technologies for sustainable tourism

In this section we provide an overview of some of the particular technologies which can be used for managing sustainable tourism. One such important technology is the Internet, which has brought about unprecedented transformations in computing and the way we communicate. Leiner *et al.* (2009: 22) define the Internet as 'a world-wide broadcasting capability, a mechanism for information dissemination, and a medium for collaboration and interaction between individuals and their computers without regard for geographic location'. The Internet has infiltrated the tourism industry, causing dramatic changes in business operations, marketing and communication. Whilst it is critical to the tourism industry, however, it cannot be classified as a technology, since it is the overarching *platform* on which these technologies for sustainable tourism are based – providing the necessary channels for the communication to take place.

Computer simulation

Computer simulation modelling is an ICT-based tool/application that can be used to manage information needs and make destinations more sustainable. This is a computer-based simplification of the real world: recent research efforts have recognised that computer-based simulation modelling can be effective in the planning and management of nature-based tourism and protected natural areas

(Wang and Manning 1999; Lawson 2006), as simulation techniques aim to envisage the proposed state of the physical environment (Williamson 2010). These models are designed to represent how a system operates over time and can be invaluable in observing and testing the different components of a system, and its interactions with its component parts, that may prove difficult to observe directly (Wang and Manning 1999). In developing the simulation models, the approaches to modelling can either be dynamic, stochastic or discrete to account for the unique traits of the destination, as described by Wang and Manning (1999) and Lawson (2006). Dynamic models represent how the internal elements of a system transform over time; stochastic simulation models are based on probability distributions to account for variation within the system; and discrete models are those that consider immediate changes in the variables at unconnected points in time.

Four main ways of using computer simulation for the planning and management of tourism sites and attractions have been identified. According to Lawson (2006), computer simulation can be used to describe existing visitor use, which is usually very difficult to observe in protected areas since they are large and have various points of entry and exit. He further explains that information about visitor use patterns (i.e. visitor use information collected at trailheads, parking areas, visitor centres, etc.). is easier to collect. This information can be entered in the computer simulation model to provide managers with precise estimates of visitors' use of the protected natural areas. Spatially and temporally explicit information about visitor use patterns can allow destination managers to recognise threats (trouble spots) to and opportunities (areas for further development) for the natural and cultural aspects of an area.

Computer simulation can also be used to monitor indicator variables that are difficult to measure (Wang and Manning 1999). Destination managers can develop management plans to shift the burden from areas with heavy usage to those with limited use, allowing them to understand how tourists account for use of time, space and place when they are on holiday (Lew and McKercher 2005). Lawson (2006: 602) cites a number of examples of this, including 'how many encounters do backpacking visitors have with other groups per day whilst hiking?' and 'how does the number of people at a popular attraction site change throughout the course of a day or visitor use season and with increasing or decreasing levels of total visitor use?'

Computer simulation can also be used to test the effectiveness of different impact conditions through simulation of hypothetical situations seeking to facilitate the best decisions being made (Wang and Manning 1999; Lawson and Manning 2003). Some issues that can be tested in this way include alleviating congestion by shifting use to other areas of the destination, the outcome of a quota on visitor numbers and revenue, and the effect of visitor use along trails by using other transportation systems (Lawson 2006). Simulating situations allows for better decisions to be made regarding carrying capacity issues. Computer simulation modelling can also be used to assist in community involvement and participation. It can be used to facilitate more practical research design for public consultation (Lawson and Manning 2003; Lawson *et al.* 2003) by providing the community with more realistic images and data about a proposed development (Lawson 2006), which can foster more informed decision-making by the community.

The true benefit of computer simulation in sustainable tourism development lies in the fact that it can simulate real-world scenarios of 'those tasks that are too complex for direct observation manipulation or even analytical mathematical analysis' (Wang and Manning 1999: 195). Some examples of computer simulation software on the market are Arena™, Simulink™ and Witness™.

Destination management system

A destination management system is the IT infrastructure that supports the activities of the destination management organisation (Sheldon 1997; Ndou and Petti 2007). Typically, a destination management system creates efficient internal and external networks and sustainable relationships with the tourist, the local community and tourism businesses, which impact on the competitive advantage of a destination by using ICT and the Internet (Collins and Buhalis 2003; Horan and Frew 2007). It is instrumental in the marketing and promotion of destinations by providing information on activities and the range of products the destination has to offer, aids in attracting appropriate market segments and increasing visitor numbers and provides comprehensive and updated information (Sheldon 1997; Buhalis 1999; Horan and Frew 2007). Destination management systems therefore allow destinations to have an effective presence online and in the marketplace (Buhalis and Deimezi 2004).

A destination management system should be the mechanism that integrates the different tourism products and services and acts as a facilitator in accomplishing a destination's objectives (Collins and Buhalis 2003). It allows a destination management organisation to partner with tourism enterprises at the destination, to co-ordinate their product offerings at the local level and offer them on the global stage (Buhalis and Spada 2000; Belbaly *et al.* 2004). Destination management systems are therefore critical in destination management since they help to manage the information needs of stakeholders, increase customer satisfaction and promote a destination as an integrated entity, rather than a number of separate products and services (Petti and Ndou 2004). In past years there has been notable work on the criteria for successful destination management systems (see Buhalis and Spada 2000).

The literature offers numerous definitions of a destination management system and little consensus on its roles and operations (Buhalis 2003). After conducting a Delphi Study with a panel of experts in the field of eTourism, the following definition of a destination management system was proposed:

> Destination Management Systems (DMS) are systems that consolidate and distribute a comprehensive range of tourism products through a variety of channels and platforms, generally catering for a specific region, and supporting the activities of a destination management organisation (DMO) within that region. DMSs attempt to utilise a customer centric approach in order

> to manage and market the destination as a holistic entity, typically providing strong destination related information, real-time reservations, destination management tools and paying particular attention to supporting small and independent tourism suppliers.
>
> (Horan and Frew 2007: 34–5)

In essence, a destination management system is a combination of websites, intranets, extranets, reservation systems, customer services and other systems that assist the DMO in the marketing, promotion and management of the destination. By having a DMS that goes beyond having a Web presence to truly engage with the customers, local community and tourism businesses, a destination management system can aid the sustainability agenda. By serving as an 'information diffusion mechanism' (Buhalis 1997: 84), a DMS can contribute to sustainable tourism development by fostering new tools for managing the valued resources (natural, economic and socio-cultural) of a destination (Buhalis 1999). A destination management system can lead to economic benefits by efficiently managing the resource inventory of a destination, providing managerial aid for small businesses and supporting the tourist experience before, during and after the visit. This system can also highlight the fragile eco-systems and resources of a destination.

The socio-cultural benefits can be improved by disseminating information to the tourists on culture, customs, history and other necessary elements that foster an understanding between the tourist and the host community. For example, a destination could include a responsible traveller guide on its website which indicates to tourists how they can act in a sustainable manner when they are on holiday and offers ways to save energy, carbon and water. A community-based information system can be developed to extend the functions of a destination management system to support the tourists and the local community (Kazasis *et al.* 2003). This system creates interaction between the tourist and the local community as, through the use of the Internet, it allows prospective tourists to be given evaluative information about a destination from members of the community, not any marketing, promotion, business-related or governmental organisation. It gives a more unbiased impression to the potential tourist and fosters a greater feeling of security through evaluations from other tourists and direct interaction with the local community (Kazasis *et al.* 2003). This is critical to a destination's image, since these comments may influence the tourists' destination choice (Staab and Werthner 2002). It also serves to sensitise tourists to the destination prior to arrival (World Bank 2006). This includes providing them with information on ground transport, directions, safety and security, events and eating places, and providing background information on the destination so that they are aware of the local culture, dress, behaviour, history and geography, and how best to experience and learn about the destination (World Bank 2006). Kazasis *et al.* (2003) commented that using a community-based information system allows for social objectives such as building community cohesion and increasing community awareness and their roles in decision-making.

Environment management information system

Environment management information systems (EMIS) are another type of ICT-based tool that can aid in managing the environmental considerations of destinations (United Nations Environment Programme 2000; El-Gayar and Fritz 2006). An EMIS is, broadly, a computer-based technology that supports an environmental management system (Moore and Bordeleau 2001). There are many definitions of an EMIS, some of which are competing and others of which are complementary (El-Gayar and Fritz 2006). A holistic definition put forth by The BTI Consulting Group (2001: 2) defined an EMIS as:

> representing a combination of computer hardware, software and professional services to manage the environmental function within an organisation. EMIS systematically gathers, analyses and reports business information related to environmental management allowing a company to track, refine and methodically improve its environmental management practice. Environment Management Information System represents all computer-driven information systems that control environmental management at a company from stand-alone PCs with a waste tracking spreadsheet to fully globally networked computer systems designed to integrate environmental health and safety functions into the company business operations information system.

Therefore an EMIS co-ordinates such activities as tracking waste, monitoring emissions, scheduling tasks, coordinating permits and documentation, conducting cost/benefit analysis and choosing among alternative materials (Moore and Bordeleau 2001). An EMIS is focused on the effective and efficient collection of performance data to sustain performance measurement and process improvement. It incorporates a variety of information technologies, which include – but are not limited to – real-time data acquisitions systems, database systems and geographical information systems (these are discussed below) as well as environmental decision support system-oriented business intelligence tools, computational intelligence and enterprise systems integration (El-Gayar and Fritz 2006). An EMIS connects scattered information about urban and environmental issues in a way that allows the end-user to analyse the information in the most appropriate fashion, with the information being stored in archives, databases and maps (United Nations Environment Programme 2000). In its simplest form it is an information system for the management of information.

All tourism businesses need to manage their internal environmental information. Through the use of an EMIS they can obtain the answers to many questions which would have been difficult before due to the incompatibility, diversity and volume of information available (United Nations Environment Programme 2000). One of the benefits of the EMIS lies in the fact that it provides cross-organisation integration of environmental data, as it aims to automate environmental management tasks (El-Gayar and Fritz 2006). It plays a functional role in implementing an environment management system and has been identified as 'the backbone for environmental management efforts by supporting the firm's internal Environment

Management System and by meeting the reporting needs for various stakeholders' (El-Gayar and Fritz 2006: 768). An EMIS can also aid disaster prevention by providing early warning signs about potentially hazardous situations (United Nations Environment Programme 2000).

EMIS have mainly been used in the pharmaceuticals, petroleum, chemical, automotive, utilities, primary metals and semiconductor industries (El-Gayar and Fritz 2006). The uses and benefits of an EMIS can be applied to tourism because of the environmental impacts that result from tourism activity. An EMIS can be used for sustainable tourism, to address the need for environmental information. It can accelerate the speed in which information is received and it can improve information integration, which can lead to sophisticated decision-making in real-time (El-Gayar and Fritz 2006). Table 2.2 identifies how an EMIS can be used for environmental information management in sustainable tourism.

Geographical information systems

A geographical information system (GIS) has been defined as 'a computer based powerful set of tools for collecting, storing, retrieving, mapping, analysing, transforming and displaying spatial and non spatial data from the geographic world for

Table 2.2 Some uses of environment management information systems for sustainable tourism

Uses	*Description*	*Technologies*
Following and complying to legislation and regulations on the environment	Adhere to regulations and rectify any violations	Legal and environmental health and safety databases Auditing systems
Energy management and preventing pollution	Reduce waste, emissions and make existing processes more efficient	Environmental cost accounting Waste management Emissions tracking
Eco-efficiency	Consideration of the economic value versus the environmental cost, which can lead to a redesign of processes	Business performance metrics Balanced scorecards Online analytical processing and query tools
Product stewardship	Company responsibility extends to consider product design and the impact on the environment	Product lifecycle analysis Impact forecasting Supply chain integration
Future consideration	Consideration of long-term impacts of the business and the implications of the triple bottom line	Large-scale systems modelling Simulation Information-sharing with stakeholders and the public

Adapted from El-Gayar and Fritz 2006.

a particular set of purposes that varies for each discipline' (Avdimiotis *et al.* 2006: 406). It is an information system that can be used to capture, store, manage, manipulate, analyse, integrate and display large amounts of geographical data (Eslami *et al.* 2011; Feick and Hall 2000; Lee and Graefe 2004; Hasse and Milne 2005; Chancellor and Cole 2008).

For tourism, a GIS operates as a decision support system for problem solving by combining database operations such as query and statistical analysis to geographically represent data (Boers and Cottrell 2006). This GIS manipulates two types of data elements: geographical or spatial data (locational aspects in the form of digitised maps with references such as latitude and longitude or postcodes and addresses) and attribute data (non-locational data such as alpha-numeric records) (Bahaire and Elliott-White 1999; McAdam 1999; Hasse and Milne 2005).

Bahaire and Elliott-White (1999) and McAdam (1999) concur that GIS are extremely useful for tourism planning and management because they can assist managers with the decision-making process. There have been several studies conducted in which a GIS has been used for tourism planning and decision-making (see Feick and Hall 2000; Boers and Cottrell 2006; Connell and Page 2008). GIS can be applied to a variety of settings, such as testing different scenarios to determine what the outcomes might be based on different variables, auditing of tourism resources and conditions, identification of locations for potential development and modelling outcomes. They can also be used to measure the geographic, environmental and socio-economic characteristics of an area, which can be used to depict socio-demographic attributes and identify possible market segments, examine the spatial relationship between resource use and distance travelled, find alternative travel routes and identify hidden areas of damage (Lee and Graefe 2004). This technology also has the potential to gauge damage from natural disasters, monitor pollution and assess the impacts of climate change (Eslami *et al.* 2011); these are all critical components in tourism planning and management.

Table 2.3 identifies the capabilities of a GIS with specific regard to tourism. This can be critical in supporting decision-making mechanisms, improving the quality and quantity of information required to make sustainability-related decisions.

GIS can assist social sustainability as structured frameworks to enhance public consultation and the community participation process for tourism planning and development (Avdimiotis *et al.* 2006; Hasse and Milne 2005; Bahaire and Elliott-White 1999). This application can be used to empower the community and make them an integral part of the planning process (Ghose 2001). The use of different types of data, such as video, sound, three-dimensional images and large-scale maps can be used to give the community more information and enable better decision-making. Hasse and Milne (2005) introduced the framework of Participatory Approaches and GIS (PAGIS) in Marahau, a small community in New Zealand. Local knowledge, historical values and emotions were integrated into the planning process through a participatory mapping exercise into a GIS (Hasse and Milne 2005). This exercise stimulated dialogue, heightened awareness, strengthened local involvement and allowed the host community to have their needs and requirements incorporated in the decision-making process.

Table 2.3 Capabilities of a geographical information system

Examples of functional capabilities of information system	*Examples of basic questions that can be investigated using system (after Rhind 1990)*		*Examples of tourism applications*
Data entry storage and manipulation	Location	What is at?	Tourism resource inventories
Map production	Condition	Where is it?	Identifying most suitable locations for development
Database integration and management	Trend	What has changed?	Measuring tourism impacts
Data queries and searches	Routing	Which is the best route?	Visitor management/flow
Spatial analysis	Pattern	What is the pattern?	Analysing relationships associated with resource use
Spatial modelling Decision support	Modelling	What if... ?	Assessing potential impacts of tourism development

Source: Bahaire and Elliott-White 1999: 161.

The use of geographical information systems in decision-making is becoming a necessity – being GIS-illiterate in the next decade would be like being someone who does not know how to use e-mail and the Internet today (Lee and Graefe 2004). GIS development is indeed a full-spectrum approach to retrieving information, developing new and existing products, ensuring quality, managing the environment, providing services such as data at information kiosks and facilitating easier and wider distribution of tourism information to the users (Raghuvanshi *et al.* 2007). As stated by Millar *et al.* (1994) and supported by Bahaire and Elliott-White (1999: 171):

> [a] Geographical Information System offers a powerful tool for providing information to support decision-making in sustainable tourism planning and management and to promote integrated management of resources based on sensitivity to their use and the needs of local communities and visitors.

Tourism is a spatial phenomenon and therefore is aligned to the uses of GIS (Avdimiotis *et al.* 2006; Boers and Cottrell 2006). It has the capability to bring the necessary information needed for decision-making to a common stage. If supported, GIS can be a fundamental tool for managing sustainability.

Chancellor and Cole (2008) commented that GIS will become more widely used as a decision-making tool in tourism due to increasing awareness of its benefits for planning and management. Data useful to GIS is becoming available and the technology is becoming cheaper and more user-friendly. There are a number of ways in which GIS can assist in sustainability, as identified in Table 2.4.

Global positioning systems

Global positioning systems (GPS) have been around since the 1970s, with (until recently) constrained accuracy. They are a series of satellites which orbit the earth broadcasting signals that are picked up by a system of receivers (Shoval and Isaacson 2006). Through triangulation of this data, GPS can be used for navigation and location. Information sent to the satellite is used to determine the geographic location of the user. This data is collected and recorded by a GPS receiver and can be transferred to a computer and displayed on mapping software such as that used by a GIS, location-based services, personal digital assistants (PDAs), mobile phones or in-car navigation (Savitsky *et al.* 2000). GPS systems are primarily made available to us through the use of networks of geo-stationary satellites courtesy of the military (it was originally a US Department of Defense project). GLONASS and Compass are the Russian and Chinese equivalents, respectively.

Use of GPS may be withdrawn if military circumstances dictate, and therefore Europe is currently developing the Galileo positioning system as an alternative. The horizontal accuracy of these systems may vary, but generally only in the region of three metres, which offers very good opportunities in relation to

Table 2.4 Geographical information system applications to sustainable tourism

Geographical information system applications for sustainable tourism	*Importance to sustainable tourism*
Integrate and manage data from numerous sources	This information can be used to ensure sustainability is accounted for in the decision making process. It also facilitates better and more informed decisions.
Indicator identification, monitoring and measurement	Data to monitor and measure indicators developed for sustainable tourism can be updated quickly. This leads to more accurate information, better analysis and decision-making.
Undertake a resource inventory for an area selected for development to determine suitability	Assist in determining suitable areas for development, those that need to be protected and those experiencing problems Identify the boundaries and the local community Demonstrate how the land is changing by identifying use and capacities Sensitise stakeholders to externalities associated with their actions.
Visualisations of areas can be produced before and after proposed developments	Local community and developers can view the results of the proposed development and how the area will change over time. Alternatives can be considered.

location-based activities. Sharda *et al.* (2006) commented that the benefits of GPS rest in their ability to produce location-specific information for both tourists and destinations and to track tourist movements, which can be useful in managing visitors' use of an area and for simulating future scenarios. GPS are therefore useful to manage information related to making decisions regarding the best use of space and time at a destination.

Nielsen and Liburd (2008) and Liburd (2005) painted possible future scenarios regarding tourists using GPS and wireless access on their mobile phones. Liburd (2005) discussed a hypothetical situation of a German family driving to Demark. Through use of the mobile phone this family was able to get directions, obtain information on suggested tours and places of interest, make reservations for accommodation and restaurants, share their experiences by uploading videos and photos of their holidays and write a blog. Additionally, whilst driving to the attraction the children were entertained by playing games related to the site on the mobile phone. They could communicate with another child who was going to the same attraction and the families were able to meet.

The case study below shows how a GIS and GPS have been combined with Wikipedia for the promotion of eco-tourism.

Case study: Promotion of eco-tourism using the practice of Wikipedia: The case-study of environmental and cultural paths in Zakynthos, Greece

Zakynthos is the southernmost and third largest, in both size and population, of the Ionian Islands. It is situated approximately 300 km west of the capital of Greece, Athens. The Zakynthos environment has become an object of international interest because the loggerhead turtle *caretta-caretta*, an endangered species protected by international conventions and by Greek legislation, lays its eggs on the island's southern shores. Also, on the steep western shores of the island, the Mediterranean monk seal *Monachus monachus* lives and breeds, a species also protected by Greek law. A big part of the coastal region of the Zakynthos has been characterised as a Marine Park (birth location of the *caretta-caretta* turtles, which are highly protected marine species). The tourism sector is of major economic importance for local community, but an effort is needed that one does not visit Zakynthos only for its beautiful beaches and crystal blue waters. The island also offers a variety of landscapes, including mountains. In the interior of the island, there are many traditional settlements and towns, whose inhabitants are engaged in cultivating traditional crops (olives, vines and vegetables).

GISs are very well suited for cartographical production (Tomlin 1991). A number of basic spatial datasets of the Zakynthos area, such as topographic maps (scale 1: 50,000), elevation data, vector data concerning administrative boundaries, hydrography, transportation networks, vegetation cover maps (scale 1: 20,000), geographic annotation and locations of meteorological stations were introduced and analysed in a GIS environment.

Continued

Every data set has a metadata code which identifies the source of the data, when the data was collected or measured or monitored or surveyed by the source organisation [...] Two Landsat 7 Enhanced Thematic Mapper Plus (ETM+) scenes have been used. Various image processing and vector GIS techniques have been used for analysis of the satellite imagery and results of the application of those techniques are presented. Finally a global positioning system, or GPS was used to accurate plot footpaths.

A complete survey of the Zakynthos footpaths was carried out. A Thales Navigation Mobile Mapper (Martinis *et al.* 2009) GPS unit with post processing capabilities was used to delineate footpaths and points of interest. Mapping was performed when ideal satellite and PDOP numbers were available. At the end of each survey, footpath data were collected into a computer and exported into the TNT maps GIS and image-processing software. The majority of the data collected during the survey was classified and stored using a wiki-based web service.

In the context of this work, the data were recorded and charted on maps for elements of particular environmental and cultural interest. These elements were grouped in categories: environmental (forests, geological information, olives groves, panoramic points, etc.) and cultural (monuments, local or traditional products). Following a spatial or thematic environmental route, visitors have the opportunity to combine vacations with [discovery] of the natural beauties and the cultural heritage. These trails are a result of networking of points of particular thematic interest, such as olive routes, wine routes, bird watching, etc. and can be combined by overnight stay and focus on sale of traditional products and the local deliveries of Zakynthos islands. All the above constitute a complete agro-tourism proposal that can combine holiday and recreation in the natural environment with environmental and cultural education focused in a specific theme or region.

The elements of particular interest that were recorded in the frame of present work in Zakynthos prefecture region, can be presented in following thematic ways: tradition and culture, olive ways, wine ways, gastronomical ways, geological ways, water ways, ways for the performance of nature, bird watching, ways of aromatic and pharmaceutical herbs, travel in the beauties of nature (Martinis *et al.* 2009).

The use of a wiki-based service proved to be a great tool for supporting the tasks of this project since it enabled different researchers to store information collaboratively in a single space. At the same time it enabled researchers and other types of users to easily search and view information enriched with multimedia material, GIS and textual information. The recording and charting of natural and cultural heritage can provide the basis for the development of alternative forms of tourism such as agro-tourism and eco. The applications that are supported by the use of new technologies are particularly effective combined with fieldwork and observations on the spot.

In this work, the registration of all particular characteristics of Zakynthos Prefecture was followed by thematic and geographic classification and the presentation of the particular identities of each region. This methodological framework manages to highlight cultural and environmental elements of the islands and make them poles of

Continued

tourism attraction. In Zakynthos Island the environmental and thematic ways can constitute a model of sustainable tourism growth that may also contribute to the environmental education and sensitisation.

The information collected in this project has been also used as the test feed data for an innovative web platform which enables visitors to seek, view and contribute information related to alternative tourism. The design and implementation of the web platform was based on the [findings] of a case study (Zins *et al.* 2004) which addressed the specific needs for searching, presenting and storing information related to alternative tourism.

The project has resulted in multiple data that are being published in paper and electronic form. An easy to use 3-page leaflet (in Greek and English) is created and distributed to local authorities and public and private Tourist Offices. This process will inform the tourists about various mountainous paths and routes, and [at] the same time will enable the authorities to gain an understanding of the work required to maintain and upgrade footpaths. Two different layouts have been organised: one for the total area of the island of Zakynthos and one for the data concerning specific footpaths. All data will be organized in [the] form of an informational Atlas, which then will be distributed in the form of a CD or on the Internet.

The web platform includes many different innovative aspects. It enables the collaborative collection of information related to alternative tourism by providing a variety of tools such as interactive map, GIS tools, adaptive tagging service, rich text, image handling etc. At the same time it allows visitors to search and view information using advanced tools which assist them on finding easily information related to alternative tourism taking also into account their personal needs. Nevertheless, the most important feature of the web platform is the ability to search and present information while following eco-touristic rules. Therefore the presented information is automatically enriched with related information that promotes the principles of eco-tourism.

This case study has been reproduced with the kind permission of Organic Eprints and can be accessed at: http://orgprints.org/19965/

We would like to acknowledge the authors of this work:

Source: Martinis, A. Halvatzaras, D and Kabassi, K. 2011. Promotion of eco-tourism using the practice of Wikipedia: the case-study of environmental and cultural paths in Zakynthos. In: Migliorini, P., Minotou, C., Lusic , D., Hashem, Y. and Martinis, Aristotelis (eds.). *Book of Abstracts. International Conference on Organic Agriculture and Agro-Eco Tourism*, DIO.

Specialist software

Specialist software can be procured by the tourism industry to help alleviate the negative impacts of tourism. Whilst there is much software worthy of discussion, this section focuses on two packages which were felt to be particularly important to the discussion. These measure the economic impacts of tourism and monitor the weather.

Economic Impact Analysis Software (EIAS)

Many destinations and tourism businesses are under pressure to demonstrate how tourism development can lead to economic benefit. Economic impact analysis can be important if properly used and interpreted (Tyrrell and Johnston 2006). This type of analysis can be used to provide information on type and amount of spending, gain public support for tourism development, ascertain which course of action best supports the community, increase economic activity and determine financial feasibility (Vogelsong and Graefe 2001).

The challenge posed is how to aggregate, analyse and make understandable these economic benefits for the wider community and stakeholders. This can be accomplished through the used of ICT-based applications. One package which can be used for this is Implan (www.implan.com). The software can be used to develop models and estimations of economic impacts. It can create detailed and comprehensible reports of tourism-related money entering a destination and how this money is being used to create further income, hence making tourism sustainable and workable for the destination.

Information management of climate

Weather and climate can affect both the attractiveness of a destination and tourism operations at the destination (Altalo *et al.* 2002), as before a tourist decides to travel, one of the first things they look at is the weather. Understanding monitoring and predicting weather and climate are critical to sustainable development. In essence, this translates to sustainable tourism, since tourism is one industry that is very dependent on the whims and fancies of the weather, climate and ocean conditions (Altalo *et al.* 2002). Accurate and updated forecasts are necessary to ensure the industry maximises its economic benefits and uses this information for tourism planning and management. The information can be useful for destinations in bidding for events, making decisions about proposed development, putting measures in place for hazards and risks associated with bad weather, providing tourists with updated information, energy management and other issues. Software applications exist that destination managers can take advantage of to manage the effects of weather, climate and ocean changes. Science Applications International Corporation (www.saic.com) provide software that can enable more advanced weather detection. This can be used to forecast and strategise the impacts of changing weather, climate and ocean conditions on tourism businesses. This weather data can be disseminated to local businesses to help them in their planning.

Wireless and mobile technology

The world as we know it has transformed from an eWorld to a mWorld (Christodoulopoulou *et al.* 2000). Wireless technology and mobile networks have advanced to such a level that people can communicate anywhere at any time (Flouri and Buhalis 2004; Buhalis and O'Connor 2006). It has facilitated the provision of 'the right service at the right time in the right location' (Nokia.com

2003, cited in Flouri and Buhalis 2004: 27). Technology which focuses on ICT and mobility includes mobile units for communication that can be built into vehicles, mobile phones, wireless telecommunication such as third-generation (3G) mobile telecommunication, radio communication and positioning technology such as GPS and GIS (Eriksson 2002).

Buhalis and Pistidda (2008) described four main types of wireless networks. These are:

- Wireless Personal Area Network (WPAN) – This is a network of wireless devices which are located within a short distance of each other (usually three to ten metres).
- Wireless Local Area Network (WLAN) – This is a network that allows the user to have access to the Internet without any wired infrastructure.
- Wireless Metropolitan Area Networks (WMAN) – This network covers large areas such as an entire city through the integration of a large number of WLANs.
- Wireless Wide Area Networks (WWAN) – This network provides Internet access around a town/city or broader areas such as a country. It can connect different WMANs, thus offering ubiquitous connectivity to mobile users.

Mobile phones are rapidly becoming the primary means of accessing the Internet. The 1980s saw the widespread adoption and use of cellular phones. This was known as the first-generation (1G) network and allowed voice but not data services. By the end of the 1980s the 1G network was being phased out in favour of the second-generation (2G) network. This became popular because it was based on digital technologies and supported good voice quality, text-based messages and international roaming. Moreover, the devices were affordable: there were huge reductions in voice tariffs and widespread use of prepaid top-ups. The major problem with the 2G network was the slow rate at which data was transferred. Consumers were demanding a faster rate, since they wanted to gain access to the Internet for browsing, downloading and sharing of files. This led to the development of the third-generation (3G) mobile network. Oliphant (1999) identified some of the requirements for 3G networks: roaming between the different 3G networks; a data rate of 144 KB/s for users moving quickly, such as in a vehicle; a data rate of 384 KB/s for pedestrians and a data rate of 2 MB/s for low mobility environments. We are now entering into an era of the fourth generation (4G) of mobile phones, which are allowing users more sophisticated access to the Internet. According to Portio Research (2012), the current number of worldwide mobile users is close to six billion and is expected to reach eight billion by the end of 2016, with this growth being driven by Asia-Pacific, Africa and the Middle East. Microsoft Tag (2011) say there are more than one billion smartphone users, eighty-six per cent of whom use their mobile phones to watch television and ninety-one per cent of whom use them for social purposes.

The tourism system is founded on mobility (Staab and Werthner 2002) and customers' preferences are strongly influenced by this mobility (Corigliano and

Baggio 2004). Tourists are using different sources to obtain information about a destination before and during a trip (Ghandour and Buhalis 2003). The implications of wireless technology and networks for travel and tourism are extremely important, and tourism presents ample opportunities to exploit these technologies (Corigliano and Baggio 2004). They are changing the means by which information-related activities are conducted since users can surf the Internet, check e-mail and undertake transactions from their mobile devices (Lee and Mills 2007). Internet-enabled technology such as cellular phones and hand-held computers allow for the free movement of the user (Wei and Ozok 2005). Through wireless access huge opportunities for interaction with the customer and the creation of personalised destination-related information are created at the destination.

Advantages offered by mobile services include 'ubiquity, localisation, awareness, immediacy, personalisation, broadcasting, portability and identification' (Lee and Mills 2007: 142). Due to these considerable advantages, research efforts are now focused on understanding how mobile technology could support the information needs of travellers, ranging from touring museums, transportation and parking information and location identification to tracking and navigation (Lee and Mills 2007). Mobile phones now have a greater reach even to communities that are digitally excluded (Buhalis and Law 2008). Different mobile devices, such as 3G and 4G mobile phones with GPS, are allowing the consumer to gain access to tourist information twenty-four hours a day, seven days a week regardless of their location.

Likewise, more transactions are also taking place on these mobile devices. This is known as mobile commerce (mCommerce). These transactions take place through a wireless device on which users of mobile services can make airline, hotel, car rental and restaurant bookings (Berger *et al.* 2003) and are now becoming a critical component of tourists' experience and satisfaction (Eriksson 2002; Lee and Mills 2007).

Forecasts indicate that mCommerce will have successful application and huge opportunities for tourism (Flouri and Buhalis 2004; Lee and Mills 2007). PhoCusWright (2012) found that more than half of all leisure travellers own a smartphone, whilst nearly seventy-five per cent of businesses travellers do so. This report also revealed that a little over one quarter of leisure travellers who use the Internet on their phones only use mobile websites, whilst just under three quarters use a combination of mobile websites and apps. It reported that BlackBerry users undertake an average of 4.5 travel-related mobile web activities per year, whilst Apple users tend to be more engaged, with 5.7 activities per year.

The future of wireless technology seems to rest with Worldwide Interoperability for Microwave Access (WiMax), since this technology is expected to offer the greatest possible coverage – up to thirty miles (Odinma *et al.* 2007). This could have a great impact in locations where wired infrastructure has not been developed or cannot be developed for economic reasons; the technology is also cheaper, simpler, smaller and more convenient to install than other types of broadband (Buhalis and Pistidda 2008). It can also support the end-user with Internet access without their having to pay expensive data roaming charges, and it is available 24/7 (Buhalis and Law 2008).

Mobile communication devices can facilitate and play an important role in sustainable tourism development (Erdmann and Behrendt 2003; Liburd 2005). Tourists are increasingly demanding information that is 'fast, flexible and convenient' (Corigliano and Baggio 2004: 16). They are also less inclined to put up with delays, poor service and lack of adequate and accurate information (Buhalis and O'Connor 2006). They expect to have access to information when and where they require it, from various handheld devices (Werthner and Ricci 2003). Using the American Customer Satisfaction Model, a positive relationship was found to exist between perceptions and experience of satisfaction for the mobile tourist (Lee and Mills 2007). Mobile services also allow personalisation of services for the tourist (Oertel *et al.* 2002). Therefore using these ICT-based applications can increase tourist satisfaction and contribute to sustainable tourism development at the destinations. Location-based services (LBS) are an important ICT-based tool for the sustainable development of tourism, which incorporates the features discussed above. The development and use of LBS can also lead to increased tourist satisfaction.

Location-related information is important in tourism, since it can influence the tourist decision-making process by swaying their choice of destination, behaviour, movements that occur at the destination and evaluation and communication of experiences gained (Nielsen and Liburd 2008). Prior to the advancement in technology and the Internet, maps were provided in the form of paper. Now, with developments around the Internet, advancement in satellite sensing and better software applications, users can access online maps from Google Earth, Virtual Earth and other mapping sites. Not only can users access online maps, but they can now also create their own maps, even if they are amateurs. The growth and availability of application programme interface allows these users to build and share customised maps detailing points of interest – where they have been or are planning to go – from websites such as Google. An application programme interface (API) is a set of functions, routines, resources, protocols and tools for developing software applications. Pictures can also be added, and these images can be geotagged. Geo-tagging refers to adding geographical co-ordinates to items such as photos, videos and websites.

Tourism is now being heavily influenced by multimedia content, such as photographs, videos, 3D virtual tourism and other graphics facilitated by the Internet. This enhances the richness of the information and allows consumers to interact with the place they may be visiting. Multimedia can aid in enhancing this virtual tourism by producing telepresence. By using a variety of technologies, telepresence increases interactivity and allows users to experience a simulated reality – that is, to feel as if they were at a location or event or experience an event, though they were not (Steuer 1992). Online maps are now commonly used to find directions as well as to provide the user with points of interest and images, opinions and comments about these places. This trend is known as neogeography. According to Turner (2006), neogeography is a unifying concept which literally means 'new geography' and refers to the wide array of techniques and tools that fall outside the realm of a traditional GIS. These maps can be created and entered either after the user has completed the activity, or as the user is having the tourist experience. The latter can occur if the user has a GPS receiver that is either linked to or built into another device (see the earlier discussion of GPS). As reliable GPS units become cheaper, a field of devices called geoware is emerging (Nielsen and Liburd 2008). These are devices that provide an awareness of location and are used to enhance performance or provide new information. Their commercial application is often referred to as use of location-based services (Nielsen and Liburd 2008).

Location-based services

LBS have been defined as 'systems which utilise the location of a mobile device in order to collect or deliver information' (Sharma *et al.* 2009: 1). LBS aim to provide the user with targeted information based on their specific requirements. When people are on vacation they think in terms of geographic location, identifying places to eat, see and stay (Eriksson 2002). LBS take account of the current geographical and spatial considerations of the tourist (Zipf and Malaka 2001; Sustainable Tourism Cooperative Research Centre 2004). This offers possibilities for ICT-based applications in the provision and delivery of location-sensitive information (Eriksson 2002).

Some applications of LBS include, but are not limited to, fleet tracking, traffic information, directions, parking, emergency services, law enforcement, sensors, monitoring, customer location for target marketing and advertising, roadside assistance, stolen vehicle recovery, object visualisation, leisure information, location-based billing, mCommerce, child tracking, navigation and directory services (Zipf and Malaka 2001; Eriksson 2002; Sustainable Tourism Cooperative Research Centre 2004). Berger *et al.* (2003) identified four main uses of LBS for tourism:

1 locating persons, objects and places;
2 discovering routes between them;
3 searching for objects in proximity such as restaurants, shops, hotels or sights; and
4 information about travelling conditions, such as traffic updates.

The use of LBS can promote greater tourist satisfaction, offering huge opportunities to optimise the tourist's experiences by personalising these services and becoming more customer-focused and flexible in their information and service delivery. This is essential for tourism to be more responsive to tourists' needs (Buhalis and O'Connor 2006; Sharda *et al.* 2006). LBS can be seen as a mechanism for providing real-time and accurate information by providing easy and quick access to tourists, as well as general information on the destination (Flouri and Buhalis 2004). LBS are transforming the tourism industry: prior to their existence, tourists depended on guidebooks, maps and tourist information centres, whereas now all the information they require whilst on holiday can be delivered through LBS (Sharma *et al.* 2009). Sharda *et al.* (2006) commented that as more people access information and data services on their mobile devices, the need for LBS will increase.

The environmental quality of a destination can be promoted by using LBS. This can lead to more sustainable production, in terms of less paper production of maps and brochures. Liburd (2005) discussed how these devices can also lead to sustainable consumption by allowing the tourist to make better decisions about which products to purchase and which companies to support.

Intelligent transport systems

Information technology can also lead to an improved land transportation system (Sheldon 1997) through intelligent transport systems (ITS). The use of ITS has been described as using a combination of IT to manage the ground transportation at a destination as well as providing useful travel information to the tourists at the destination (Sheldon 1997; Diagle and Zimmerman 2004). ITS use telematic systems which provide detailed information on traffic, individual information, information from independent locations, traffic guidance and dynamic routing via GPS (Erdmann and Behrendt 2003). A number of different technologies can be included in ITS; with regard to tourism, these include route guidance systems, traveller information systems, automated vehicle locations, fleet management systems and automated traffic management systems (Sheldon 1997). In cars, ITS can help a driver navigate, find the best routes and avoid traffic and collisions; in trains and buses they can be used for managing and optimising fleet operations and offering passengers automatic ticketing and real-time traffic information; and on the roadside they can be used to co-ordinate traffic signals, detect and manage incidents and display information for drivers, passengers and pedestrians (Eriksson 2002). As traffic increases at a destination, the local movement of tourists becomes more challenging (Diagle and Zimmerman 2004). Using ITS can increase tourist satisfaction by avoiding 'frustration, delays and accidents' (Sheldon 1997 p. 72) and allowing them to have 'have safer, faster, and more enjoyable journeys' (Diagle and Zimmerman 2004: 151).

Community informatics

An ICT-based tool/application that can be used for sustainable tourism development is community informatics (CI). The aim of CI is to increase community participation in decisions that affect them through the 'wired world' (Milne *et al.* 2005: 122). Gurstein (2000) describes it as a set of principles and practices that are focused on designing and delivering ICT for the enhancement of community development (through personal, social, cultural or economic development) and the lives of the residents. Communities have untapped potential and through the use of ICT they can become enlightened as to what they possess and what they are capable of, thereby developing local commitment, resources and skills (Taylor

2004). Therefore ICT is seen as having an important facilitating role in community processes and community transformation, through bridging the digital divide and dealing with community fragmentation and the inclusion of previously excluded communities (Gretzel *et al.* 2009). Milne *et al.* (2005) identified five areas in which ICT can enhance the quality of life of a community: the promotion of democratic participation, development of social capital, empowerment of individuals (especially marginalised groups), strengthening of community and its identity and the creation of sustainable community economic development.

CI models have been developed by using e-mail bulletin boards and community networks, all based on the Internet (Milne *et al.* 2005). For example, the Internet has been used for citizen participation in the rebuilding of New York City's Lower Manhattan area following the 11 September 2001 attacks (Green and Murrmann 2005). Similarly, Gretzel *et al.* (2009) used CI for heritage tourism development in Hearne, Texas.

Carbon calculators

Recently there has been a proliferation of carbon calculators seeking to measure our carbon footprint based on our activities. Tourism is no exception to this, especially with air transport being one of the heaviest contributors to carbon emissions. Data now exists which can be used to measure tourism's contribution to carbon emissions. It is estimated that seventy-six per cent of fossil fuels are used for air travel and the remainder used for destination consumption (Gössling 2000). Airline emissions have therefore been given special consideration, because they are emitted in the upper troposphere and lower stratosphere and therefore have a larger impact on climate change than emissions released on the earth's surface (United Nations Environment Programme 2003), and ninety per cent of energy consumption in tourism is spent on transportation (Gössling 2000).

In tourism, ICT could be used to lower greenhouse gas emissions if the following was developed:

> ICT-supported cost-effective monitoring and reporting schemes that enable transport to be included in emissions trading schemes and prioritised ICT-based demand-side management measures making it possible to adjust energy consumption and transport demand to a sustainable level using economic instruments.
>
> (Erdmann and Goodman 2004: 44)

South West Tourism in the UK, in partnership with the Stockholm Environment Institute (SEI), has developed and launched web-based software called the Resource Energy and Analysis Program (REAP). This online tool was designed to track materials' carbon dioxide emissions and the environmental impact of different visitor markets and various tourist activities (www. resource-accounting.org.uk). REAP can also calculate impacts on the environment considering the entire supply chain, a service and an associated unit of demand, such as a visitor day (Mintel 2011). Using additional software such as a GIS, REAP can help to simulate future scenarios and map tourist movements through a particular area (www.resource-accounting.org.uk).

Virtual tourism

Virtual tourism refers to a tourism experience in an electronic environment, which acts as a substitute for the actual experience or physical journey. This type of tourism will allow participants to travel to places via new technologies, free of the usual restrictions of time, distance, cost and human frailty. Irrespective of the actual shape of the future, demand for travel will continue to exist, although perhaps in forms different from those we understand at present. It is argued that one day virtual tourism will replace the industry as we know it today (Milne and Ateljevic 2001; Teo 2002). With virtual reality, once a tourist has online access he/she can experience a destination's culture, history and other points of tourist interest in a visual and interactive manner (Christodoulopoulou *et al.* 2000). Virtual reality can be used for destinations which have exceeded their carrying capacity; for a destination that is fragile and in danger of being damaged by tourism; to sensitise tourists about a destination prior to their visit; as a substitute for activities which might be seen as socially unacceptable, such as hunting or sex tourism; for tourists who enjoy dangerous activities such as rock climbing or high altitude skiing and to rejuvenate declining resorts (Swarbrooke 1999). If virtual tourism can become a reality it could be used to reduce tourist transport and hence have a positive effect on carbon emissions. Virtual mobility could decrease passenger transport by six to eight per cent (Erdmann and Behrendt 2003). Virtual tourism could reduce the demand for transportation to and from a destination, but this can only happen if the virtual models of destinations are highly similar to the real thing and if virtual tourism can advance beyond what it is today and become mainstream.

These virtual worlds exist as simulated environments where avatars are used to represent the user. An avatar is used by a computer user to represent himself/herself in an online environment and can be personalised to the user's preferences. Two existing examples of virtual worlds are VirtuyMall and Second Life. VirtuyMall is a 3D online mall where visitors, represented as avatars, can walk through the mall, go shopping and chat with others. Second Life, which has gained popularity amongst users and the media in the past few years (Bellotti *et al.* 2009), is organised as a set of virtual worlds: avatars can have a variety of experiences by interacting with each other in the virtual space. The virtual world could be used by the tourism industry so that tourists can create their dream vacation.

A key question is: 'will virtual travel alter the desire for people to travel and the ultimate seduction of "real" place'? (Milne and Ateljevic 2001: 385). Virtual tourism may never surpass the actual experience of what a destination is really like, but what it can do is assist the tourist in getting a feel of what they are going to encounter on their trip. It can simulate those experiences, provide the tourist with an idea of what the actual experience will be like and allow tourists to experience a destination or part of a destination that they might never be able to travel to.

Social media

Social media has evolved as the development of the Internet has provided new software tools, which allow consumers to generate content and engage in conversations based on this content. Some examples of social media are social networks, such as Facebook and MySpace; wikis – for example, Wikipedia; blogs, such as Blogger; podcasts, like those which can be found on iTunes; social news sites, such as digg; social bookmarking sites, for instance del.icio.us; and content sharing sites, like YouTube and flickr. Many tourism providers engage with social media primarily for the marketing and promotion of their product; however, social media can be a powerful tool for sustainable tourism. These online conversations can be a way for communities to find their voice in order to discuss how tourism is developed in their locale. It allows them to share information with the tourists, providing the latter an avenue for better interpretation of the destination. It can also be used by businesses as a mechanism to share information with each other and the communities within which they operate, to develop sustainable business practices. Social media will be covered in greater detail in Chapter 7.

Radio frequency identification

Radio frequency identification (RFID) uses radio frequency technology for the transfer of data. This is done by attaching a RFID tag or label to real-world objects that contain an integrated circuit connected to an antenna which can be read by special readers (Isaksson 2010). This exchange of data and energy occurs without any contact between the tag and the reader. The reader emits electromagnetic waves that create a magnetic field, powering the tag circuits, which modulate the waves and send them back to the reader to convert into digital data (Oztaysi, Baysan and Akpinar 2009). RFID tags can be either passive or active. Passive tags get their energy from the radio frequency signal sent from the reader, as they do not have a power source. They are cheaper, smaller and have a short-range frequency of about three metres and a storage capacity of 128 bytes. Active tags possess batteries which serve as their source of energy. They are not reliant on the reader and therefore have greater range capability and a larger capacity for data storage. In tourism, RFID has a broad range of applications, such as tracking and control systems, contactless payment systems and information provision. RFID has huge potential for sustainable tourism development because it can monitor goods through the supply chain to deal with sustainable consumption and provenance concerns, whilst tourists can use it for easier transactions at their destination through payment systems and information gathering.

Gamification

Gamification is normally understood to involve the process of taking approaches, techniques and technologies developed in the sphere of game design and applying them to non-game functions, typically to engage the gamers in real-world applications. It is an approach perfectly suited to the environments of Web 2.0 and is beginning to thrive on social networks. There are now a number of destinations embracing gamification. An interesting example is the Thailand Tourism game to be found on Smile Land (http://www.socialgaminghub.com/smileland-social-games-tourism-thailand), where players are encouraged to take a tour of Thailand, visiting up to 200 locations. Destinations and businesses can play a significant role here in taking advantage of this gaming disposition and connecting both locals and tourists to local goods and services through reward systems. It may be that such a system could reward good, sustainable behaviours, such as using public transport, by awarding badges or points with perhaps some tangible benefit, such as discounts. Equally, behaviours deemed to be negative in relation to tourism sustainability could be penalised by deducting points.

Conclusion

Some researchers have stated that the environment is the lifeblood of tourism, whereas others have stated that information holds this role. Likewise, ICT has also been identified by some as a necessity for destinations to remain competitive and literally to survive (Milne and Ateljevic 2001; Gratzer *et al.* 2004), whereas other researchers have stated that the competitiveness of a destination is based on its sustainability (Laws 1995). It can be concluded that both ICT and sustainability are key to the longevity and future prosperity of a destination. What better way, then, to develop the best destination in the global market environment than by forming a synergistic relationship between these two – that is, using ICT to manage the sustainability of a destination? In the words of Middleton and Clarke (2001: 457), 'no view of the future makes sense without reference to ICT'. This was expressed over a decade ago and is still appropriate today.

Today's world is increasingly focused on the use and application of ICT, and the tourism industry must use this to their advantage. The strategic implementation of technology has already become necessary and will continue to be important for businesses to survive in an age of globalisation and commoditisation. Stamboulis and Skayannis (2003) comment that the use of ICT in tourism has been defensive, with most attention paid to the areas of increasing information provision, business transaction processes and cost savings. The role of ICT has to move beyond its traditional functions.

The debate on how tourism can become more sustainable continues, but despite this, sustainable tourism practices have been implemented worldwide (Choi and Sirakaya 2006) and there have been numerous case studies of sustainable tourism in action. This text is seeking to broaden existing knowledge and understanding of mechanisms for the sustainable tourism development of destinations by applying ICT. Large amounts of pressure are being placed on destinations today to consider the environment in their business operations (Moore and Bordeleau 2001). Tourism will always have impacts; to reduce these impacts to zero, tourism would have to cease. Instead of limiting numbers, sustainable tourism should consider how to better manage the resources that are available and modify tourist behaviour, rather than specifying a limit to the number of visitors using resources.

Tourism stakeholders therefore need to adopt ICT and become technology-aware, eco-efficient and environmentally innovative in their operations with reference to sustainable tourism development. Not doing this will cause tourist destinations and businesses at the destinations to suffer both environmentally and economically. For this to occur, first one needs to understand the benefits that ICT can offer. Once this is realised, ICT will become part of routine operations, and the resultant effect will be higher levels of ICT use and implementation (Yuan *et al.* 2006). Furthermore, the importance of ICT to the tourism planning process will continue to grow (Gretzel *et al.* 2009). Tourism can create revenue without risking negative effects on the environment (Krozer and Christensen-Redzepovic 2006). There is neither a one-size-fits-all, nor a simple and easy solution for sustainable tourism development; however, the application of ICT for sustainable tourism can create a 'frictionless' destination (Berkhout and Hertin 2001: 4) and make the approach to sustainable tourism development more practical and reliable.

Chapter 2 questions

1 Discuss the ways in which consumer preferences and tourist behaviour have been changed in recent years by the adoption of new technologies.
2 Increasingly tourism businesses are identifying specific staff responsibilities in relation to scanning the Internet for reviews, blogs, etc. relevant to their organisation, with a view to understanding this information and positively responding to criticism. How might the emergence of the Semantic Web change this approach?
3 Why do you think virtual communities offer a sense of security and trust? Can you think of some examples?
4 The text discusses the use of computer simulation in assisting destination managers' attempts to balance 'traffic' loading at a destination. Can you find other specific examples of destination management use of computer simulation?
5 Location-based services are becoming ever more widely used in tourism. Can you identify some examples from sports tourism?

3 Destinations and sustainable tourism

Learning outcomes

This chapter focuses on how destinations can engage with technology for sustainable tourism development. After reading this chapter you should be able to:

- understand the relationship between sustainable development and sustainable tourism;
- discuss the current approaches to managing sustainable tourism;
- examine the opportunities for destinations to use technology for sustainable tourism; and
- identify some of the technologies which can be used by destinations for sustainable tourism development.

Introduction

Before any discussion can be entered into on how destinations may use or are already using technology for sustainable tourism, it is necessary to provide a review of sustainable development, sustainable tourism and the concepts and tools currently used for managing sustainable tourism. This starting point is necessary to show how technology fits with the existing sustainable tourism research and contributes to the wider sustainable development agenda. Sustainable development is considered here because the concept of sustainable tourism, derived from its application to tourism, has its wider foundations in, and an intimate relationship with, the concept of sustainable development (Bramwell and Lane 1993; Swarbrooke 1999; Hall 2000; Hardy and Beeton 2001; Saarinen 2006). This chapter first pays attention to the metamorphosis of the concept of sustainable tourism and current management approaches. It then considers the areas in destination management where technology can be used and identifies some of the technologies that destinations may invest in to help alleviate their sustainable tourism development concerns.

Background to sustainable development

The concept of sustainable development resulted from a series of worldwide political processes with the aim of uniting the most important needs of our times. Some of these needs included overcoming poverty, environmental protection of natural resources, social justice and cultural diversity (Yoon and Lee 2003). Today, with pressure on the world's finite resources growing daily, interest in sustainable development has been rekindled, with many businesses 'going green' and defining a sustainable agenda as part of their corporate strategy.

Hardy *et al.* (2002) provide a valuable historical account of sustainable development, tracing concerns about the human impact on the environment back to the days of ancient civilisation. These researchers discussed the concept's evolution in three forms: conservation vision, economic theory and community vision. The conservation vision highlighted that in early times, even though sustainability was not precisely defined as it is today, human beings did appreciate that resources needed to be conserved for future use (Hardy *et al.* 2002). After World War Two sustainability awareness increased due to the rapid rate of economic growth, which did not take into account ecological and social processes (Miller and Twining-Ward 2006). It was becoming apparent that economic development was destroying the environment, with some forms of destruction being irreversible. From the mid-1960s emphasis was placed on the relationship between the concepts of growth, economic development and the environment. Perspectives varied as to whether growth and development were compatible with protection of the environment. Economic models were failing to tackle the issues of poverty and inequality and there were increasing calls for sustainable growth with environmental considerations (Bernstein 1973; Hardy *et al.* 2002). Communities were not reaping the full benefits of development and it was felt that they should be consulted in matters that affected their interests. Measures were therefore needed to protect and preserve the environment.

One noteworthy development at this time was the United Nations Conference on the Human Environment held in Stockholm in 1972, which resulted in the viewpoint being taken that the environment and development were compatible (Page and Connell 2006). In March 1980, the publication of the World Conservation Strategy further promoted the idea of sustainable development (Bramwell and Lane 1993; Hall and Lew 1998). The World Conservation Strategy emphasised the notion of fusing conservation with development: ensuring fundamental human needs were fulfilled; protecting invaluable species, ecosystems and ecological processes; and ensuring fairness, social justice and cultural diversity (International Union for the Conservation of Nature and Natural Resources 1980). With the publishing of the World Conservation Strategy, sustainability was now a major talking concept in the international arena, uniting the concerns of the conservationists with the aims of developers (Bramwell and Lane 1993).

Sustainability accrued large support because it sought to strike a balance between the environmental, social and economic aspects of development (Coccossis 1996). Economic sustainability refers to creating prosperity for all levels of society and focusing on the costs and benefits of these economic activities. Social sustainability refers to protecting the rights of individuals and ensuring equal opportunities for all, and environmental sustainability pertains to protecting and managing our renewable and, especially, non-renewable resources to ensure continuity for future generations. It reinforces the viewpoint that economic growth and environmental development can work hand in hand (Pezzey 1992) – economic development cannot be considered in isolation from the concerns of the environment and society; as they share a mutually dependent relationship.

The concept was later defined further: the most renowned and widely used definition of sustainable development originated from the Brundtland Report, which defined sustainable development as 'meeting the needs of the present without compromising the ability of future generations to meet their own needs' (World Commission on Environment and Development 1987: 43). In this report the term 'sustainable development' was first used to merge the two conflicting concepts of economic growth and environmental conservation (Hardy and Beeton 2001; Altinay and Hussain 2005); it brought public attention to a debate from many years before (Miller and Twining-Ward 2005; Choi and Sirakaya 2006; Cole 2006).

Sustainable development rests on the fundamental principles of futurity, equity and holism, as identified by Sharpley's (2000) model of sustainable development in Table 3.1. Futurity denotes that sustainable development is a long-run process of change, where short and medium-run targets are set in accomplishing this long-run goal. Equity is concerned with ensuring that all people, especially the poor, get a fair share of resources. There are two main types of equity: inter-generational and intra-generational. The former is concerned with the current generation using resources in such a manner that they are maintained or enhanced for use by future generations – that is, fairness between present and future members of society. The latter, on the other hand, focuses on the community sharing equitably in the costs and benefits, with the winners compensating the losers – that is, fairness between the members of the current society (Collins 1999). Holism implies that sustainable development can only become a reality if it takes into consideration the global, political, socioeconomic and ecological contexts (Sharpley 2000).

Sustainable development is of course an amorphous concept which can be fashioned to fit a variety of perspectives, and is not without its problems with respect to its definition, its complexity and its attempt to cover a wide scope of interests (Bramwell and Lane 2000; Saarinen 2006). It has been criticised for being vague, contradictory and subject to various interpretations by different groups, with some regarding the term as an oxymoron (Sharpley 2000). In pursuing sustainable development policies, differing conditions have to be considered, such as stages of economic development, management objectives, ethical considerations and host population concerns. This allows for a wide variety of applicability to different settings according to the circumstances presented. Sustainable development is therefore a 'moving' goal (Lee 2001: 315).

Despite these shortcomings, sustainable development has acted as a mechanism through which the numerous stakeholders can cooperate, negotiate and reflect on their actions and impacts on the environment (Saarinen 2006). Therefore it is invaluable. The principles of sustainable development have been applied to many businesses, with tourism no exception. Tourism's interest in sustainable development is understandable and logical, since what tourism sells is the environment (Murphy and Price 2005). The response from the tourism industry has been to

Table 3.1 A model of sustainable development: principles and objectives

Fundamental principles	Holistic approach: development and environmental issues integrated within a global social Futurity: focus on long-term capacity for continuance of the global eco-system Equity: development that is fair and equitable and which provides opportunities for access to and use of resources for all members of all societies both in the present and future
Developmental objectives	Improvement of the quality of life for all people: education, life expectancy, opportunities to fulfil potential Satisfaction of basic needs; concentration on the nature of what is provided rather than income Self-reliance: political freedom and local decision making for local needs Endogenous development
Sustainability objectives	Sustainable population levels Minimal depletion of non-renewable natural resources Sustainable use of renewable resources Pollution emissions within the assimilative capacity of the environment
Requirements for sustainable development	Adoption of a new social paradigm relevant to sustainable living International and national political and economic systems dedicated to equitable development and resource use Technological systems that can search continuously for new solutions to environmental problems Global alliance facilitating integrated development policies at local national and international levels

Source: Sharpley 2000: 8.

incorporate the principles of sustainable development into tourism policy planning and delivery. According to Butler (1999: 8), 'if there is a single factor that has the potential to change the nature of tourism more than any other it is the introduction of the concept of sustainable development'. This quote is still pertinent today.

Sustainable tourism

In the late 1980s and early 1990s, tourism professionals began considering the implications of sustainable development for tourism (Berno and Bricker 2001). Today the concept is widely researched, with policy and research approaches focusing on various topics, including historical development (Hall and Lew 1998), framework for progression of sustainable tourism (Clarke 1997), definitional issues (Hunter 1995, 1997; Butler 1999; Garrod and Fyall 1998; Sharpley 2000), differing interpretations (Hunter 1995; 1997; Coccossis 1996), conceptual and operational progression of sustainable tourism (Hardy *et al.* 2002), principles of sustainable tourism and policy perspectives (UNWTO 2005), consumer awareness and practices for responsible tourism (Harrison and Husbands 1996), eco-tourism and protected areas (Agardy 1993; Ceballos-Lascuráin 1996; Farrell and Marion 2002), rural tourism development (Hetherington 1991; Sharpley and Sharpley 1997; Wilson *et al.* 2001), parks and green spaces (Mertes and Hall 1995), the adverse ecological effects of nature tourism (Lindberg 1991) and indicator development and monitoring (UNWTO 2004a; Miller and Twining-Ward 2005; 2006).

Clarke (1997) proposed a framework that identified four positions – polar opposites, continuum, movement and convergence – on how sustainable tourism has grown and continues to be interpreted by the tourism industry. Polar opposites was the earliest view held, in which sustainable tourism and mass tourism were seen to be conflicting, because mass tourism was seen as bad whilst small-scale tourism was viewed as good. In the 1990s this position was denounced and one of continuum was adopted, after it was realised that small-scale tourism had the capacity to grow into mass tourism if not properly managed. This led to the third position of movement, in which mass tourism was no longer seen as bad but rather as something that can be developed into more sustainable forms of tourism. The last position in the framework was convergence, in which the current understanding of sustainable tourism is 'a goal that all tourism regardless of scale must strive to achieve' (Clarke 1997: 229). The research completed by Clarke (1997) demonstrated how the concept of sustainable tourism shifted from its early popularisation to our understanding of it today. Another dimension, the perception of scale, was added to Clarke's (1997) framework by Hardy and Beeton (2001). These researchers observed that sustainable tourism has changed over time and can now be applied to a variety of landscapes and settings in different contexts and different scales of operations.

In the tourism literature there have been two main streams of approach to defining sustainable tourism. The first stream has defined sustainable tourism as a very sector-specific, tourism-centric approach. These types of definitions are very inward-looking and are centred on tourism maintaining its business viability over a period of time (Miller and Twining-Ward 2005). They are usually tailored to meet the needs of conservationists, governments, communities and developers (Page and Connell 2006), with sustainable tourism viewed as separate from sustainable development. Hunter (1995, 1997) argued that this view limits our understanding of the scope and scale of resources used in tourism and is unsuccessful in identifying the links that exist between tourism and other activities. Moreover, in defining sustainable tourism, additional information is necessary to determine what is an acceptable limit for tourism – exactly what should be sustained for whom, for how long, and under what conditions (Berno and Bricker 2001; McCool and Lime 2001; Liu 2003).

The second approach seeks to define sustainable tourism in terms of a broader multi-sectoral context, whereby sustainable tourism is viewed in light of its parental paradigm, sustainable development (Hunter 1995, 1997; Collins 1999; Sharpley 2000; Sheldon *et al.* 2005). Hunter (1995: 156) termed this 'an extra-parochial contributory sense'. This approach speaks of recognising and mitigating tourism's impacts as part of achieving the bigger goal of sustainable development.

Tourism is not the only user of resources in an area; therefore, it should complement other resource users at the destination (Butler 1999).

The above discussion displays the diversity and complexity of this subject. Defining sustainable tourism has therefore become 'something of a cottage industry' (Garrod and Fyall 1998: 199) and today the concept is still unclear, despite the numerous definitions which can be found in the literature (Farsari *et al.* 2007). This lack of a widely accepted definition has led to confusion about what sustainable tourism truly means (Swarbrooke 1999), and this vagueness is most often attributed to the failure to implement sustainable tourism for destinations (Ioannides 2001; Ko 2005; Choi and Sirakaya 2006; Farsari *et al.* 2007).

One can elaborate extensively on the numerous definitions of sustainable tourism, but the important point to note is that despite varying interpretations, there are certain fundamental features and commonalities in these definitions. They encourage an understanding of tourism's impacts on the natural, cultural, human and economic environment. They also stress that in developing and maintaining tourism, one must ensure that tourism does not damage the natural and built environment and must make sustainable use of environmental resources. Sustainable tourism should also be economically efficient in reducing over-consumption and waste. It should generate employment and bring benefits to the local economy. Tourism should be aligned to the cultures and values of people affected by it and involve the host community in its development. It should be integrated into overall destination planning, with continuous research, monitoring and implementation, and should provide benefits for all members of society. All of these commonalities in the definitions underpin the notion that the economic viability of a destination should be ensured without sacrificing the natural and socio-cultural environments.

However, in adopting this multi-sectoral perspective, some challenges still exist, since some researchers view sustainable tourism as needing to strike a balance between these three elements (economic, environmental and socio-cultural) in order for tourism to be considered sustainable. One example of this is Müller's (1994) magic pentagon, which states that an ideal situation will exist when a balance is reached amongst the following elements, which all carry equal weight: economic health, wellbeing of the locals, unspoilt nature, protection of resources, healthy culture and optimum satisfaction of guest requirements. According to Müller (1994), harmony must be established within this magic pentagon in order to maximise benefits and minimise costs.

Finding this balance between the economic, environmental and socio-cultural resources of a destination whilst competing for international tourism arrivals has become a leading challenge and a preoccupation for destinations worldwide (Organisation of American States 1997). Other conceptualisations of sustainable tourism discussed by researchers such as Hunter (1997), Garrod and Fyall (1998) and Weaver (2006) offer a spectrum of interpretations of sustainable tourism, ranging from very weak to very strong. Economic sustainability was viewed as a very weak interpretation, whilst a very strong interpretation places precedence on the natural environment (Hunter 1997; Garrod and Fyall 1998).

Striking this balance has always been a vital component of sustainable tourism; however, efforts to achieve it fail to take account of the reality in that in everyday life, trade-offs do take place. Likewise, Teo (2002) argued that exactly what is required to achieve this balance has never been investigated in the tourism literature and it is often assumed that tourism development is in a state of imbalance, which must be resolved.

The aim of achieving this acceptable balance between economic, environmental, social and cultural elements is idealistic, since in any tactical and strategic operation, trade-offs must take place in favour of one or more aspects of sustainability (Collins 1999; McCool and Lime 2001). As Hjalager (1996) rightly points out, balance is easily said but not easily done. Johnston and Tyrell (2005) argue that it is doubtful whether all the elements of sustainable tourism can be sustained concurrently. Moreover, there is a growing amount of literature which states that achieving sustainable tourism is a utopian goal and a concept that lacks integrity (Hardy and Beeton 2001). This supports the view that sustainable tourism may never be truly achieved, but destinations can work towards becoming more sustainable. Opportunity costs do exist and all elements cannot be necessarily sustained simultaneously.

Furthermore, some of the literature discusses the notion of limits being inherent to the concept (Butler 1999; Hardy and Beeton 2001), whereas others have argued against such limits (Johnston and Tyrell 2005). Rather than focusing on restricting growth, the issues one should concentrate on are implementing policy and prescriptions to make sustainable tourism a working reality. If progressive action is not taken, negative outcomes could be near at hand, with the result being the end of the tourism industry.

Gilbert *et al.* (1998) recognised that the environmental degradation of a tourism destination ultimately results in this destination losing its drawing power. This translates into declining tourism revenues, and if returns decrease then the compelling force for sustaining and developing the community is lost. Likewise, the sustainable tourism agenda will only be a triumph if the stakeholders involved can gain a profit through pursuing sustainable tourism (Organisation of American States 1997). Realistically, unless the doctrine of sustainable tourism becomes integrated with a 'business model' it appears questionable that it will have any worthwhile value or benefits (Sheldon *et al.* 2005: 56).

Sustainable tourism, as demonstrated, is plagued with many shortcomings and has been the source of many arguments in the literature. Despite these problems, the concept has provided a unified platform where tourism stakeholders can 'interact, negotiate and reflect on their actions' consequences for the environment' (Saarinen 2006: 1124). It is not our purpose to labour over these disputes; rather, we acknowledge that they do exist, but concentrate on a more pragmatic perspective of the concept. Swarbrooke (1999) criticised academics for being narrow-minded by focusing on defining and debating the concept, with this process only leading to uncertainty amongst stakeholders and not aiding in putting the concept into practical application. Since 1998 Garrod and Fyall have argued for a move away from definition to operationalisation. Some progress has been made; however, a whole lot more is required, and new approaches are needed if the industry is to confront the mammoth challenges ahead.

A key point to note is that sustainable tourism is an approach to tourism management. It is not the only way that tourism can be developed – other options are available – but it is hailed as the best approach to adopt in tourism planning, since it is seeking to ensure that the foundation of the tourism industry is maintained for the future. It is agreed that further discussions and research are required to assign a widely accepted meaning to sustainable tourism, but operationalising of the concept is needed (Butler 1999). Discussing sustainability is simple; implementation is difficult: therefore efforts must be made to avoid sustainable tourism becoming an empty cliché.

For this purpose of this book, sustainable tourism will be seen as a positive, comprehensive and integrated approach to tourism development which involves resource management and working together with stakeholders for the long-term viability and quality of the social, economic and environmental resources (Prosser 1994; Hunter 1997; Murphy and Price 2005; Miller and Twining-Ward 2005; Ayuso 2007). It is about conservation and managing change to support a bright, prosperous and long-term tourism future (Swarbrooke 1999). Sustainable tourism will be considered a process moving towards fulfilling the larger goal of sustainable development. It should therefore seek to integrate tourism into a balanced relationship with wider economic and conservation goals (Mycoo 2006) and stress that tourism should be viewed in a holistic manner and developed to become part of the natural, social, cultural and human environment. Achieving sustainable tourism is not an end goal, but rather should be seen as a progressing one that changes as the tourism system changes, and which all destinations must aspire to achieve (Lee 2001; Swarbrooke 1999).

The plethora of literature that exists on sustainable tourism has failed to acknowledge technology as a means of mitigating tourism's negative impacts. Destination managers are charged with the task of making their respective destinations profitable entities. This will depend heavily on well-maintained and conserved primary resources. There has been a paradigm shift towards sustainable tourism development in which stakeholders are becoming involved and sustainability is being embedded in the creation, distribution and delivery of the tourism product (Gilbert *et al.* 1998; United Nations Environment Programme 2003). Destinations can become commercially viable entities by adopting an environmental approach to managing their destinations in which they contribute positively to conserving and adding to the environment in which they operate. Careful policies, remedies, business strategies and management tools are required to sustain tourism's resource base, which has already been despoiled and will continue to be degraded as a result of the promise of quick returns.

Managing sustainable tourism

This section will provide a discussion of the main concepts and tools used by destinations in achieving sustainable tourism development. 'A concept is an idea of how to achieve sustainability' (Schianetz *et al.* 2007: 372), whereas a tool/mechanism is something that is used to implement the concept. Table 3.2 identifies the main concepts and their primary objectives in sustainable tourism. This is followed by a discussion of the current tools/mechanisms that are used. It should be noted that the terms tools, mechanisms and instruments will be used interchangeably for stylistic reasons.

Visitor management techniques

Specific techniques known as visitor management techniques have to be used when carrying capacity is determined to be reaching its threshold (Mason 2005) in order to monitor visitor flows and control tourist numbers (Page and Connell 2006). Some of these techniques include queues, reservations, pricing, timed entry, zoning permits and setting up of protected areas. Queues, reservations, lottery pricing, permits and timed entry are used to control visitors by limiting their numbers or dispersing them throughout the year. The revenue accrued from pricing can be used for preservation and upkeep of the site (Organisation of American States 1997; Swarbrooke 1999). Permits are used to control visitor demand and have been used at national parks as well as mass tourism exhibitions and tourism sites in Italy and Britain (Beeton and Benfield 2002). Zoning limits visitor access to specific areas and allows the area to be used for diverse recreation opportunities (Lawson 2006). The setting up of designated protected areas worldwide aims to prevent degradation of natural resources and also ensures that economic benefits continue to be accrued (Mason 2005). In addition to these visitor management techniques, several alternatives to carrying capacity have been developed.

Alternatives to carrying capacity

McCool and Lime (2001) proposed alternative approaches to tourism carrying capacity by using planning frameworks that focus on sustaining social and biophysical resources rather than setting limits to tourist numbers. These frameworks are: limits of acceptable change (LAC), visitor impact management (VIM), visitor experience and resource protection (VERP), environmental impact assessment (EIA) and cumulative effects assessment (CEA). These are briefly discussed below.

LAC is a planning procedure designed for recreation settings based on how much change is acceptable to managers and users (Wright 1998; Simón *et al.* 2004; Murphy and Price 2005). This decision is arrived at after a series of sequential steps that define the conditions desired at a destination, the level of change considered reasonable and the management actions required to maintain or reinstate these acceptable conditions (see Stankey *et al.* 1985; Wright 1998). LAC differs from carrying capacity in that it does not look at establishing a particular number as the limit, but rather looks at the conditions required in the area (Stankey *et al.* 1985; Ahn *et al.* 2002). LAC has been applied to Calhoun County, Texas (Ahn *et al.* 2002), Wet Tropics World Heritage Area in Australia (Page 2003) and Kangaroo Island in Australia.

Table 3.2 Concepts for managing sustainable tourism development

Concepts	*Definition*	*Main objectives in tourism*
Carrying capacity	'The number of visitors that a destination is able to absorb without damage to the environment community or visitor experience' (United Nations Environment Programme 2003: 20)	Prevention of environmental degradation caused by excessive tourist numbers
Government intervention	A central authority takes mandatory measures to reduce environmental degradation (Gilbert *et al.* 1998)	Pollution prevention and control
Economic approach	Instruments such as taxes and financial incentives are used to persuade tourism businesses to engage in more sustainable activities	Pollution prevention and control and the encouragement of sustainable practices
Self-regulation	Tourism industry taking responsibility for its own action	Pollution prevention and control and the encouragement of sustainable practices
Education	Educating the tourist on developing and displaying more sustainable behaviours at the destination	Encouraging sustainable consumption patterns by educating the tourists to see the effects of their actions on the environment and to modify their behaviour
Monitoring	Regular assessment of an issue with regards to specific goals objectives and expectations set based on this issue (Miller and Twining-Ward 2006)	Provide a clear measurement of progress updated information and enhanced knowledge to assist in the movement from sustainable tourism theory to practice
Marketing and information services	Destinations market segment in order to attract the types of tourists they want	Promote particular forms of tourism, influence tourists' behaviour, promote product offerings and reduce seasonality by promoting off-season opportunities
Environmental management	'Process of decision making about the allocation of natural and artificial resources that will make optimum use of the environment to satisfy at least basic human needs for an indefinite period of time and where possible to improve environmental quality' (Barrow 2006: 164)	Environmental objectives are integrated into the tourism policy and planning

Table 3.2 Continued

Concepts	*Definition*	*Main objectives in tourism*
Cleaner production	'The continuous application of an integrated preventive environmental strategy to processes products and services to increase overall efficiency and reduce risks to humans and the environment' (United Nations Environment Programme 2006: 3)	Pollution and prevention control

VIM, on the other hand, uses a sequential process which aims to reduce or control the impacts that threaten the quality of outdoor recreation tourism areas and experiences. It requires two separate elements: description (of the relationships between specific conditions and use and the impacts associated with these conditions) and evaluation (of the acceptability of various impacts). The VIM planning process helps to address three issues inherent to impact management: problem identification; determination of potential causal factors that affect the occurrence; and severity of unacceptable impacts and selection of potential management strategies to address these unacceptable conditions (Wright 1998). VIM has been used on Prince Edward Island, Canada and in Vera Cruz, Mexico (Page 2003).

VERP is a management tool that focuses on desired ecological and social conditions rather than on visitor numbers, and provides a logical process for managing carrying capacity at national parks. In this respect it is similar to LAC and VIM, since it involves public consultation and maintains that management goals should be translated into objectives through the use of indicators and standards (Wright 1998). However, VERP differs from LAC and VIM in that its use is intended solely for parks rather than wilderness areas, with modification needed for its use outside the park setting (Wright 1998).

EIA provides useful information about impacts of proposed environmental developments (United Nations Environment Programme/United Nations World Tourism Organisation 2005). It has been used as a planning tool in projects for some years, determining the approach to sustainability by assessing whether a project's perceived economic benefits are aligned with the environmental, social and cultural consequences (Wright 1998). EIA has been defined as:

> a process which attempts to identify and predict impacts of legislative proposals, policies, programs, projects and operational procedures on the bio-geophysical environment and on human health and well-being. It also interprets and communicates information about those and investigates and proposes means for their management.
>
> (Canadian Environmental Assessment Research Council 1988: 1)

Little has been discussed in the literature regarding how EIA should be conducted for tourism. It can be a useful tool in tourism planning (Simpson and Wall 1999; Barrow 2006), however, since it accounts for impacts at all stages of a proposed development and considers alternative development options (United Nations Environment Programme/United Nations World Tourism Organisation 2005).

Lastly, CEA is 'an assessment of the incremental effects of an action on the environment when the effects are combined with those from other past existing and future actions' (Hegmann *et al.* 1999: 10). CEA has been used in tourism because of the different sizes and diversity of tourism developments. It is 'holistic and integrative' (Wright 1998: 81).

Sustainability indicators

The use of indicators has existed for a long time and has been generally used to guide decision-making (Li 2004). Numerous governmental, non-governmental and international organisations such as the European Environment Agency, European Union, Organisation for Economic Co-operation and Development, United Nations Development Programme, United Nations Environment Programme, United Nations World Tourism Organisation and The World Bank have all taken steps to develop indicators (Miller 2001; Rebollo and Baidal 2003; Choi and Sirakaya 2006). Some of these indicators include population growth rate, gross domestic product and trade balance (Li 2004).

Indicator development has been identified as an integral part of destination planning and management in promoting sustainable tourism development at all levels of a destination. In the tourism literature there has been widespread discussion of the use of indicators for better monitoring of the tourism system and progressing the goal of sustainable tourism (see Ceron and Dubois 2003; Choi and Sirakaya 2006; Miller 2001; United Nations World Tourism Organisation 2004a; Miller and Twining-Ward 2005).

Dubois (2005: 141) defined an indicator as 'a variable which can take a certain number of values (statistical) or states (qualitative) according to circumstances (temporal, spatial)'. Indicators for sustainable tourism are 'measures of the existence or severity of current issues, signals of upcoming situations or problems, measures of risk and potential need for action and means to identify and measure the results of our actions' (United Nations World Tourism Organisation 2004a: 8). The development of indicators is not new to tourism, with the industry having recorded its economic performance for many years, but its application to sustainability is growing (Miller and Twining-Ward 2006).

In this realm, indicators are used to monitor, measure and analyse changes and resultant impacts on the tourism system (Weaver 2006). Additionally, indicators can assist destinations in determining their sustainable tourism objectives, establish and track progress and prioritise for the future (McCool and Lime 2001; Miller and Twining-Ward 2006). They can be used for baseline assessment of a condition or need-target setting for policies and actions, assessment of actions and evaluation review and modification of policies (United Nations Environment Programme/United Nations World Tourism Organisation 2005). Indicators are intended to provide information in a straightforward, numerical and easy to understand format (Choi and Sirakaya 2006). For tourism, the best indicators are those that respond to threats regarding sustainability (United Nations World Tourism Organisation 2004a).

The United Nations World Tourism Organisation has led the way and defined a new approach to indicator development (Miller and Twining-Ward 2005). In 2004 the United Nations World Tourism Organisation produced a comprehensive guidebook to help tourism managers develop the most appropriate indicators for their respective destinations. Instead of core indicators or ecosystem-specific indicators, a set of twelve baseline issues and twenty related indicators were suggested. The baseline issues and indicators were considered the most common and suitable for almost all destinations allowing for international comparison. Including the baseline issues, United Nations World Tourism Organisation (2004a) developed a total of nearly fifty issues each, with ten to fifteen sub-issues and twenty-five suggested indicators applied to eighteen different types of destinations, from small islands to theme parks. This provided an immense and rather overwhelming monitoring resource of more than one thousand potential indicators. This 2004 guidebook described the issues and indicators in much more detail than previously existed and included a number of practical examples of implementation (Miller and Twining-Ward 2005).

In line with United Nations World Tourism Organisation's (2004a) guidebook, Miller and Twining-Ward (2005) produced a book that discussed the history and development of indicator and monitoring systems for sustainable tourism development. This text investigated the reasons for public and private sector adoption of sustainable tourism policies and how indicators and monitoring could help this goal be achieved. It also looked at the principles and techniques involved in indicator development, as well as providing case studies of indicators in action.

Sustainability indicators are now being actively pursued in tourism as a measure to deal with sustainable tourism. The literature demonstrates a variety of approaches to the use of indicators for sustainable tourism development. For example, Lozano-Oyola *et al.* (2012) provided an indicator system for the evaluation of sustainable tourism at cultural destinations, Park and Yoon (2011) developed indicators for the measurement of sustainable rural tourism, Choi and Sirakaya (2006) focused on indicators for community tourism, Miller (2001) established indicators that tourists could use in the selection of their holidays, Li (2004) developed indicators based on the Pressure–State–Response Model for Tianmushan Nature Reserve in China and Ioris *et al.* (2008) designed and applied indicators for water management in Brazil and Scotland.

Indicator development is not without its pitfalls. Despite its perceived benefits, several researchers have criticised the development and use of indicators for sustainable tourism development. These criticisms include difficulties in assessment, scale, interpretation, proper selection and adequate measurements, as well as the accusation that they are costly and time consuming (Miller 2001; Hughes 2002;

Dubois 2005; Miller and Twining-Ward 2006; Choi and Sirakaya 2006). Indicators are not a solution, nor can they alone create a tourism that is more sustainable (Ceron and Dubois 2003). They do, however, provide valuable information to encourage informed decision-making and aid destination managers in developing and implementing action plans and increasing the general level of awareness of sustainable tourism (Miller and Twining-Ward 2006).

Certification, accreditation and eco-labelling

Certification is a process which ensures that there are some bases or principles which organisations can conform to in order to ensure they meet certain requirements or standards (Font 2005; United Nations Environment Programme/United Nations World Tourism Organisation 2005). It is described as a voluntary procedure which accesses, monitors and gives written assurance that a business, product, process, service or management system conforms to specific requirements (Honey and Rome 2001). The certification process can be implemented by a national, regional or international certification body that sets the standards and assesses the organisations (see Font 2005: 213–214). This process ensures continuous improvement of tourism and preservation and protection of the environment (United Nations Environment Programme 2003). Accreditation, on the other hand, ensures that the 'third party' providing the certification operates according to the highest standards and 'guarantees [...] the competency of certification programmes and the validity of the standards they work to' (Font *et al.* 2003: 213).

Most certification criteria are based on Agenda 21 (United Nations World Tourism Organisation 1996) and ISO 14001 (www.iso14000-iso14001-environmental-management.com). They include the minimum acceptable criteria for reducing, re-using and recycling waste, energy, efficiency, conservation, sustainable purchasing and consumption patterns, social and cultural development, efficient hazardous waste disposal, transportation policies, land use planning and management and protection of environmental/natural/historic sites (Mycoo 2006). An example of a certification programme currently in operation is ISO 14001, an international certification for all sectors that sets standards for an environmental management system. Being a global scheme, each country has a body that has been accredited to audit and certify local businesses with the ISO standard (Bambrook and Murphy 2008).

The end result of certification is a marketable logo/seal, which identifies that a minimum standard has been met or exceeded (Font 2005). This logo/seal is commonly known as an eco-label. Certification can therefore be seen as the process and the eco-label the product. Mihalic (1998: 33) defined eco-labels as 'an effective market-based instrument capable of reducing the negative impacts of tourism products, production methods, services and processes on the environment whilst at the same time improving the environmental quality of tourism places'. The principal aims of these eco-labels are to minimise the negative impacts of tourism and continuously enhance the quality and image of a destination (Sasidharan *et al.*

2002). They bestow upon a destination, or tourism businesses at a destination, a sign of approval, showing that it has reached and is maintaining a certain environmental approach (Nair *et al.* 2003). This increases tourist satisfaction, gives a destination a competitive advantage (Kozak and Nield 2004) and serves as a benchmark for tourism operators (United Nations Environment Programme 2003).

Eco-labels tend to vary in scale, activity, content, context and organisation (Buckley 2001; Kozak and Nield 2004). Today there are numerous eco-labels (over 100), with no single one having worldwide acceptance. Some of the more popular ones include Destination 21 Denmark, Green Globe Worldwide, Nature and Ecotourism Accreditation Programme Australia and Blue Flag Worldwide.

Awards

Awards are usually presented to tourism businesses by some recognising body as a reward for their efforts in becoming more sustainable. The receipt and recognition of receiving awards are both important since, in competing for these awards, destinations are showing that they are trying to be more sustainable. Even though the competition may be useful in getting establishments to be more environmentally friendly, Mihalic (2000) argued most of these awards are not objective and lack transparency and credibility, therefore rendering judging of environmental quality difficult. She observed that awards are an excellent starting point and promote a good image for the destination, but a more co-ordinated systematic approach is needed.

Legislation, regulation and licensing

Legislation, regulation and licensing can be used by a government authority to aid in sustainable tourism development by ensuring requirements are complied with and enforcing penalties if they are not. Legislation gives the authority to enforce requirements which are defined and elaborated by regulations and is a process of checking and showing compliance with imposed regulations, standards or permissions (United Nations Environment Programme/United Nations World Tourism Organisation 2005).

An example of this is land use planning and development control. This can be used to shape the type and location of tourism development and prevent unnecessary or harmful developments from occurring. Land use planning includes integrated area management and zoning for tourism development. Other command and control mechanisms used are public regulation and effluent and emissions standards, among other techniques.

Taxes

Tourist taxes can be used in two primary ways for sustainable tourism development: to reduce demand and by channelling the generated tax revenues into destination maintenance and development (Swarbrooke 1999). The European Commission has supported taxes since they bring compliance into line with the

'Polluter Pays Principle' (Palmer-Tous *et al.* 2007). Taxes can be levied on a tourism business, on the tourist or on the resources, such as an effluent or waste charge (United Nations Environment Programme/United Nations World Tourism Organisation 2005). Tourist taxes can be important in sustainable tourism development if they change the tourists' behaviour to the benefit of the environment (Palmer-Tous *et al.* 2007). In addition to being an economic instrument, tourist taxes can be a visitor management technique, since they can be used to influence demand.

This technique, however, has its disadvantages, with Swarbrooke (1999: 13) identifying several issues about using tourist taxes. These include tourist discrimination, lack of information about tourists' willingness to pay, the suggestion that the complex and costly mechanism required for tax implementation may not lead to responsible behaviour, constant variation of taxes due to seasonality and, based on the limitations of carrying capacity, the question of how taxes can be used to influence demand if the right 'limit' is not truly known. Taxes can also be used in a different manner, whereby tax incentives can be given to organisations engaging in sustainable tourism development projects or being proactive in environmental stewardship. For example, the UK government has recently increased the air passenger duty tax by eight per cent, leading to an increase in air fares.

Codes of conduct

Agenda 21 established the development, adoption and implementation of codes of conduct (COC) by industries as a main priority for reaching goals of sustainable development (UNWTO 1996). COC in tourism act as guidelines for the industry's operations within non-statutory requirements. They are public statements that demonstrate a commitment to sustainability (Ayuso 2007). These codes are not enforced, nor are they enforceable. There are different types of codes and these can range from the general tourism industry that address specific sectors and activities, for tourists and the host populations (Mihalic 2000; Mason 2003). Tourists are generally the largest audience for COC, since it is hoped that these codes will modify their behaviour and hence reduce their perceived negative impacts (Mason 2003; Cole 2007). COC also exercise control and provide useful guidance to different stakeholder groups (United Nations Environment Programme/United Nations World Tourism Organisation 2005).

There are various reasons for adopting COC in tourism. They serve as a vehicle of communication between government agencies, industry sectors, community interests and environmental and cultural stakeholders (Mason 2003; Cole 2007). COC also generate awareness within the industry and governments of the importance of sound environmental policies and management, and encourage them to promote a quality environment and a sustainable industry (Mason 2003). They increase awareness among international and domestic visitors of the importance of respecting both natural and cultural environments (Cole 2007). Moreover, the use of COC can help to sensitise the host population to the importance of environmental protection and host–guest relationships and encourage co-operation among industry sectors and government agencies, host communities and non-governmental organisations to achieve the goals of sustainability. The adoption of codes can result in improvements to the natural environment and the sustainability of the tourism industry. It can lead to an improved image for the destination, attract tourists who are seeking environmentally responsible forms of tourism, reduce costs because of more environmentally efficient practices and lead to an improved quality of life for the host community.

Some notable examples of COC are Agenda 21 for the Tourist and Travel Industry (United Nations World Tourism Organisation 1996), the United Nations World Tourism Organisation's Global Code of Ethics for Tourism (United Nations World Tourism Organisation 2001), and World Travel and Tourism Council's Corporate Social Leadership in Tourism (World Travel and Tourism Council 2003).

COC appear to be impressive, but they have their flaws (Mason 2003). Very few attempts have been made to evaluate the effectiveness of codes, and Cole (2007) found that the implementation of a tourist code in Ngadha, Indonesia was found to be neither cheap nor easy. Wheeller (1994: 651) describes COC as 'laughable' and 'futile' and questions their true effectiveness. The processes by which COC are produced have been criticised, since they are usually developed by concerned groups and do not involve a larger public consultation (Sirakaya 1997). They do not really offer any great benefit because they present limited value for decision-making and action, they cannot direct environmental action or determine the nature of it, and there are too many of them in existence (Cole 2007). Codes are usually poorly implemented and hardly monitored for progress and corrective action. Therefore better co-ordination is needed, since any one destination can have several COCs for different groups with diverse aims (Mason and Mowforth 1996).

De-marketing

Another tool that has been used to manage sustainable tourism at the destination level is de-marketing. De-marketing is defined as 'that aspect of marketing that deals with discouraging customers in general or a certain class of customers in particular on a temporary or permanent basis' (Kotler and Levy 1971: 75). These researchers discussed three types of de-marketing: general de-marketing, where there is a desire to reduce the total level of demand; selective de-marketing, where demand from a certain market segment is decreased; and ostensible marketing, where there is an appearance of reduced demand as a result of scarcity but this in turn generates greater demand for the desired product.

With reference to sustainable tourism, de-marketing is also an action strategy aimed at dissuading tourists from visiting a destination (Gunn and Var 2002). Reducing the total level of demand can be aligned to the visitor management techniques discussed earlier. Effective market segmentation can be a key tool for sustainable tourism (Kastenholz 2004). If destinations identify the right segments that they want to attract then a 'destination-fit' can be achieved, which leads to the long-term goal of sustainable tourism.

De-marketing has not been actively pursued in tourism as a means of reducing demand and controlling supply, but this approach can be used as a part of a destination's marketing mix to allow the destination to achieve its strategic objectives (Beeton and Benfield 2002). De-marketing has been used in Italy at the site of The Last Supper (1495–97), at Sissinghurst Castle Garden in Kent, England and at Wilsons Promontory National Park, Victoria, Australia (Beeton and Benfield 2002).

Destinations

So far we have discussed sustainable development, sustainable tourism and the tools/mechanism used for managing these complex phenomena. Our discussion now focuses on defining what we consider to be a destination, destination management, destination management organisations and a destination manager. Setting this scope is important as we progress to understanding destinations' uses of technology for sustainable tourism and the technologies of which they may avail themselves.

Destinations can be regarded as any well-defined geographical area, such as a continent, a region, a country, a town or an attraction (Youell 1998; Hall 2000; Ritchie and Crouch 2003; Sainaghi 2006; Tourism Sustainability Group 2007), or a perceptual concept construed by the tourist, such as a cruise ship (Buhalis 2000). They are an important symbol and a means of attracting tourists (Ko 2005; Tsaur *et al.* 2006). They are considered 'away-from-home' places (Ryan and Cave 2005) where people travel to enjoy the products and services (such as accommodation, attractions, events and other tourist facilities) that provide different experiences for them to enjoy (Youell 1998; Buhalis 2000; Ritchie and Crouch 2003). These destinations are therefore critical to tourist experiences (Vukonic 1997; Bornhurst *et al.* 2010).

We will define a destination as a physical space/geographical area which contains tourism products and services to be consumed by the tourists as part of the experience and which are managed and marketed by destination authorities/organisations. These destinations hold the attracting power for tourists and are the central point for all the stakeholders in tourism (Carter 2005; Ko 2005), but they are also the areas in which the main tourism impacts (economic, social and environmental) ensue and are felt most powerfully (Murphy 1985; Medlik 2003; Wall and Mathieson 2006). Therefore they are also the places where preventative and remedial measures should be implemented for tourism to be managed in a sustainable manner.

Destinations are therefore vulnerable, complex and problematic interrelated entities (Prosser 1994; Saarinen 2004), where changes in one area result in consequences for other parts (Presenza *et al.* 2005). They present assorted challenges for management, who must cater to a variety of stakeholders – tourists, businesses and local communities (Howie 2003). In these times of uncertainty, increasing competition, easy substitution of destinations by the consumer and change, successful management of destinations will present greater complexity.

There needs to be a coordinated approach to managing a destination, with strategic planning of the component parts maximised to the benefit of stakeholders. An organisation must be established to take this lead for the successful development of a destination (Lebe and Milfelner 2006). The desire to fulfil this need has resulted in the emergence of destination management and destination management organisations.

According to the United Nations World Tourism Organisation (2004b: 3), destination management organisations are the organisations responsible for the management and/or marketing of destinations and generally fall into one of the following categories:

- National Tourism Authorities or Organisations responsible for management and marketing of tourism at a national level.
- Regional provincial or state destination management organisations responsible for the management and/or marketing of tourism in a geographic region defined for that purpose sometimes but not always an administrative or local government region such as a county state or province.
- Local destination management organisations responsible for the management and/or marketing of tourism based on a smaller geographic area or city/town.

Traditionally destination management organisations were thought of as destination marketing organisations (Presenza *et al.* 2005): 'The concept of a destination management organisation where the 'M' emphasises total management rather than simply marketing is a somewhat recent conceptualisation of the organisation function of destination management' (Ritchie and Crouch 2003: 73). The role of destination management organisations is evolving and there is an increasing recognition that it should extend beyond marketing to include other elements that are key to the success of a destination (Presenza *et al.* 2005). From the United Nations World Tourism Organisation's (2004b) definition there appears to be no clear distinction between a destination management organisation and a destination marketing organisation. A clear distinction will be identified between these two, and this text will focus on destination management organisations' management rather than marketing.

Ritchie and Crouch (2003) developed a model of destination competiveness in which several components of destination management were identified. These were: organisation quality of service/experience, information/research, human resource development, finance and venture capital, visitor management, resource stewardship and crisis management. Presenza *et al.* (2005) expanded upon Ritchie and Crouch's (2003) work and categorised the activities of the destination management organisations as falling under two main functions: external destination marketing and internal destination development. The external activities included marketing and promotion, aiding local firms in increasing their competitiveness and producing a competitive advantage for the destination through positioning

(Sainaghi 2006). The internal destination development included all other activities besides marketing and promotion. Destination management organisations are also convenors, since they ensure that various stakeholders' interests are integrated and are working together in a productive and meaningful manner (Carter 2005; Presenza *et al.* 2005). Clearly the operations and functions of a destination management organisation are more than purely marketing and promotion.

A destination management organisation should ensure sustainability for the visitor, the host community, the destination and the industry (Gilbert *et al.* 1998), as environmental quality is critical in attracting and sustaining tourists who are the linchpin of a developing and growing tourism industry. A destination management organisation must promote a tourist destination but at the same time maintain its social, cultural, environmental and economic assets (Werthner and Klein 1999).

Destination management organisations can take different forms, being perhaps a governmental division, a quasi-governmental organisation, a public–private partnership, a non-governmental organisation, a not-for-profit organisation or a private organisation (Youell 1998; Ritchie and Crouch 2003; Presenza *et al.* 2005). Additionally, destination management organisations' revenue can be gained from different sources, such as government (Ritchie and Crouch 2003; Sheehan and Ritchie 2005), tourist taxes and levies, membership fees, advertising and promotional campaigns and commissions for booking conferences (Ritchie and Crouch 2003). All of this collectively demonstrates that the role of a destination management organisation is a daunting one. Carter (2005) states that whilst destination managements have no god-given right to exist, they must endeavour to increase value and achieve higher standards in activities performed by the private sector.

Based on the above definition of a destination and discussion of destination management organisations, the term will be ascribed to an organisation responsible for the holistic management of tourism at the destination level, which encompasses range of tourism development planning and marketing activities and can fall under one of the following categories:

- Continental destination management organisation, responsible for the management of tourism in a continent defined for that purpose.
- Regional destination management organisation – also known as Regional Tourism Organisation – responsible for the management of tourism in a geographic region defined for that purpose.
- National destination management organisation, also known as National tourism organisations, and responsible for management of tourism of a country.
- Local destination management organisation, responsible for the management of tourism based on a smaller geographic area or city/town.
- Local attraction destination management organisation, responsible for the management of tourism based on an attraction or local feature of a geographic area or city/town.

More specifically, destination management organisations are considered the chief management and organising body at a destination because:

- they are established with the main purpose of managing tourism development at a particular destination;
- they adopt an integrated and holistic approach at the destination – that is, a system approach;
- they are usually the primary body responsible for sustainable tourism development in the area;
- they represent the interests of and are an important liaison between all the major stakeholders in tourism development;
- no other destination organisation has the capability to develop strategies to deal with the diversity of stakeholders (Bornhurst *et al.* 2010);
- even though the specific institutional arrangements may vary in countries, almost all destinations have a destination management organisation (Werthner and Klein 1999);
- they are frequently part of government and therefore possess the political, legislative and financial power to manage resources for strategic stakeholder benefit (Buhalis 2000); and
- many destinations have established a destination management organisation to ensure successful leadership management and stewardship (Bornhurst *et al.* 2010).

Destinations exist which are not managed by destination management organisations, as identified above. These destinations may be managed by a government, a Ministry, part of a Ministry, a local body, a private entity, a public–private partnership, or some other type of management arrangement. Additionally, other agencies besides the destination management organisation, such as environmental agencies, may be responsible for managing the sustainable tourism development of a destination and can employ the technologies discussed. However, as destination management organisations are ascribed to be the key body responsible for managing tourism at the destination level, the use of technologies will be viewed from their perspective.

Destination management organisations and technology use

It can be seen that sustainable tourism has progressed a long way since its inception. Several techniques are currently being used by destination management agencies for managing sustainable tourism development. In the discussion of the above tools/mechanisms it can be seen that there has been no mention of technology in the literature as a concept, nor of any technology-based tools/mechanisms for managing sustainable tourism development.

Adopting technology as part of their business strategy can have huge positive implications for destination management organisations. As has been noted, technology has been used primarily for the marketing and promotion of products and services, portraying an image of the destination and communicating their messages to the tourists (Yuan *et al.* 2006). It can also, however, assist them in improving their business processes and facilitating better destination management and planning (Buhalis 2000; Ma *et al.* 2003; Yuan *et al.* 2006). By taking advantage of intranets (internal systems that are accessed by employees), organisations can re-engineer internal processes, whilst extranets can support the development of close relationships with trusted partners, which can lead to online transactions, expansion of the distribution channel and extension of the value chain (Buhalis 2003; Buhalis and Deimezi 2004). The reality today is that if a destination management organisation fails to adopt technology, they are choosing to fail (Buhalis 2003).

In 2004 the United Nations World Tourism Organisation undertook a survey of destination management organisations with regards to technology use. The results of this survey identified that destination management organisations with an eBusiness strategy used ICT mainly for marketing and promotion, information collection, reservation services and product-related activities. Tourism is no newcomer to using technology – it is used by destination management organisations mainly for marketing and promotional activities and enhancing their online presence through bookings and product offerings. Many destinations have engaged with a destination management system (DMS) and have sought to co-ordinate small and medium-sized enterprises and offer their products and services through a one-stop online shop. Destination management organisations have also used ICT for product development. There is no mention, however, of ICT being utilised for sustainable tourism development. Little research exists on the specific applications of the use of ICT for sustainable tourism development; therefore ICT can be seen as a new and innovative approach for sustainable tourism development. By using ICT creatively and imaginatively, destination management organisations can be more transparent in associating a true environmental cost to the tourism product. They can also fill the information gaps that exist with regard to the environmental information needed for proper monitoring and decision-making. They can make 'intelligent use of intelligent systems' (Berkhout and Hertin 2001: 2).

Technology-enabled sustainable destinations

In Chapter 1 the importance of the tourism–environment relationship and the technology-sustainable tourism relationship was discussed and analysed. A destination can be considered sustainable if an appropriate balance is achieved in the environmental, economic and socio-cultural aspects of tourism development (United Nations World Tourism Organisation 2004a; Edgell 2006). Operating a sustainable destination is a weighty challenge for destination managers as they are continuously being tested to develop competitive destinations to increase visitor numbers, to have appealing and innovative product offerings, to provide the necessary infrastructure, superstructure and support systems, to create lasting and memorable experiences for the tourists and to satisfy and to co-ordinate stakeholders' needs. From a destination manager's perspective, the central issue for him/her is making the most optimal decision in terms of resource allocation and ensuring the environment is maintained, preserved and protected. For this to happen the destination manager requires support in the form of timely, concise and accurate information for tourism planning and development, co-operation of stakeholders, mechanisms to solicit and incorporate stakeholder views for the tourism development process, and means of providing and maintaining tourist satisfaction. The use of technology can help destination managers in this process. There are a number of areas in tourism development and management where destination managers can use technology: namely, information management, tourist satisfaction, interpretation, enabling partnerships, community participation and energy consumption.

Destination managers require vast amounts of information for decision-making and long-term planning. Some of these information requirements include business planning, establishing compliance with regulations/standards, product development, partnership identification, quality management and assurance, personnel management, market planning and evaluation, feasibility assessment, investment, monitoring, policy making and evaluation, research problems, communication and extension and identification of core competencies (Carson and Sharma 2002). Fuchs and Höpken (2005) observed that in tourism there is weak use of information for decision-making, and the potential for ICT in supporting tourism managerial decision-making is largely unexplored and unexploited. This can be attributed to the diversity and fragmentation of data sources, resulting in limited access and lack of know-how in relation to data analysis and the most appropriate use of this information.

Tourism as a service industry has both an informational and a physical component. Technology can be used to help destination managers manage this information content with regards to sustainable tourism; they will then be on a better path to ensuring sounder decision-making. Destination managers need to find out if the information they require is available, where it is located, how to gain access to it and determine the form the information exists in, how to make sense of it, and how to store and distribute this information. Moreover, too much information can be overwhelming and confuse the decisions which destination managers have to make.

At the heart of sustainable tourism development lies the process of decision-making, which is focused on the best allocation of resources within a limited period of time that satisfies all stakeholders involved. Not all tourism development is worthwhile and destination managers must be able to effectively sift through the necessary information, make sense of it (develop possible scenarios) and reach a workable decision in a suitable time period. If a destination manager has sound methods of monitoring and analysing environmental data (El-Gayar and Fritz 2006), the routes tourists use, their frequency of use and timings and how tourists account for time, space and place (Lew and McKercher 2005), they can better plan for tourism and make it more sustainable for destinations. ICT can provide 'concise, timely and to-the-point information which is directly usable' for decision-making (United Nations Environment Programme/United Nations World

Tourism Organisation 2005: 9). In short, information is power, and being able to use this information wisely and effectively will definitely be to a destination manager's benefit. Some indicative technologies that can be used to support this are environmental management information systems, geographical information systems, global positioning systems and DMS.

Another important area in which technology can be used is satisfying the tourist. Tourist satisfaction is regarded as critical in whether a tourist returns to a destination or encourages others to visit or not visit. Satisfaction has been found to be a relationship between expectations and experiences. This is the difference between expectations and perceived outcomes (Truong and Foster 2006). It is a subjective concept determined by many influencing factors, such as the safety, security and quality of sites and attractions, accommodation, the cleanliness of a destination, its water quality and the hospitality of the destination. The United Nations World Tourism Organisation (2004a) identified tourism satisfaction as a baseline issue for sustainable tourism development, since sustaining tourism satisfaction is important to whether tourists return to the destination and therefore plays a critical role in influencing the economic environment. One of the most important determining elements of satisfaction is receiving accurate and comprehensive tourist information (Buhalis and O'Connor 2006). Tourists can access information from numerous sources and the Internet has made access to this information easier. Today's tourists expect to have ubiquitous access to information, which is customised to their requirements, and are able to access it through different devices, such as mobile phones, laptops or PDAs (Höpken *et al.* 2008). However, there is a lot of information on the Internet, some of which is poorly organised and unstructured. Tourists can suffer from information overload and thereby may be unable to make the best decisions regarding activities to undertake at the destination in order to maximise their experiences and satisfaction levels. Destination management organisations can provide accurate and updated information to the tourists when and where they need it through the use of ICT. Some of the technologies that can be used in this way are location-based services, intelligent transport systems, virtual tourism, DMS and global positioning systems.

Technology can also be used to assist in the interpretation of a destination. Tilden (1957), one of the earliest commentators on interpretation, suggested that it is an educational process with the primary aim of revealing meanings and relationships. Interpretation has been defined as 'an activity that creates the image that a specific territory and community will disseminate among visitors and that will contribute to community education, pride and sense of place' (World Bank 2006). It informs tourists about the significance of a destination and gives them insights into places at the destination so that they have better enjoyment of it, fostering a positive demeanour towards conservation, preservation, history, culture and landscape (Mason 2005). Interpretation therefore plays an important role in sustainable tourism, as improving visitor experience, knowledge and understanding and helping with the protection and conservation of places and cultures have been identified as the main functions of interpretation with regard to achieving sustainable tourism (Moscardo 2000; Moscardo and Walker 2006). Interpretation can be achieved through a variety of methods, which include, but are not limited to, education, objects, media, signage, trained tour guides, maps and first-hand experiences (Mason 2005). Technology can play and influential role in allowing better interpretation of a destination. This can contribute to sustainable tourism in that tourists are given better information before and during the experience. This can lead to increased tourist satisfaction, as well as protection and preservation of the environment. Some of the technologies which can be used for this are location-based services, virtual tourism and DMS.

One of the critical challenges for tourism is how to plan for and manage an industry that is fragmented and diverse. Bramwell and Lane (2000) commented that some sort of mechanism is required to overcome this fragmentation for tourism to be sustainable. Involving different stakeholders in tourism planning is now being seen as an essential part of the planning process (Swarbrooke 1999; Bramwell and Lane 2000; Hardy and Beeton 2001; Tourism Sustainability Group 2007; Currie *et al.* 2008), since tourism is heavily dependent on effective partnerships (Buhalis and O'Connor 2006), which are linked to its sustainability (Milne and Ateljevic 2001). Developing partnerships and co-operation is a well-documented topic in tourism research (see for example Hall 2000; Bramwell and Lane 2000) and since the 1980s many governments have stressed the importance of partnerships, particularly between the public and private sector, in tourism (Bhat and Milne 2008).

Bramwell and Lane (2000) proposed four ways in which partnerships and collaboration can aid sustainable tourism development. Collaboration might promote greater consideration for natural and socio-cultural resources; it can lead to a more holistic approach to tourism planning and policy making; it may foster a more equitable distribution of costs and benefits and policies which have fairer outcomes; and greater participation of stakeholders can to lead to empowered decision-making and capacity building and promote a sense of ownership amongst stakeholders (Bramwell and Lane 2000). The co-operation and involvement of stakeholders can be connected to stakeholder and collaboration theory. The emergence of ICT allows networks to be created and enhanced (Milne and Ateljevic 2001). The use of ICT enables stakeholders at the destination to become more efficient in their communication strategies and supports greater co-operation in the delivery of tourism products and services (Buhalis and O'Connor 2006). It can enable more pragmatic approaches and change the way sustainability was previously managed at the destination. Destinations can use DMS to aid with this.

Community participation has been identified as a critical issue for sustainable tourism (Bramwell and Sharman 1999; Hardy and Beeton 2001; United Nations World Tourism Organisation 2004a) and has become a crucial aspect of public policy decision-making since the 1960s (Keske and Smutko 2010). There have been many suggestions that tourism should reap benefits for the local community, but limited means of explaining how this can be accomplished (Din 1996). Community-based approaches to tourism are popular as they explicitly describe processes for involving local stakeholders, understanding the tourism development process and participating in decisions about the types, locations and benefits of such proposed developments. Moreover, the increasing recognition of tourism impacts has led to calls for the community to be more involved in tourism development (Feick and Hall 2000). Mowforth and Munt (1998) observed that more community involvement in tourism planning and decision-making could be important in allowing the host population more control over development decisions. Involving the local community would also lead to increased environmental awareness, maximise local economic benefits (Milne 1987) and lead to workable long-term decisions (Murphy and Murphy 2004). Moscardo (2007), however, commented that the local community needs to have a sound understanding of tourism in order to effectively engage in tourism discussion and in the decision-making process. Likewise, the community should be involved in processes and issues which affect their lives (Wall and Mathieson 2006). For the local community to truly benefit from tourism, it needs to be part of the decision-making process.

A good example of stakeholder involvement was demonstrated in Canada by Tourism Montreal, which was the first city to sign the National Geographic Geotourism Charter in 2007. This charter promoted and encouraged sustainable tourism development and as a result of this Montreal developed a GeoTourism Map Guide, which was launched in 2009 (http://www.geomontreal.com/). In developing this guide, the city did not want to focus solely on the main tourist attractions, but rather on those which were unique and held deep meaning for the city. They asked community members to submit attractions which they felt were distinctive, had heritage value and were sustainable. This led to the design of a map including over 100 places of interest and attractions, portraying the natural, cultural and historical value of the city.

Technology can aid in this respect, thereby making tourism more sustainable, through online community tourism planning. Technologies such as computer simulation, geographical information systems and community informatics can be employed.

Travel and tourism does indeed consume large amounts of energy (Lin 2010), with estimates showing that tourism is thought to be responsible for five per cent of CO_2 emissions (Gössling 2009). Energy usage has become a grave concern for tourism, especially in relation to climate change. The tourism industry requires large amounts of energy in order to execute its product services and ensure that visitors have satisfying and lasting experiences (Kelly and Williams 2007). Tourists' requirements are undoubtedly changing as they are demanding more unique experiences, which require greater energy to facilitate. Energy is required for transportation to, from and at the destination, as well as to provide the facilities and services required at the destination (Gössling 2000; Becken 2002). To limit the impact, destination managers should develop well–thought out visitor transport networks (Gunn and Var 2002).

Air travel consumes the largest portion of energy at a destination (Gössling 2000), and from a global point of view transport is the most relevant sector in terms of the environmental sustainability of tourism, accounting for an estimated seventy-five to ninety per cent of all greenhouse gas emissions caused by tourism

(Gössling 2002; Ceron and Dubois 2003). The Intergovernmental Panel on Climate Change estimate that aviation will increase by thirty per cent by 2050 and could contribute fifteen per cent of total carbon dioxide (CO_2) emissions (Dubois and Ceron 2006).

Energy consumption has resulted in greenhouse gases being emitted that have reduced destinations' air quality and environmental health. If these emissions are not addressed they will undoubtedly have drastic implications for tourism (Kelly and Williams 2007). It is estimated that a two-week vacation can create over 3,385 kilograms of fuel consumption per tourist in a developing country (Gössling 2000). Destination planners therefore need to be vigilant and proactive and adopt energy management strategies and policies (Kelly and Williams 2007). Some strategies which are already in place include innovative planning, design and management practices associated with transportation, building design and construction and energy supply (Kelly and Williams 2007). There are no clear and easy strategies for dealing with minimising energy use through technology-based tools/applications (Erdmann and Goodman 2004). Solutions proposed to regulate and control emissions in tourism include charging passengers for emissions based on country of origin (Becken 2002), developing measures of economic-environmental accounting (Becken and Patterson 2006) and afforestation programmes (Gössling 2000). Managing the uses and impacts of energy is beyond a destination manager's control (Kelly and Williams 2007). Some indicative technologies which can be used to support them are carbon calculators, intelligent transport systems and geographical information systems.

Technologies which can be engaged with by destinations

Table 3.3 provides a concise snapshot of the technologies which can be used by destinations to support sustainable tourism development. These were explained in detail in Chapter 2.

Conclusion

The areas in destination management where destinations may consider technology use, and some of the indicative technologies which they may select, have been discussed above. Destinations do not develop in a uniform fashion; they have different aims and objectives in terms of their tourism policy and planning and have limitations placed on them in terms of, for example, government legislation, funding and lack of a skilled workforce. The ways in which destinations engage with technology will largely depend on these influencing factors, which will be discussed in depth in Chapter 8.

In implementing these technologies there are short to medium-term steps that destination managers can take. It was demonstrated that a DMS can help with all three aspects of sustainability; economic, environmental and socio-cultural. Since most destinations have a DMS, perhaps the most logical progression would be to develop more sophisticated uses of it. Additionally, geographical information systems (GIS) have vast potential to help achieve the principles of sustainable tourism

Table 3.3 Collection of ICT-based tools/applications for sustainable tourism development

ICT-based tools/ applications	*Definition*	*Uses for sustainable tourism*
Carbon calculator	Used to determine carbon emissions based on the type and amount of energy consumed. The result of this calculation is known as the carbon footprint and is measured in tonnes of CO_2	Environmental benefits result from the monitoring of emissions Economic benefits can be realised if destinations demonstrate to the tourists that they are willing to pay more attention to the environment. They will gain more support from the environmentally-conscious traveller Socio-cultural benefits are created by having a cleaner environment for the host community through the monitoring of emissions
Community informatics	Focused on the design and delivery of technological applications for enhancing community participation and development through the use of e-mail bulleting boards and networks all based on the Internet	Socio-cultural benefits are enhanced through increased community participation in the decision making process This develops social capital by empowering individuals, strengthening community identity and creating opportunities for economic development
Computer simulation	A simulation of real world settings where models are designed to depict how a system operates over time	Issues too complex for direct observation, manipulation or mathematical analysis are simulated to investigate the effectiveness of alternative management practices. This leads to better decision on impacts on the economic, natural and socio-cultural environments Realistic images are produced for public consultation concerning visitor use of the community's space rather than just identifying a hypothetical situation. This leads to better relationship with the tourist, tourist planner and host community and facilitates community participation in decisions which affect them

Table 3.3 Continued

ICT-based tools/ applications	*Definition*	*Uses for sustainable tourism*
Destination management system	A system that consolidates and distributes a comprehensive range of tourism products through a variety of channels and platforms	Facilitates the establishment of platforms for promoting economic benefits for the local communities, reducing socio-cultural tensions and negative impacts and highlighting the fragile eco-systems of destinations By providing co-ordinated online information anywhere, anytime, DMS can lead to increased levels of tourist satisfaction by reducing search time and providing pertinent information about a destination
Economic impact analysis software	Software used to monitor the economic impacts of tourism by providing information on the type and amount of spending	Information can be used to determine financial feasibility, choose among alternatives, increase the level of economic activity and lobby public support for tourism development
Environment management information systems	A combination of computer hardware, software and professional services that integrates disparate information about environmental issues to manage the environmental function within an organisation. It systematically gathers, analyses and reports business information related to environmental management such as waste tracking and emissions. This allows a company to track, refine and improve its environmental practice	Disparate information about environmental issues such as tracking, waste monitoring, emissions and conducting cost/benefit analysis is connected and integrated by the EMIS for analysis. This leads to better decisions on impacts on the economic natural and socio-cultural environments
Gamification	A process of taking approaches, techniques and technologies developed in the sphere of game design and applying them to non-game functions typically to engage the gamers in real-world applications	Can be used to connect the tourist with the local community Encourage sustainable behaviours and consumption

Continued

Table 3.3 Continued

ICT-based tools/ applications	*Definition*	*Uses for sustainable tourism*
Geographical information systems	Information systems that can capture, store, manage, manipulate, analyse, integrate and display large amounts of geographical data	Indicators for sustainable tourism can be identified, defined and measured. Information provided for identifying and designating suitable locations for development and three-dimensional images can be produced for proposed developments to evaluate proposals
Global positioning system	Satellite-based navigation system that provides positioning navigation and timing services to users in any weather conditions around the world 24 hours a day	By tracking tourist movements plans can be developed to distribute tourists throughout the destination or at different times of the year so that the impacts on the environment can be managed and minimised
Intelligent transport system	Telematic systems which provide detailed information on traffic information from independent locations, traffic guidance and dynamic routing	A better ground transport system allows tourists to be more aware of their exact travelling times at the destination. This leads to wider usage of public transport rather than hiring private cars at the destination. This leads to energy savings and protection of the environment A better transport system also benefits the local community. This reduces traffic congestion at the destination. Host-tourist antagonism can decrease since locals may no longer be resentful of the tourist crowding the roads with their rentals or not understanding the driving rules and regulations of the destinations. People will feel more at ease since transport is relatively hassle free. ITS also provides information about accidents and the safest routes to take so it increases both the safety of the visitor and the host community

Table 3.3 Continued

ICT-based tools/ applications	*Definition*	*Uses for sustainable tourism*
Location-based services	This can collect and deliver information to and from a mobile device depending on the automatic location of the user. The aim of LBS is to provide targeted information to the user based on his/her geographic location. Such information include but is not limited to places to visit, eat and stay as well as emergency and health services	Information can be provided on the LBS thereby reducing the need for print material Messages can be sent to the tourists to create awareness and familiarise them with the culture and customs of a destination. This information can help the tourists make sustainable choices about which products to consume whilst at the destination. It not only makes them environmentally aware but also more conscious of the socio-cultural environment. This information helps them to develop a better respect for the local community and their culture and heritage Information can be provided on promotions, places to visit, accommodation and other general information such as safety and security and weather. This increases tourists' decision-making capacity and contributes to greater tourist spend leading to economic benefits for the destination It also reduces the volume of print material since maps and information on the destination can now be retrieved through location-based services
Virtual tourism	Anyone can experience the culture, history and other points of tourist interests in a visual and interactive manner without actually visiting the destination. An example of this include on-line guided tours of museums and heritage sites where the visitor can experience the destination without actually visiting the destination	It can be used as a substitute for destinations that have exceeded their carrying capacity are fragile and in danger of being damaged by tourist activities. Tourists can be informed about a destination prior to their visit by having them do virtual tours of the destination. It can also act as a substitute for activities which are usually regarded as socially unacceptable

Continued

Table 3.3 Continued

ICT-based tools/ applications	*Definition*	*Uses for sustainable tourism*
		Reduce tourist transport and hence have positive effect on carbon emissions
Weather, climate and ocean change forecasting software	Software used to monitor changes in the weather climate and ocean	This information can be useful for bidding for events, making decisions about proposed development, putting measures in place for hazards and risks associated with bad weather, provide tourists with updated information, energy management and other issues

development, but this ICT-based tool/application is not being used by destinations to its full potential. Some destination management organisations are already engaging with GIS, but mainly for mapping tourist movements and route identification. Since destination management organisations already have this technology at their disposal, the way forward will be to investigate other uses of the GIS and put this into action for destinations.

In the long term, destination management organisations need to be educated on sustainable tourism, what it means for their destinations and how these ICT-based tools/applications can help to better manage tourism impacts. It is fair to postulate that destination management organisations are concerned with the bottom line, and economic concerns tend to outweigh environmental and socio-cultural effects. However, as demonstrated, most of these tools do impact on the economic environment, both directly and indirectly. If destination managers truly understand the value of using technology for sustainable tourism, it will have greater use in the tourism industry.

Technology, if adopted by destinations for use in sustainable tourism development, can lead to great improvements in how sustainability is managed. It can be used to monitor, report and measure tourism's impacts. Destination managers could be provided with readily available and concise information on key issues for sustainable tourism decision-making. With this information easily accessible to them, they could then focus on truly developing the destination in a sustainable manner. Using technology for sustainable tourism will enhance communication between visitors and tourism businesses by building platforms where the community, tourist businesses and tourists can share interests and contribute information on sustainable tourism-related matters that benefits the destination. This not only leads to tourist satisfaction, but also serves as a way of educating all parties. This facilitates the co-ordination and engagement of diversified stakeholders in sustainable tourism and supporting relationships.

Technology can also be used to implement existing approaches to managing sustainable tourism development. For example, computer simulation and GIS can help with measuring and monitoring indicators, whilst location-based services and DMS can be used to market and de-market destinations and educate tourists.

The value of this chapter is its provision of a greater understanding of the opportunities that exist in destination management regarding the use of technology for sustainable tourism development, the possible technologies that can be used and the contribution of these technologies to the sustainable tourism development agenda.

Chapter 3 questions

1 Why do authors find it so difficult to produce a precise definition of sustainable development?
2 Discuss the view that ultimately, sustainable tourism development may be unachievable.
3 Why is the development and implementation of sustainability indicators important?
4 Is de-marketing a viable tool in support of sustainable tourism development? Can you give examples of its use by destinations?
5 Is there any real evidence that destination marketing organisations are being replaced by or becoming destination management organisations?
6 Reduction in energy use at a destination is seen by many as a key component of developing a responsible approach to tourism management. Can you find examples where destinations have taken significant steps to reduce energy use related to tourism?

4 A business perspective on sustainable tourism

Learning outcomes

This chapter focuses on tourism businesses' applications of technology for sustainable tourism. At the end of this chapter you should be able to:

- understand how businesses can engage with technology for sustainable tourism development; and
- discuss some of these technologies and their uses.

Introduction

Tourism businesses face continuously increasing pressure to be innovative and reinvent how they conduct their trade in order to satisfy customer demand, but also to keep abreast of changes to their operating environment – such as economic, social, demographic and technological changes – which threaten their competitiveness and survival. Service businesses, such as those in tourism, have tended to adopt affirmative action for sustainable development at a slower rate, due to their environmental impacts not being highly visible and less pressure being exerted by governments for them to do so (Ayuso 2006). Even though adoption is gradual, businesses are beginning to engage as awareness of the environmental implications of their activities has increased. Dwyer *et al.* (2009) comment that research efforts have begun to focus on how tourism can assist in reducing the degradation of the environment and its demands on resources, whereas before this the focus was on tourism development. This has spurred tremendous growth in tools for sustainability in the past decade, with stakeholders recognising that sustainable practices make business sense (Cornell Hospitality 2010).

Sustainability should be a top priority given tourism's intimate relationship with the environment, which is a key determinant in keeping a destination growing, attractive and competitive. In meeting the needs of their customers, businesses should ensure that their practices are in harmony with the destination's sustainability objectives and strive to reduce the negative impacts of their operations (Dwyer *et al.* 2009). Many tourism businesses struggle to make sustainability a priority due to lacking an understanding of what is required, knowledge, concern, finances and support, and an inability to translate academic research into workable options. In the literature, however, it is acknowledged that businesses which are environmentally friendly can increase their profits, lower costs, increase efficiency, improve their image, enhance stakeholder loyalty, improve product and service differentiation and increase employee morale (Kassinis and Soteriou 2003). Linked to this, Ayuso (2006) argued that competitive advantage, stakeholder theory and the human cognition process can be used as theoretical frameworks to analyse why businesses adopt environmental practices and the benefits that can be derived.

This chapter concentrates on tourism businesses at a destination, and how they can use technology in making their businesses more sustainable. Tourism consumers are engaged in the production and consumption process and are co-producers of environmental practices such as energy use and water saving measures; their presence in this process renders a lack of flexibility for tourist businesses and may coerce the businesses into enforcing more advanced approaches to environmental practices (Kassinis and Soteriou 2003). All tourism businesses engage with technology in some form and the pervasiveness of the Internet has contributed to increased uptake and use. Some of the main areas where technology has been applied by tourism businesses are: marketing and promotion, sales and distribution customers, supplier relationship management and ensuring smooth and efficient business operations. Not all technologies will be suitable, and therefore tourism businesses need to evaluate the available technologies to ensure that those invested in contribute to the business. Specifically, we will focus here on the main businesses at the destination – namely, visitor attractions, transport, accommodation and food and beverages – and how they can use technology in their business operations for sustainable tourism development.

Visitor attractions

Visitor attractions are undeniably a principal reason for tourists to visit a destination: whether it is for the blue-water beaches, fantastic ski slopes or rugged mountains, attractions drive tourists to a destination. Whether these attractions are man-made or natural, tourists' use of them has an impact on the environment. Many attractions are natural, however: tourists often visit a destination to enjoy nature trails, sun, sand and sea, climb rugged mountains and generally experience nature. If these attractions are not properly managed then their future use will be degraded, as is already the case for many destinations, such as those with coral reefs which are now dead due to overuse or coastlines that have eroded due to improper development. These heritage and attraction sites need to be managed, as they are used in the marketing and promotion of destinations, so tourists are buying into an idea and anticipate that their expectations will be realised. When a destination can no longer meet a tourist's requirements they will move on to another destination, and therefore businesses must make the utmost effort to ensure that the environment which tourists come to experience is preserved, protected and maintained for continued prosperity. Environmental threats challenging visitor attractions – especially natural ones – include climate change, depletion of resources, changes in the landscape and habitat loss.

Managers of visitor attractions are concerned with how to ensure their attractions continue to make a profit. To do so they need to ensure they are still appealing to the visitor, but also that they are managed in such a fashion that they can continue to be enjoyed for a sustained period of time. It is vitally important that visitor attraction managers seek to implement sustainability principles. Technology can indeed provide the impetus required to make visitor attractions more sustainable. Some of the specific technologies which can assist visitor and heritage attractions are geographical information systems, global positioning systems, environment management information systems, location-based services, carbon calculators and virtual tourism.

Geographical information systems (GIS), which were discussed in Chapter 2, can be used by visitor and heritage attractions for tourism planning and decision-making. GIS can be used to map how the tourists travel through the attractions at a destination. This is important as it allows decision makers to have a better understanding of the popularity of the attraction and when it is used most. This will help in addressing seasonality concerns, but can also focus on overuse so that planners might be able to plan site staff levels, the amount of investment needed to maintain the attraction and ways to dissipate or deal with tourist numbers and the impacts they may bring. GIS can also be used to track tourist movements at the attraction itself. This would be useful in order to see the areas that are most used, after which appropriate routes and modes of transport to these areas can be planned. This tool can also assist in landscape monitoring, to see how the land changes over time with tourists' use.

Planning and management of visitor attractions can indeed be supported by the use of a GIS. Its uses include measuring the geographic, environmental and socio-economic properties of an attraction, identifying the spatial distribution of the social and demographic aspects of the area, determining new markets and examining the spatial relationships between existing recreational or natural resources and distances travelled from the origins of potential tourists (Lee and Gaefe 2004). It has been argued that protected areas are at the core of tourism development (Boers and Cottrell 2007). To ensure that these attractions continue to meet tourist approval and satisfaction (demand), planners must have an understanding of the resources and what must be done to maintain them, to ensure they are not overused or depleted beyond repair (supply). GIS technology has the potential to model tourists' itineraries and map tourist flows. Researchers such as McKercher and Lew (2004) and Page and Connell (2007) have advocated the necessity to understand tourist itineraries and tourist movements. Itinerary mapping is useful in determining the routes that tourists use in particular locations, the flows of tourists and the types of activities they engage in, which is important in understanding tourist impacts and resource use (Page and Connell 2007). A global positioning system (GPS) can be used similarly to a GIS to produce location-related information tracking tourists' movements, to understand their use of time and space. GPS technologies enable users to know where they are and to use this information in constructing personalised maps for communication and navigation purposes. A study by McKercher *et al.* (2012), using a combination of GPS technology and

GIS software, confirmed previous findings: first-time visitors to a destination tend to be wider travellers throughout the destination, whilst repeat visitors tend to prefer to spend their time in a smaller number of places.

This has implications for sustainability. The use of this technology can help businesses understand tourist movements at various times and in different locations at the attraction. It can also be of use in determining seasonality and developing the necessary approaches to mitigate this. By having a better understanding of how tourists are using the attraction, business planners can allocate resources more efficiently in order to balance resource use for sustainable tourism development. Sites and attractions can be developed to appeal to tourists with divergent interests in order to cope with the environmental pressures. GIS can identify new attractions for development, thereby easing the use of places which may be reaching their capacity points.

GIS also has the potential to help with the economic aspect of sustainability, as it can assist in marketing of the visitor attractions. Once the tourist data has a spatial element to it, GIS analysis can take place – for example, if a business possesses customers' addresses, they can be used to map their distance to the business and, through clustering of tourists by location, selected marketing techniques can be used in these areas or new target markets can be identified (Chancellor and Cole 2008). This type of analysis is founded on the concept of geodemographics, which is based on the assumption that people living in the same area tend to share similar demographic profiles (Elliott-White and Finn 1998). Having an understanding of where people live can provide marketers with inferences about the people in that area and allow them to take a more targeted approach to marketing.

Environment management information systems (EMIS), which were discussed in Chapter 2, can also be used to monitor and manage the environmental functions of tourist attractions. An example of an EMIS in action is the Xanterra Parks and Resorts Ecometrix System, which this business uses to track and monitor its environmental performance.

Case study: Xanterra Parks and Resort Ecometrix – measuring environmental performance

For over 130 years Xanterra Parks and Resorts have engaged in lodging, restaurants and other operations in the USA. Today the company is well known for park and resort management, having the responsibility for managing some of the most beautiful and well-known parks such as Yellowstone National Park, Grand Canyon National Park and Mount Rushmore National Park, to name just a few.

Xanterra is of the belief that you cannot conserve what you cannot measure. This business has therefore sought to implement an Environmental Management Information System, Ecometrix, which assists them in diligently evaluating their environmental performance to determine if systems are actually producing effective results.

Xanterra's Ecometrix is a computerised tracking system, which monitors:

- consumption of electricity, natural gas, gasoline, diesel, propane, fuel oil and water;
- generation of renewable energy;
- generation of solid waste;
- recycled materials, waste diverted from landfills, hazardous waste, and recycled hazardous waste;
- sustainable cuisine; and
- greenhouse gas emissions, compliance violations, pollution prevention, and Clean Air Act Criteria Air Pollutant emissions.

Hazardous waste tracking also includes Universal Wastes such as batteries, electronics, fluorescent lamps and mercury switches. The generation of this type of data allows this business to remain compliant, reduce liabilities but also ensure that they are being sustainable throughout their operations and make changes where it is required.

By using the data from Ecometrix, the business was able to:

- switch from diesel fuel to 100% recycled, waste vegetable oil in powering steam locomotives during the 5–7 trips they run per year. This vegetable oil came from the cooking at the Grand Canyon Restaurant and other local food service providers;
- install a wind turbine which generates 17,000 kWh of clean renewable energy at Maumee Bay State Park;
- develop the tourism's industry first green retail store; and
- implement the national park system's first complete ban on water bottle sales replacing them with water stations and reusable containers.

This information was published with the kind permission of Xanterra Parks and Resorts. More information on Xanterra Parks and Resorts can be found on their website at www.xanterra.com

Managers of visitor attractions can also make use of location-based services to provide updated and personalised information about product offerings to visitors at the attraction. This serves a two-fold purpose. It may lead to increased visitor satisfaction due to the customised and real-time delivery of information. By delivering information through this medium, visitor attractions' managers can encourage more sustainable product consumption through the use of fewer paper-based products. It can be used to assist the visitor in interpreting the attraction, especially if it is a cultural and heritage attraction, by sensitising them to the attraction and making them more aware of the culture and customs. It can increase cultural exchanges, since the tourists are aware of differences and similarities beforehand and can adapt to the culture and gain a more thorough understanding of the history, lifestyles, customs, sacred sites, rituals, language and other valued traditions where they are visiting.

Carbon calculators can also be built in as part of the visitor attraction's offer to the tourist. They can be placed on the website or built as an application for mobile phones for the visitor attraction. The benefit of this is that it would allow the visitor to see what their carbon footprint is at the attraction, so they have a better understanding of their impacts. Using this information, the attraction could develop marketing offers around low-carbon offers and provide discounts to visitors choosing this. Likewise, virtual tourism can be used to help visitors simulate the implications of their actions on the environment. This gives them a better interpretation of their impacts. Virtual tourism can also be used as part of the attraction product to allow visitors to experience parts of the attraction that may no longer be fit for use by the general public. Combining this with the actual attraction provides a greater product offer for the visitor, whilst at the same time preventing damage and destruction to sensitive parts of the attraction.

Transport

'Transport is a vital facilitator of tourism' (Page 2011: 80). In the 1930s airlines developed into a commercial business, propelled by technology developments that allowed organisations to provide regular passenger freight and postal services (Page 2003). In the modern era, airlines have been the main form of transport in the tourism industry. Travel is now established as an important part of lifestyle, with much of this driven by changes in air travel, which now allow access to more destinations, faster access, more comfort and the prospect of cheap air fare. Cheap air fares are provided by budget airlines that have established successful business models based on Internet use, and this has challenged full-service and chartered airlines to change their pricing strategies. The trend appears to be for lifestyle travellers to take several short trips per year, rather than one or two long trips. Adams (2005) observed that air travel has evolved from a luxury good to a form of hypermobility, whilst Gössling and Peeters (2007) commented that the functions of air travel are now wide-ranging as they cater to different groups in society with different purposes. For many types of movement and mobility, air travel is now the given practice (Gössling and Hall 2006). Gössling and Peeters (2007) estimate that air travel will come to outpace land and sea travel, whilst Peeters *et al.* (2004) indicated that in the European Union the approximate distance covered by a tourist will grow from around 1,150 kilometres in 2000 to about 1,600–1,700 kilometres by 2020.

In the tourism industry, airlines have been accused of having significant negative impacts (see for example Sausen *et al.* 2005). A lot of this discussion relates to airlines' contribution to CO_2 emissions and, in effect, climate change. Some of the notable impacts of climate change are rising sea levels, melting of the glaciers, decreasing snow cover on ski slopes, changes to rainfall patterns and fluctuation in temperatures (International Panel on Climate Change [IPCC] 2007). Estimations show that tourism as an industry contributes an overall average of five per cent of CO_2 emissions and approximately fourteen per cent of all emissions when other greenhouse gases are accounted for. About three-quarters of this amount can be attributed to the airline industry (McKercher *et al.* 2010). Airborne emissions can be between 1.9 and 5.1 times more dangerous than surface-based emissions, since the height at which they are released means they do a greater level of damage to the environment (Gössling and Peeters 2007). Tourism which involves air transport is seen as the most destructive to the environment because of its implications for climate change (Gössling *et al.* 2005), and airlines will continue to come under pressure for solutions to reduce not only their CO_2 contribution, but also their other negative environmental impacts, such as congestion and safety and security.

There have been calls to reduce the level of air travel through raising air fares, introducing green taxes, decreasing the number of flights, limiting long-haul travel or encouraging people to use alternative forms of transport. Becken (2007) found that tourists generally rejected the proposition of reducing their ability to travel by air. She surmised that even though air travel plays a functional role, such as travel to holiday destinations, it also is a critical part of an individual's position in society. In the introductory chapter it was stated that the premise of this text is that the tourism industry can proceed on a path to sustainability once the industry is managed properly. Our approach is not to limit visitor numbers or cut air transport; rather, we suggest that through the proper management of these areas, sustainability can be achieved through technology.

The biggest challenge for airlines in terms of sustainability is how to reduce their contribution to carbon emissions. Primarily driven by spiralling fuel costs, most carriers are paying ever greater attention to reducing fuel utilisation and improving economies of use of fossil fuel-propelled transportation, or substituting it altogether. This would accrue for the business money to invest in research and development for cleaner technologies and more competent and fuel-efficient design for their aircraft. Aircraft manufacturers are developing more efficient aircraft as there is pressure to direct tourists, where possible, towards mass transit options such as trains and away from aircraft; again, governments are increasingly using legislation to seek to alter behaviours. A recent example of the complexity of this area can be illustrated by considering the European Union Emissions Trading Scheme. This is a well-intentioned scheme to penalise airlines for each tonne of carbon dioxide emitted where carbon allowances have not been surrendered. More than ten years of talks through the International Civil Aviation Organisation have failed to provide consensus. Whilst international agreements and disagreements continue, governments independently and collectively strive for action and carriers look to their costs, there are a number of technologies which may provide help.

A large part of Continental Airlines' fleet is now more energy efficient, which saves fuel and reduces emissions by five per cent. EasyJet plan to install energy-efficient engines on their Airbus A319s, and the most fuel-efficient airline on the market has been developed: this is the Boeing 787 Dreamliner, which Virgin Airlines has ordered fifteen of. They should become part of the Virgin fleet by 2014 (Mintel 2011). In 2010, Virgin Airlines started to use Airbus A330s; this is expected to reduce the company's fuel consumption and carbon emission by fifteen per cent per seat (Virgin Atlantic 2011).

Due to the nature of the airline business, the multiple facets involved, such as government, and the large scale of operations, one of the best ways in which technologies can be of use in making the airline sector more sustainable is by allowing them to use technology to keep updated and to form partnerships, whether this be through an online forum, e-mail, websearch or a special dedicated network for partnership and information sharing. Airlines are concerned about reducing their carbon contribution. Given the costly nature of their assets and the high cost of fuel and maintaining their operations, it cannot be expected that airlines solely invest in finding ways to solve these issues; rather, engaging in a partnership approach would be best. For example, some airlines have already begun to enter into partnerships with organisations such as the Carbon War Room and Sustainable Aviation Fuel Users Group to help develop alternative fuels which are more environmentally friendly. The use of technology can allow them to keep updated and share and provide information in a common space. Virgin Atlantic, for example, is working with Sustainable Aviation's Operational Improvements Group to determine better flight routes, as straighter routes save time and energy.

Airlines can also maintain carbon/fuel use by using their reservations and scheduling computer systems to analyse their bookings to ensure they are running at peak levels, as a full aircraft reduces the amount of CO_2 per passenger. By using expert software systems they can monitor loads and bookings and therefore make adjustments to ensure they are at the best load per flight. Airlines can avail themselves of carbon calculators, and many have already done so. Travellers could be aware of their carbon footprint and be provided with alternative routes and options to allow them to reduce their footprint and offset their own journey. Many airlines, including British Airways, KLM, Delta and Continental, now offer apps for smartphone users. These apps cover key areas such as flight check-in, boarding pass download, flight status tracking, arrival and departure information, mileage checking and upgrades. Additional features could be added to these apps, providing information about carbon offsetting and their carbon contribution.

Airlines could also use technology to make their internal operations more efficient. For example, an EMIS, discussed above, could be used to help them track and monitor waste throughout the process. Airlines are also considering the benefits of RFID (see Chapter 2 for a discussion of the technology) as a more efficient means of baggage handling than the commonly used barcode system. IATA (2007) reported that twenty bags are mishandled per thousand airline customers, of which 9.7 per cent is due to inefficient barcode reading and eleven per cent is due to poor baggage handling. This report indicated that airlines could save US$733 million per year through RFID deployment, which allows the business to be more efficient and effective in its baggage operations. Curtain *et al.* (2007) observed that through the use of RFID, any object in the organisation can be tagged, which allows it to be a mobile, intelligent and communicating aspect in the business information environment. Lost baggage results in time and money lost by both customers and the airline, as time has to be invested in providing information about the luggage, calling to see if the luggage was found and trying to locate the luggage. Cost is incurred by customers purchasing items before baggage is returned, as well as by the airline in compensation and the labour costs of searching for the lost items. Using RFID reduces the need for manual luggage inspection and routing, as readers on the conveyor belt communicate with the tags placed on the luggage to ensure correct routing (Nath *et al.* 2006).

RFID could have other uses for airlines, in addition to optimising their baggage process. It could be used to tag and track items in cargo operations, as well as the vehicles transporting the cargo. Airline assets such as computers and other movable inventory could be tagged and employees could be provided with RFID-enabled identification cards. Airline staff could also be tagged to allow for more efficient staff scheduling. This would lead to improvement in customer satisfaction and increased airport safety and security, which are critical components of the sustainable tourism process.

There are other modes of transport that tourists can use to reach a destination, and which can also be used for travelling whilst at the destination. Such modes of transport include rail, car, bus, coach, cruise, cycling and transport on inland water routes. In recent times emphasis has been placed on reducing journeys by car and encouraging tourists to use other forms of transport. In domestic tourism, cars are the most significant form of transport for tourists both going to and at a destination (Page and Connell 2008). Cars have allowed tourists to be more flexible with their travel plans, but this has also led to overuse of sites, with many attractions having to reconsider their planning strategies to account for the impact of cars (Page 2011). The use of cars is being discouraged due to overcongestion, traffic noise, emissions and the need for fuel. One of the ways to encourage sustainable travel is for tourists to use more environmentally friendly forms of travel, which are public forms of transport such as buses, coach and rail. However, tourists like to have accessibility at their fingertips: given the limited time they may spend at a destination, they want to arrive and leave when it is convenient to them. For other modes of transport to be used, different transport networks need to be integrated for seamless travel, so that the tourists can easily connect and access the areas they want to reach at their convenience. The challenge for transport in tourism is that it is usually controlled and regulated by the government or other agencies, and therefore tourism has to lobby to effect systems for more sustainable forms of transport.

Additionally, ground transport is not used only for tourism; it also serves the local population's day-to-day transport requirements. Intelligent transport systems, as discussed in Chapter 2, could encourage tourists to use more public transport if they have real-time information at their fingertips; however, this initiative cannot be driven by the tourism industry alone. Ground transport providers have also begun to experiment with clean technology. For example, at the end of 2010 the UK launched its first hydrogen-powered bus in London. There needs to be co-operation with the government, transport service providers, the tourist industry, the local population and other affected stakeholders. Here technology can play a key role in providing a means of communication and a forum for this issue to be debated.

Accommodation and food and beverage suppliers

When tourists visit a destination they require a place to stay; this is commonly referred to as lodging or accommodation. Page (2011) commented that accommodation services are at the core of destinations' hosting of guests and visitors where there is the exchange of money for stipulated services, a particular type of accommodation and other services such as food and beverage. The key components of the accommodation product are: the location, the facilities offered, the service level, the image, the price and product differentiation for different customer bases (Page 2011).

There are numerous forms of accommodation provision, such as hostels, guesthouses, bed and breakfasts and hotels. The type of accommodation we will largely focus on in this section is the hotel sector. Hotels cater to the needs of various types of travellers by offering rooms, but also ancillary facilities and services such as rooms for event hire, catering, laundry and entertainment. We will not explore and provide an overview of the accommodation sector, as this has been well documented in other publications.

Accommodation providers are faced with the challenge of making their business operations sustainable in areas such as energy usage, consumption, water usage, purchasing and waste. The sector has responded to these challenges by implementing a number of voluntary measures to demonstrate its commitment to sustainable tourism (Kirk 1998). Some of the most widely used are codes of conduct, certification, adopting best practices such as linen re-use policies, use of eco-friendly cleaning products, implementing more efficient design – such as aerated showers, low flush toilets, use of more natural light – and development and engagement with environmental performance indicators. Moreover, there has been development of the concept of a 'green hotel'. According to the Green Hotel Association (2008), these are environmentally friendly businesses where the management is keen to develop and implement programmes to save water and energy and deal with solid waste whilst saving money and protecting the environment.

However, hoteliers are still encountering difficulties in making their businesses sustainable. It has been estimated that the energy consumption per bed per night in hotels is around 130 megajoules, with a hotel emitting an average of 20.6 kilograms of carbon dioxide per night and using more energy per visitor than the local community due to energy-intensive facilities such as pools and gyms (Gössling *et al.* 2005). Hotels are also big producers of waste and consumers of water. Bohdanowicz (2005) estimated that one kilogram of waste per guest per day is produced by the average hotel.

The expanding capabilities of technology are empowering businesses to meet the challenges presented by changing consumer behaviour. We will soon see a proliferation of *carbo-tourists*, who check a property's carbon emission levels before making a decision to stay. For greater and more rapid engagement, accommodation providers can use technology with customers to educate them and make them more aware of the environmental policies of the property, but also their duty to the environment. This can be done by putting easily accessible information on the business' website, e-mailing potential guests as part of their booking confirmation or through social networking sites such as Facebook or Twitter. Technology is also providing accommodation providers with tools for advanced database management, whereby these businesses can respond to the personalised needs of the customers based on customer preferences. These add value for the customer, with the resultant effect of customer satisfaction and repeat purchases. Many hotel companies are also creating applications for mobile phones. These can be used for information dissemination and guest communication before they come to the property, but also for providing messages and information to them whilst they are at the location. Guests can also use these media to communicate with accommodation providers to share knowledge and further develop their understanding.

In making their business sustainable, accommodation providers can engage with technology in a number of ways. Hoteliers are already using technology for sustainable tourism, these aspects relate mainly to sustainable consumption. Many properties have implemented systems for recycling greywater and waste disposal and energy management systems to assist in managing and optimising their energy consumption and greenhouse gas emissions, as well as developing software to cut down on labour costs and to improve communication and the guest experience. Additionally, they could use an environmental management system, as discussed above, to manage multi-property organisations. Special software can be bought which can help businesses. For example, Village Green Global Inc. (VGG) has developed energy reporting and carbon accounting software which is being sold as 'Software as a Service'. This helps businesses to monitor and report their carbon emissions. They could also invest in new tools such as Waterpebble, a device which monitors and memorises the amount of water going down the drain. It memorises a person's first shower, which it uses as the benchmark, and then, via a traffic light system, flashes from green to red to tell the user when to finish showering (www.waterpebble.com). Technology can also be used in 'greening' the supply chain, which is discussed further in Chapter 5.

Technology, in this situation, means faster communication with staff and business partners. It provides new ways to deliver staff training. It can reduce the time taken to perform tasks such as banking, regulatory compliance, monitoring tax and payroll management and personnel recruitment (Carson and Sharma 2001; Milne and Ateljevic 2001). This is particularly important for regional businesses, who may have limited physical access to banks and government offices and may be distant from business partners and sources of labour. It also allows more flexibility in time management, a critical issue when dealing with tourists whose times of arrival and departure are hard to predict (Schmallegger and Carson 2007). In short, the potential of technology for business management includes better knowledge of markets, better design of products and packages and greater flexibility in how business administration tasks are conducted.

Accommodation providers are also investing in clean or green technology which is designed to reduce use of non-renewable resources such as fossil fuels, make a smaller environment impact and also produce products which can be reused and recycled in order to reduce the level of waste in the production and consumption process. Such investments by hoteliers include solar power, which can be used to provide light and heat and lead to decreased energy costs; motion sensors for heat and light; water recycling and rainwater harvesting; green roofing; and the use of devices such as environmentally friendly televisions, hair dryers, refrigerators and hot-water distribution systems.

For example, The Aurum Lodge in Alberta, Canada uses photovoltaic panels which allows it to generate one hundred per cent of hot water requirement in the summer and more than eighty per cent of electricity. This property has invested in a solid waste management system with a composting toilet which collects and processes more than fifty per cent of human waste and food waste. This allows the business to reduce water by more than 150 litres per day, leading to savings of more than 135 kilowatt hours of electricity per year. They have implemented a GFX Heat recovery system from used water. Energy is lost when hot water goes down the drain; this system allows them to capture the heat from that hot water and re-use it (www.aurumlodge.com).

The Savoy Hotel in London invested £2.4 million in green technology before its reopening in October 2010. Energy-efficient improvements, which included a Combined Heat and Power (CHP) unit, led to a forty per cent reduction in energy use and saved more than 3,000 tonnes of carbon emissions (Mintel 2011). The business also invested in a £1 million data centre to track all electricity sources and outgoing water in the hotel and an infrared detector to monitor room energy use and automatically turn off energy sources when guests are not in their rooms (Mintel 2011).

The certification and eco-labelling process discussed in Chapter 6 is being used by hotels to improve their green credentials. Many of these tools are web-based and therefore hoteliers can easily use them to check whether their businesses are meeting requirements, or what they can do to improve. Some examples are the Green Hotel Association, The Audubon Green Leaf Programme, Green Globe, the Green Tourism Business Scheme (GTBS) and the CERES Green Hotel Initiative.

The types of technology used will depend on a number of factors, including the size and scope of the organisation. To be a sustainable accommodation operator this type of thinking must be disseminated through all levels of the organisation, no matter the size of the business. A small or medium-sized (SME) operator may not find it necessary to use an EMIS, as compared with a large chain operator with a number of properties based over the world. This SME may well be able to manage the major aspects of its sustainable businesses without significant use of technology. However, many SMEs have not even begun to engage with technology, with some having no web presence and a manual process for reservations. For these businesses at the low end of technology adoption, the uptake of technology – and particularly use of the Internet – could be a significant step in helping them become more sustainable, as they would gain access to a wealth of information. They could use this to enhance and develop their knowledge about making their operations more sustainable, but also share and communicate information with their colleagues and customers. The use of computers could help with day-to-day monitoring of the business, such as keeping track of inventory, keeping notes about suppliers and undertaking research on partners in order to make their operations more efficient and sustainable.

Food and beverage consumption is a big part of a tourist's experience when visiting a destination; however, restaurants have been labelled as one of the biggest producers of waste. Arthur Potts Dawson, speaking at TED Talk 2010, indicated that every calorie of food consumed in the UK takes ten calories to produce. The majority of waste occurs through unused food, improper cooking of food, wastage in food preparation, poor supply chain procedures and customer wastage. However, there are several new technologies that restaurants can engage with to make their businesses more sustainable. Restaurants could invest in composting systems which treat unused and raw food to convert it into a substance that can be used as a biofuel or soil. For example, the 4foods USA composting system disposes of all food and packing waste in a restaurant and turns this waste into drainage water, instead of having waste sent to a landfill (QSR 2010). These businesses can also make use of water filtration systems for water re-use. Restaurants are investing in iPads to allow customers to order without the need for a server, but also to trace where their food comes from, the ingredients used and the amount of carbon used in producing the food. This enables more sustainable consumption and increases customer satisfaction through more sustainable sourcing.

Food and beverage providers can also benefit from RFID, to manage their inventory and stock control processes but also measure their carbon footprint with regard to food production. RFID can be used to track the source of the food, but also to monitor temperature during transport and routes being used for transport and determine the amount of stock required.

Conclusion

Sustainability is a critical consideration for the longevity of tourism businesses, and this can be affected through the use of technology. The uptake of technology also adds value and may produce a competitive advantage for a business. Business managers must be astute in understanding the nature of their business and its impacts on the economic, natural and social environment, and gauge how technology can assist them in making their businesses better and more sustainable.

Chapter 4 questions

1 To what extent do you agree with the assertion that 'protected areas' are vital to tourist development?
2 Discuss the tensions faced by local destination planners dealing with a large-scale resort development and discuss how ICT may facilitate the process and contribute to sustainability.
3 What tools are available to businesses at a destination to support traffic management?
4 Give an example of good practice in tour operations traffic handling.
5 How might accommodation businesses have to adjust to increased customer demands for green 'credentials'? Give examples.

5 Technology-supported supply chain management for sustainable tourism

Learning outcomes

This chapter investigates the relationship between technology and sustainable supply chain management. After reading this chapter you should be able to:

- understand the importance of sustainable tourism supply chain management; and
- examine how technology can be used to support sustainable tourism supply chain management.

Introduction

The study of supply chain management was initiated in the manufacturing sector and has now grown into a relatively mature field. In spite of this being a well-developed research area, most of the supply chain literature has concentrated on how to manage tangible products and the procurement of goods in the manufacturing sector, resulting in a lack of research on service supply chains (Giannakis 2011). Service industries possess certain qualities that make them unique. These are, mainly: intangibility, heterogeneity, simultaneous production and consumption and inability to be stored. One such service industry which is now beginning to be noticed by supply chain management is the tourism industry.

A supply chain comprises a series of value-added processes maintained by one or more organisations, which starts with a supplier and ends with the consumer. They exist to co-ordinate activities between suppliers in the chain and match supply with the demands of the market (Tan *et al.* 2000). The main functions of supply chain management include reducing costs, improving services and enabling better communication and interaction with partners in the supply chain and increased flexibility with regards to delivery and response time (Ranganathan *et al.* 2004). There is no unified agreement on defining supply chain management but the most frequently used definition has been proposed by Simchi-Levi *et al.* (2000: 1), who defined it as

> a set of approaches utilised to efficiently integrate suppliers, manufacturers, warehouses and stores so that merchandise is produced and distributed at the

> right quantities to the right locations and at the right time in order to minimise system-wide costs while satisfying service level requirements.

This explanation has its foundation in the manufacturing sector and therefore must be modified to suit the tourism industry.

Supply chain management in tourism is not controlled by a single, large manufacturing entity; rather, it consists of intricate networks of many small businesses working towards the creation of a unified tourism product (Rusko *et al.* 2009). Gratzer *et al.* (2004) identified more than thirty different industrial components catering to the needs of tourists. This is a multi-disciplinary field and a business made up of many entities with differing dimensions which are generated by the major forces of demand and supply (Gunn and Var 2002). Tourism bears many distinct features which separate it from other industries. It is an intricate amalgam of both tangible and non-tangible aspects that include tourism, non-tourism, local community tourists and varying levels of authority (Shaw and Williams 2004). Its spatial nature leads to wider social and cultural experiences. Therefore tourism is not a physical commodity but combines various interests, activities, stakeholders and businesses that work together to form a distinct supply chain to cater to the needs of the tourists (Page 2003). Suppliers include airline, ground transportation, hotels, restaurants, visitor attractions, rental car agencies, tour operators, travel agents and tour guides.

Moreover, tourism can be viewed as a system and therefore must be analysed from an integrated perspective, which can be considered to be a network of tourism supply chains (Zhang *et al.* 2009). Rusko *et al.* (2009) argued that managing an entire tourism destination may be more complex than managing separate goods, as destinations exist in both physical and mental forms in the minds of the consumers and understanding what actually exists and what is believed to exist is important. Therefore the tourism supply chain is a wide range of linkages of horizontal, vertical and diagonal relationships between businesses (Michael 2007). At each link in the tourism supply chain, there is simultaneous production and consumption – unlike the manufacturing sector, in which consumption comes after the production stage (Harewood 2008). Supply chain management is far more intricate and complex in the tourism industry than it is in the manufacturing sector, because of the interconnected nature of a large number of suppliers, tourism's relationship with the environment and the nature of the product (Rusko *et al.* 2009).

Zhang *et al.* (2009: 347) proposed the following definitions for tourism supply chain management and the tourism supply chain. Tourism supply chain management was viewed as

> a set of approaches utilised to efficiently manage the operations of the tourism supply chain within a specific tourism destination to meet the needs of tourists from the targeted source market(s) and accomplish the business objectives [...] a tourism supply chain is defined as a network of tourism organisations engaged in different activities ranging from the supply of different components of tourism products/services such as flights and accommodation to the

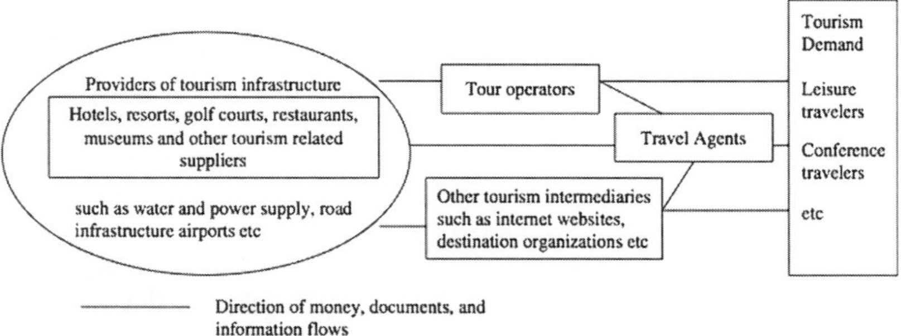

Figure 5.1 Tourism supply chain.

Source: Sigala 2008.

distribution and marketing of the final tourism product at a specific tourism destination and involves a wide range of participants in both the private and public sectors.

Therefore some of the central components of the tourism supply chain are accommodation, transport, food and beverages, sites and attraction, tourism services, activities and events at the destination. In essence, the tourism supply chain involves two main groups. The first is the suppliers who are involved in the creation and delivery of tourism goods and services; the second is the tourists – as identified in Figure 5.1, they are co-producers, as they share in the production and consumption process (Sigala 2008).

In the tourism industry the research on supply chain management is still in its infancy. It has been researched from the perspective of tourism distribution channels, with the main focus on promotion and marketing; however, the supply side has been relatively ignored and many of these studies have failed to consider the complete tourism product and tourist experiences at the destination (Zhang *et al.* 2009; Rusko *et al.* 2009). There has also been limited published work on tourism value or the tourism industry chain, and research in tourism supply chain management has not kept pace with the rapid acceleration of the industry (Zhang *et al.* 2009). Another facet that has been largely unaccounted for in the research on tourism supply chain management is sustainability and the contribution of technology to sustainable tourism supply chain management.

Senge (2010) observed that 'sustainability issues are often supply chain issues'. Sustainable supply chains have become a mainstream issue (Corbett and Klassen 2006). A sustainable supply chain should be one which performs well in all aspects of sustainable development – economic, environmental and socio-cultural. This is commonly known in the tourism literature as the triple bottom-line approach. Pagell and Wu (2009) indicated that if a supply chain performs well on the three elements of the triple bottom line, sustainable supply chain management will refer to the particular managerial action taken to make the chain more sustainable, with the long-term aim of creating a fully sustainable chain.

There has been some research into sustainable tourism supply chain management: for example, Font *et al.* (2008), Sigala (2008), and Budeanu (2009) focused on the role of tour operators in this process. Tour operators are an integral component of tourism supply chains as they play a critical role in distribution. Sigala (2008) observed that these tour operators direct large volumes of tourists to destinations and that suppliers have a persuasive influence on the attitudes and practices of tourism suppliers, delivering low-cost packages to large amounts of people – which can have a damaging environmental impact if not properly managed.

There has been some research into the potential of technology for supply chain management, which addresses planning, forecasting and information sharing. In the tourism industry the technology-related research on supply chain management has primarily focused on how technology – and especially the Internet – has altered the tourism distribution channel landscape, especially for tourism suppliers (see for example O'Connor and Frew 2002, 2004), the implications of using these technologies and how they can be manipulated for tourism supply chain marketing (see for example Go and Williams 1993). The emphasis of technology use for sustainable tourism supply chain management is virtually non-existent. Sustainability is a key concern of destinations, as they rely on their environments to remain in business. Nagel (2000) commented that to develop sustainable supply chains there should be a focus on technological innovations in the supply chain. Technology can assist in finding the right balance in managing the destination resources between use and preservation, benefiting tourism supply chain management, is a key enabling factor in making tourism supply chains more sustainable.

The purpose of this chapter is to focus on how technology can be used to support supply chain management in tourism with the aim of encouraging sustainability. We will first focus on what sustainable supply chain management is and why there is a need for sustainable supply chains in tourism. We will then move on to look at how technology can be used to support tourism supply chains. Two case studies will be presented to demonstrate such technologies in action for sustainable tourism supply chain management.

Sustainable supply chain management

As resources are beginning to approach their finite point, we must consider the implications of the supply chain on the wider environment (economic, natural and socio-cultural) and how supply chains can be managed to ensure ideal use of such limited resources. The sustainable supply chain, more commonly known as 'green supply chain' or 'environmental supply chain', focuses on the whole supply chain, from producing, consuming and delivering customer service to disposal of the product (Linton *et al.* 2007). Sustainability in supply chain management is not only about the start-to-end phase or the product or service; it must also assimilate matters which go beyond the core of supply chain management, such as product design, spin-off products, product life extension, product end-of-life and recovery processes at end-of-life (Linton *et al.* 2007).

Making supply chains sustainable focuses on how to strike a balance between market performance and environmental and social issues in order to have concurrent improvements in both economic and environmental performance through developed supplier–buyer relationships (Zhu and Cote 2004). This approach is ideal not only for the organisation but also for the environment (Cognizant 2008). As the environmental dilemma unfolds, especially the threat of climate change, tourism businesses may be held accountable for the environmental impacts of their suppliers and therefore must consider the environment throughout all elements of the entire supply chain. Carbon emissions for supply chain products and services purchased by industry are estimated to be three times greater than direct industry emissions (Matthews *et al.* 2008).

Definitions of a sustainable supply chain vary, from relating to collaborative partnerships (Zhu and Cote 2004) to consideration of the operation setting of the product and production (Murphy and Poist 2003) or the long-term benefits of enhanced environmental performance (Stevels 2002). Seuring and Muller (2008: 1700) provide a broad definition for sustainable supply chain management, they say it is

> the management of material, information and capital flows as well as cooperation among companies along the supply chain while taking goals from all three dimensions of sustainable development, i.e., economic, environmental and social, into account which are derived from customer and stakeholder requirements.

For the tourism industry, sustainable supply chain management can be understood as the management policies and practices employed and relationships formed to efficiently manage the economic, environmental and socio-cultural concerns related to the tourism supply chain within a specific tourism destination, in order to meet the needs of tourists and the host community and to realise the business objectives in the short, medium and long term. It involves continuous learning and improvement in all stages in the supply chain management process (Sigala 2008). Table 5.1 shows the stages of sustainable supply chain management in tourism.

In the tourism industry there has been a desire for destinations and businesses at the destinations to become more sustainable, and this can be achieved partly through the ways in which their supply chains are managed. There are several driving forces behind supply chains becoming more sustainable in the tourism industry.

Government legislation, regulation and licensing are propelling the need for tourism businesses to become more environmentally friendly in their operations. Through these approaches a government pushes a business into sustainability, by enforcing penalties if stipulated requirements are not met.

Table 5.1 Stages in sustainable supply chain management in tourism

Stage of supply chain	*Activity*
Sustainable product design	Design and creation of the trip to ensure it is in harmony with the environment. For example, this involves using businesses which are GreenGlobe certified
Sustainable procurement	Selecting entering into contractual arrangements and managing suppliers and stakeholders who are pursuing environmentally sensitive policies
Sustainable production	Due to simultaneous production and consumption in the tourism industry it involves the destination and the stakeholders (the businesses and the tourists) in delivery of a sustainable product. For example, this can involve staff training and tourist education
Sustainable delivery – distribution Sustainable reverse logistics	Sustainable management of the distribution chain, which consist of feedback mechanism and learning. For example, this can involve reporting of activities for transparency and accountability

Source: Adapted from Sigala 2008.

The tourism industry has also taken it upon itself to become more self-regulatory and develop standards of industry best practice for sustainable tourism. This is due to increasing recognition that the environment is at the heart of the tourism industry and that continued degradation would leave many destinations without an industry and many people without a livelihood. Tourism businesses are also very conscious of their appearance to customers. Through the use of social media, information about a business can be dispersed quite rapidly, and this can lead to long-term negative consequences. McWilliams and Siegel (2000) deem that businesses consider what consumers think about their sustainability practices. These businesses want to be seen as actually implementing green policies rather than being accused of 'greenwashing'. Additionally UNWTO, the leading international agency for tourism, stresses the issue of sustainable tourism development; this is a powerful force that can propel action by destinations and tourism businesses. One approach to self-regulation is developing codes of conduct (see for example Cole 2007).

Mefford (2011) notes that businesses tend to be of the opinion that consumers are more concerned about pricing rather than environmental product sourcing. However, consumers are also demanding that businesses be greener in their actions, and research undertaken by PhocusWright (2009) on US travellers found that just under a third of these travellers indicated a willingness to pay some sort of premium for green travel products. These consumers are invoking greater interest in the impacts of businesses on socio-cultural environments and are motivated to purchase goods and services that are environmentally friendly from beginning to end. As Yeoman (2005) commented, consumers who are more affluent are focusing on ethical consumption; Tapper and Font (2004) also stressed that businesses are being forced to adopt sustainable supply chain practices, as tourists are increasingly concerned with the environment. There is a growing disapproval of manipulative corporate behaviour and a welcoming response to responsible businesses. There has also been an increasing focus on the provenance of goods and services, with customers' legislative bodies and partner businesses demanding information about where products come from. They are keen to know about the 'quality, safety, ethics and environmental impacts' (Harvard Business Review 2010: 77) of these products.

Businesses may be doing themselves a disservice by not engaging in sustainable supply chain management, as they may face revenue losses due to negative publicity and consumer boycott (Mefford 2011). Consumers are demanding products of greater quality and which are more customised; engaging in sustainable supply chain management can offer this. Sustainable business practices can induce customer preference for an organisation's goods and services and this can lead to increased brand equity, increased sales and more profit (Mefford 2011). Budeanu (2009) found that German and Finnish tour operators adopted environmental supply chain management practices due to customer demand for holiday products that integrate quality with sustainability.

Sustainable supply chains are also seen as a means for improving strategic performance, sustaining long-term competitive advantage and allowing tourism businesses to become leaders in environmental initiatives (Budeanu 2009). Competition is no longer focused on individual businesses, but rather on rivalry amongst chains (Dewhurst *et al.* 2000). Sustainable tourism supply chains can offer benefits such as reduced distribution, increased time efficiency, cost effectiveness, greater internal co-ordination, stimulating organisations' innovation capabilities and new competences. Tourism businesses must therefore appraise their suppliers for risk reduction and product differentiation in a market which is easily saturated (Budeanu 2009). Businesses may end up having lower long-term production costs and be able to charge higher product prices and develop stronger brand equity through pursuing sustainable supply chain approaches (Mefford 2011).

Sigala (2008) adopted the Cigolini *et al.* (2004) model in developing a theoretical framework for making sustainable supply chain management in tourism achievable. The Cigolini *et al.* (2004) model focused on two areas for supply chain management implementation, which were supply chain techniques and supply chain tools. Supply chain techniques focused on the arrangement of the supply chain and its management, with the aim of achieving different activities and aligning the process amongst supply chain members (Sigala 2008). Supply chain tools supported the implementation of one or more of the supply chain techniques. Sigala (2008) argued that sustainable supply chain management can be viewed as a supply chain management technique, as it involves the tourism suppliers integrating and co-ordinating their supply chain management practices. This approach will also be adopted in understanding how technology can be used for sustainable tourism supply chain management, as this approach builds on the literature in both supply chain management and tourism; therefore it is logical to build on this research domain.

Three of the supply chain tools proposed by Cigolini *et al.* (2004) which were adapted by Sigala (2008) for sustainable tourism supply chain management were information tools, co-ordination and control tools and organisation tools. These are depicted in Table 5.2.

The central point to be derived from this is that effective sustainable tourism supply chain management is dependent upon collaboration through information sharing and synchronisation between the members of the supply chain. This can lead to effective decision-making, increased organisational performance, creative and innovative products and increased customer satisfaction, which in turn leads to competitive advantages for these businesses. The use of technology, particularly information and communication technology, can assist in this process, as it consists of tools designed to help the user in collecting, examining, diffusing and sharing information. Dwyer *et al.* (2009: 66) commented that 'successful tourism managers must be able to imagine, perceive and gauge the effects of oncoming science and technology upon demand, supply and distribution'. Technology can also help in co-ordination and control and managing organisation communication internally and externally. This is explored further in the next section.

Technologies for tourism supply chain management

There are a number of vital areas where technology can be put into effect to foster a more sustainable tourism supply chain. One of the principal ways in which such technologies can be used for sustainable tourism supply chain management is in overcoming fragmentation. Zhang *et al.* (2009) categorised the tourism supply chain management relationships into four types – many-to-many, one-to-many, many-to-one and one-to-one relationships – with these relationships taking various forms, such as arm's length, strategic alliance, vertical integration, co-operation, co-ordination and competition, and decisions spanning the strategic, tactical and operational aspects of the businesses.

In Chapter 2 we discussed how overcoming fragmentation can lead to the development of a more sustainable tourism industry. Technology can play a vital role in managing the activities of stakeholders in the tourism supply chain by enabling them to co-operate and to overcome the dispersion that exists in the industry, which can lead to performance gains. Various suppliers in the tourism supply chain make independent decisions regarding price and market allocation of resources but, due to the interdependent nature of the networks, choices made by one member of the chain can influence the gains accrued by the other members (Harrison and Van Hoek 2008). In tourism the varying degrees and components of tourism packages make it critical for suppliers to collaborate with each other, with competitors and with consumers (Kernel 2005).

Collaboration with suppliers, consumers and competitors is indeed a component of developing a sustainable supply chain (Pagell and Wu 2009), and integration of these suppliers in the tourism product development processes can lead to increased competitiveness (Zhang *et al.* 2009), quicker responsiveness, flexibility and less waste (McLaren *et al.* 2002) in the industry. This collaboration can lead to more

Table 5.2 Supply chain tools' uses and benefits

Supply chain tools	*Uses*	*Benefits to the supply chain*
Information tools	To gather, analyse, transmit and share data regarding customer data, end-to-end inventory status and locations, order status, cost-related data and performance status	Members of the supply chain can use this shared information to help design and deliver products that fulfill customer requirements more quickly and effectively
		Having available performance metrics allows members to address production and quality issues more quickly by permitting more responsive demand planning
Coordination and control tools	To monitor and influence the decision-making process by measuring performances and setting rewards based on the achievement of certain results	Information sharing amongst members of the supply chain which leads to trust and accountability of members
		Development of integrated supply chain performance metrics based on commonly agreed goals aligned to internal suppliers' performance systems
		Sharing of information leading to concise, relevant and updated information for sound decision-making by supply chain partners
		Continuous sharing, monitoring and enforcement of the performance metrics, which helps in the identification of bottlenecks and allows continuous improvements of the supply chain performance
		Sharing to risks and costs and fairness in compensation amongst supply chain members' results in greater motivation of members
Organisational tools	To support communication and coordination across all levels of the organisation	Aligns the strategic, operational and tactical decisions of the organisation

Adapted from Sigala 2008.

than simply information exchange and integration; it can allow tourism suppliers to make valid decisions relating to planning, forecasting, designing, distribution of their product (Kumar 2001) and reducing waste. Technology can be used to facilitate this process.

Many firms in tourism collapse because they cannot satisfy market demands. The tourism demand forecasting literature has benefited from considerable research, with Li, Song and Witt (2005) providing a comprehensive review of this area. Despite the many sophisticated quantitative demand forecasting models present in the literature, tourism professionals are either unfamiliar with these updated forecasting approaches due to lack of interest or access to the literature, or do not have the time to engage in designing and developing models for more correct forecasting (Zhang *et al.* 2009). Approximating future demand is a critical component of tourism supply chain planning and information sharing and collaborative forecasting amongst partners in the chain is necessary, as this allows for the mutual flow of information and improvements in accuracy (Zhang *et al.* 2009). Technology can be the solution to this, as it can help design the forecasting process and provide the support systems required in facilitating and developing these processes. It is also a useful means for information sharing amongst stakeholders, which benefits the tourism industry, as forecasts are more accurate and there is a better flow of information amongst partners. Technology can only enhance this.

Information sharing is important in working towards sustainable tourism supply chains. Tan (2000) commented that information sharing is a key ingredient of supply chain management, as the thrust of research focus in this area has changed from making manufacturing processes more efficient to activity co-ordination in the supply chain network through knowledge management. Stakeholder interactions and co-ordination can be improved through better and more co-ordinated information sharing. Linton *et al.* (2007) argued that if all the sequences of steps along the supply chain were optimised in producing and delivering the services, the greatest value would be achieved at the lowest possible cost. Integrating technology into tourism supply chain management can lead to better co-operation amongst partners (Veronneau and Roy 2009).

Tourism supplier co-ordination can lead to an enhanced end product for tourists, which in turn can result in increase tourist satisfaction. It has been argued that the fundamental goal of tourism supply chain management is tourist satisfaction (Zhang *et al.* 2009), and this has been recognised as important to sustainable tourism development. One way of achieving this satisfaction is through supply chain transparency, which reveals the materials and processes used in the supply chain and where this happens (Bonanni *et al.* 2010). Many customers feel it is important to know the provenance behind the products they receive, and technology can be a means to disseminate this knowledge – as documented in the case study below.

Web-based technologies can be used to allow suppliers to have an overarching view of the whole tourism supply chain, enabling them to make more informed decisions in order to satisfy customer demands. The use of web-based technologies has made co-ordination and collaboration in supply chain management a workable option, as they can be fairly cost-effective, have greater flexibility, allow the timely sharing of information and lead to reductions in the costs involved in changing suppliers and customers (Ranganathan *et al.* 2004). Supply chain integration relates to the information flows, physical flows and financial flows between a firm and its partners in the supply chain (Rai *et al.* 2006). The use of technologies allows tourism businesses to share information with their partners, which informs planning of the supply chain network. The timely sharing of information is important in faster decision-making. Deveraj *et al.* (2007) noted that information sharing can be separated into demand-oriented and supply-oriented information sharing, where 'demand-oriented' refers to sharing of data such as sales, customer profiles and customer relationship management and 'supply-oriented' pertains to inventory levels. Collaboration must be aligned with information sharing to determine the full picture of the supply chain, but it is the capability for collaboration which will give businesses a competitive edge (Devaraj *et al.* 2007). The use of technology also generates sustainable performance gains, as it allows tourism businesses to have higher order supply chain integration (Rai *et al.* 2006). This aligns to the resource-based view of firms (Barney 1991) and research has revealed that sustained competitive advantage can be achieved by a business that is willing to develop and make the most of new technologies, which leads to greater capability of the organisation (Zhu 2004). These technologies are also important in providing provenance data to customers. Harvard Business Review (2010) highlighted that in the future, customers will expect to have easy access to this information, which will be influential in businesses establishing trust and reputation.

The benefits of web-based technologies for supply chain management should not be viewed in isolation from the challenges. Ranganathan *et al.* (2004) identified that success depends on the smooth integration of a number of organisational, functional and technological factors and on the extent of internal integration and diffusion with business partners in the supply chain. As with tracking technologies and technology tags, the issue will be how much data should be revealed to customers. The case study below provides evidence of how such web-based technologies can be used.

Case study: Beacon Green Hotel by Beacon Purchasing

You can't stay there and you won't find it in any hotel guide, but the virtual Beacon Green Hotel by Beacon Purchasing is an innovative initiative to promote the best sustainable practice to its hotelier members. Beacon Purchasing UK provides purchasing services for hotels throughout the UK, buying for around 2,000 hotels and using up to 130 suppliers. The company is using its role in the industry to facilitate sustainable practices in UK hotels via its award winning Green Hotel website, which takes the visitor on a virtual tour of a hotel, systematically showing the steps a hotel can take to make the operation more environmentally friendly.

Diane Webster, Head of Sales and Marketing at Beacon UK, who launched the site, tells Footprint: 'We were looking for the right way to get information about green

Continued

products to our customers, but also wanted to find a way to pass on the huge amount of information that we and our suppliers have on green issues. The virtual hotel was the right solution for this and it's a fun, interactive learning tool for users. Next year we want to add more areas such as the exterior of the hotel where we will explore solutions for recycling and waste management, and winning the Caterersearch Web Interactive/Innovative Award has spurred us to get started on the next stage now.'

The virtual tour of the hotel covers the lobby, meeting rooms, bar/restaurant, guest rooms, bathrooms and kitchen, showing all the green practices and purchasing behaviours that can be implemented. In the kitchen area alone there are more than 15 energy saving initiatives that can be implemented, and many of these examples can be clicked on to disclose further information. These links also provide access to specific suppliers that supply energy efficient kitchen equipment and lighting. There are further links to other organisations which assist hotels in becoming more green through providing a range of sustainability products and services. Suppliers range from those buying 90 per cent recycled pens to those who can provide bulk toiletry supplies rather than individual packets. Service suppliers offer waste tracking and also a service that calculates and educates guests on the carbon footprint of their trip.

Visitors to the site can also look at one particular hotel and see what it saved in one year in waste to landfill and by implementing a range of other initiatives. Other hotel case studies show how energy consumption can be reduced throughout each part of the hotel as well as ecologically sound waste and water management, leading to reduced operational costs. As Beacon and its supplier partners enhance their green credentials, so will the hotel develop, providing a strong foundation for the future promotion of green products and information.

However, it was very important to Beacon to ensure that it was not perceived to be a purchasing expert for green products; rather, its aim was to use the website to share its own journey towards becoming a more environmentally friendly business while encouraging members to do the same. Initially focusing on a core range of products, with 11 suppliers, enabled Beacon to launch the hotel with enough content to be interesting – but without appearing to have all the answers. The hotel opened with five areas to explore and had a clear core range of information and easily accessible products available to purchase.

A secondary challenge has been to overcome the perception that going green is expensive – a major concern during a time of economic instability. As a purchasing consortium whose business model is to leverage collective volume to drive best price for its members and therefore save money, getting members to purchase greener products at a perceived higher price was an interesting challenge. This was overcome by demonstrating that affordable solutions are available and that sometimes small steps can have a significant effect. For example, installing Hippo bags in the toilet cisterns does not mean significantly increased expenditure but does mean that a hotelier can save money and reduce their impact on the environment. 'It's not all about installing wind turbines or solar panels,' says Webster.

Green Tourism is a key partner in the endeavour, identifying and accrediting those products and services that meet their sustainable business scheme criteria. Beacon's association with GTBS is further strengthened through its sister brand, Best Western GB, which selected Green Tourism as its preferred 'green' accreditation body

Continued

in 2007. Promoting the scheme through the 280 hotels in the UK, Best Western has identified green champions within each of their properties to support – individuals who are important links for Beacon, in the scope, launch and ongoing development of the Green Hotel.

Beacon has also developed relationships with a number of organisations and agencies, specifically Envirowise and WRAP. The conference room in the Green Hotel website displays an Envirowise video case study which outlines best practice for sustainability within a hotel. An association with Red Tractor is also being explored by Beacon to promote licensed Red Tractor suppliers through the Green Hotel website. Further partnerships have been developed with industry leading bodies such as the Considerate Hoteliers Association (CHA), an association of like-minded hoteliers who encourage, assist, motivate and cajole fellow hoteliers to adopt sound and sustainable environmentally friendly and socially responsible policies and practices. This year, putting its money where its mouth is, Beacon is sponsoring the Considerate Green Marketing Initiative of the Year, in conjunction with CHA – to drive awareness of sustainability and to promote the green hotel website as a source of information, suppliers and green products.

The CEO of Interchange and Consort Hotels, David Clarke, is chairman of the Sustainability Committee for the British Hospitality Industry (BHA) and is a key figure in the promotion of the company's CSR aims, and the approach it is taking to put this at the heart of its business. 'It's not always easy to know what practical and commercially viable steps can be taken to become green. It's more complex than we think,' says Webster. 'It's easy to come up with a simple CSR statement but we wanted to bring our values alive and get our different stakeholders involved. Any small change in purchasing behaviour can have a huge impact on the environment. We aim to give people information about where they can become more green and then, if they choose, direct them to a directory of green products in that particular area,' she says.

This case has been reproduced through the kind permission of the Footprint Media Group, and we would like to acknowledge Foodservice Footprint as the source of the information. It can be accessed at http://www.foodservicefootprint.com/features-2/virtual-greening.

Computer simulation, which was discussed in Chapter 2, can be used to support sustainable tourism supply chains. Several studies have been completed on simulation for supply chains (see for example Cigolini *et al.* 2011; Umeda and Zhang 2006). The simulated supply chain provides rich information that allows for detailed analysis of supply chain partners' activities in the chain to determine the chain's environmental impacts, inefficiencies and gaps, and how energy can be saved.

Tracking technologies such as RFID tags will play an increasingly significant role in sustainable tourism supply chain management. It will serve as a means of allowing companies to gain information about where their goods come from and how they pass through the supply chain and to measure their environmental footprint (Harvard Business Review 2010). Even though the essence of the

Table 5.3 The uses of RFID in the sustainable supply chain

Procurement	*Production*	*Distribution*	*Reverse logistic*
RFID, along with sensors, can enable measurement of emission rates and energy efficiency of products before purchasing	It can enable measuring and diagnosing of the carbon emissions related to the product at different processes RFID coupled with appropriate sensor can record the flows of wastewater and solid waste	It can enable accurate measurement of emissions during transport and transportation utilisation	The RFID could record data about the material of different parts of the product. The data from the RFID tag is later used in the reverse logistics to assist in deciding which components can be re-manufactured, refurbished or sent to landfill or incinerator

Adapted from Dukovska-Popovska *et al.* 2010.

nature of the tourism product is intangible, there are tangible elements which are necessary in delivering and creating memorable guest experiences, such as the materials needed in the construction of accommodation, furnishings, linens, amenities, cutlery and food and beverages. As provenance becomes a wider concern, these technologies will be instrumental in allowing tourism suppliers to track the sustainability of their suppliers. For example, many food products today are labelled as organic or fair trade. However, how can we verify that the product is what is actually said on the label? Customers and other stakeholders are asking now to see where this product was sourced to ensure it is actually organic. Technology tags allow the supplier to store vast amounts of information on the tag, update this information and track the product through the supply chain. Table 5.3 shows how RFID can support sustainable supply chains.

This information can be easily uploaded to the web for customers to access. Bonanni *et al.* (2010) developed a web-based software tool called Sourcemap, where the entire supply chain can be viewed at a glance and information is provided about products and their origins. The case study below describes how this technology can be used by small hoteliers. This allows for transparency in operation. Also, this data can be easily passed from one supplier to the next in the chain, allowing low-cost data exchange for co-operation and collaboration. This tracking also allows suppliers to gauge their carbon footprint.

Case study: Sourcemap: A web tool for sustainable design and supply chain transparency

The Hotelier owns and operates a three-star vacation hotel and restaurant on the banks of Loch Ness. Much of the tourism to the area is driven by its scenic landscapes and her approach reflects an investment in the area's natural wealth. In recent

Continued

years she has taken steps to increase the environmental sustainability of the hotel installing a wood chip heating system and participating in national and international green initiatives. She tracks how far guests have travelled to reach the hotel and offsets their carbon footprint by planting trees in nearby forests. She sources produce from local and organic farms whenever possible. The hotel's philosophy and sustainability efforts are documented on its website which she updates daily along with a number of accompanying social networks. The hotel website includes embedded Tripadvisor widget showing unbiased (but largely positive) reviews from her guests (www.tripadvisor.com); she is also considering a Facebook presence.

Figure 5.2. The hotelier inspired the design of a travel template which creates a badge of the carbon footprint of an event to which many people travel.

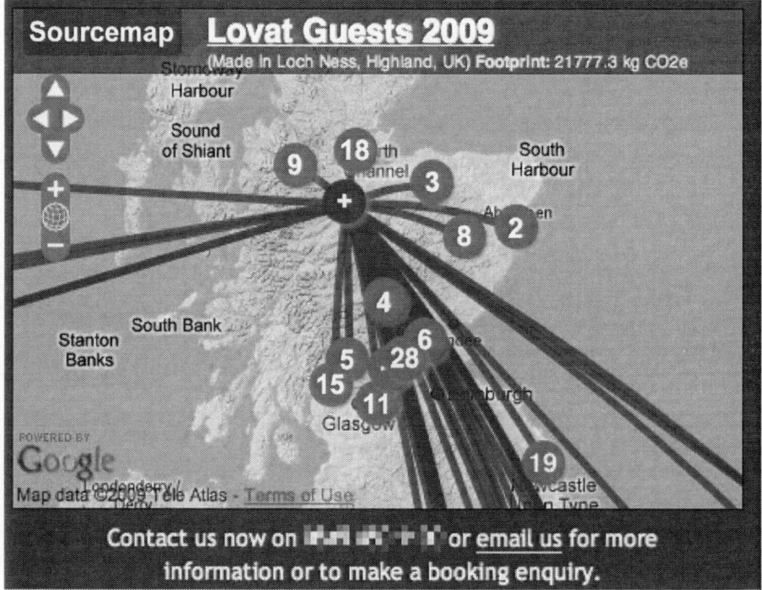

Figure 5.2 The hotelier inspired the design of a travel template which creates a badge of the carbon footprint of an event to which many people travel.

When the Hotelier first heard of Sourcemap she suggested using it to visualize the paths travelled by her visitors and to use the visualisation on her website as a way of explaining her efforts to offset carbon footprint. This led to refining an embeddable widget and to develop a template specifically for visualising travel (see Fig. 5.2). She included a Sourcemap embed of yearly travel footprint on the hotel's website, along with a description of the carbon offsets she has chosen to purchase. Based on her suggestions, the capacity to include offsets was added to the Sourcemap interface so that conscientious businesses can present a badge of reduced global warming

Continued

contribution alongside a description of their efforts. Her hotel now represents a carbon-neutral travel destination for all of her guests.

Later the Hotelier proposed that the map could be used to assist in strategic planning for the hospitality industry of the region. Visualising where guests originate, from where food is sourced and which sites are visited could assist the region in overall development. Finally she requested a streamlined input method whereby information could be directly exported from her existing database of guests to Sourcemap. These expanded functions further motivated the development of an extensible architecture with multiple points of entry to the Sourcemap calculators and visualisations.

Source: Bonanni L. *et al.* (2008). Small business applications of Sourcemap. Proceedings of the 28th international conference on Human factors in computing systems – CHI '10. Atlanta Georgia USA 2010. ACM

Tourism suppliers can also share the necessary framework for these technology solutions by using cloud computing, also known as 'software as a service'. By sharing applications on the cloud, less hardware will be required and energy will be saved, resulting in a reduction in carbon emissions.

Additionally, tourism supply chains can avail themselves of a destination management system, as discussed in previous chapters. This can be a strategic tool for building and strengthening relationships, networks and communities that can transform the tourism supply chains and enhance economic development at the destination level. Several types of software have been written about for use in supply chain management, including enterprise resource planning and advance planning systems. The uses of this specialist software can provide an overview of the supply chain and assist in managing demand and supply. It is argued that for this software to be of full value, data is required for planning and forecasting. This is indeed true, but in this turbulent business environment which constantly changes and shifts, limited demand history will be needed (Kumar 2001). Decision support systems allow supply chain managers to perform scenario analysis for assistance in decision-making (Bechtel and Jayaram 1997). Simulation software can also be used to help tourism suppliers visualise the different supplier relationships and consider the impacts of these relationships for the business and the consumer.

Conclusion

In the future, customers, governments and other stakeholders will exert stronger demands on tourism supply chains for them to account for the environment. As a critical component of any tourism business, sustainability should also be incorporated into how supply chains are formed, developed and managed. The biggest challenge in developing sustainable tourism supply chains is ensuring co-operation, co-ordination and tracking procurement by supply chain members. Technology can be a driving force in making this process more effective and efficient.

Chapter 5 questions

1 What are the main features which distinguish supply chains in tourism from those in manufacturing?
2 How can managing supply chains contribute to more sustainable destinations?
3 Give some examples of how ICT is utilised in addressing and overcoming fragmentation issues in the supply chain.
4 Discuss what you understand by the term ‘co-opetition’ and give some examples where the practice contributes to the sustainable tourism agenda.
5 In what ways do you see good supply chain management connecting tourist satisfaction to sustainable tourism?

6 Tourist use of technology for sustainable tourism

Learning outcomes

This chapter provides an overview of the motivations for and barriers to technology adoption and use by the tourist. It emphasises the importance of awareness, education and motivation both in broad sustainability issues and in focused areas. After reading this chapter you should be able to understand:

- the technology-enabled sustainable choices available to the tourist; and
- examples of use of these technologies at different trip stages from varying tourist perspectives.

Introduction

In the preceding chapters we looked at the background to sustainable tourism and the emergent and increasingly broad role which ICT may play. This introduction was followed by a tour of technologies used in support of sustainable tourism development from a destination management perspective, and subsequently a look through the eyes of the supply chain stakeholders at how technology can come to play a part, in thinking and in practice, in implementing approaches to support sustainable tourism. A particular focus of the earlier material was to not only take a holistic view of the place of ICT-mediated sustainability within the tourism system, but also to highlight the central role of the destination. In this chapter, whilst still considering the full gamut of stakeholders, we put the consumer – the tourist – centre stage, and look at uses and trends in tourists' use of ICT and its relation to the goals of sustainable tourism. The tourist will necessarily, in many – if not most – cases, encounter the destination's perspective on sustainability mainly through the destination management system's (DMS) main website and support channels; however, of course, there are also technologies and channels available to the tourist beyond the destination offer. This chapter addresses the spectrum of consumer use of ICT-mediated or supported information and decision-making in relation to sustainable tourism.

In considering the relationship between ICT, sustainability and tourism, we must recognise that there is a constant and complex interplay of drivers influencing the ultimate paths which tourists take. Elsewhere in the text we have reflected on the wider issues of sustainable tourism; it is important to now also think of the perceived place of sustainability in the mindset of the tourist and ask questions such as whether and, if so, to what extent it may feature at each stage of a trip's decision-making process, and what facilitators and barriers may exist in developing awareness and engagement with sustainable tourism. This chapter will therefore focus more specifically on the ways in which tourists engage with ICT in this context, and will continually underline the ever-increasing importance of information in all aspects of tourism. This centrality of information is transforming tourism at all levels. We are currently experiencing seismic shifts in the structures, paradigms and business models of tourism and how we, as tourists in the system, interact with them.

Before engaging with technologies, perhaps a reasonable place to start is by reminding ourselves about tourists. Who is a tourist? Why do they do it? What do they want? The type of tourist under consideration relates closely to the reasons for a trip and we become tourists for many and varied reasons: visiting friends and relatives, a vacation to a favourite destination or a visit to a new destination as a business traveller. We undertake these trips as solo travellers with a partner or friend, with a group or with family, and we may have both physical presence and potentially virtual personas in each case. As we shall see later, even physical presence is evolving through technologies such as augmented reality (AR), in which there is a degree of blurring across physical online and virtual worlds. Of course, there is also the fully virtual world, which may enrich, complement or indeed potentially substitute for really being there. The things we take into consideration when planning a trip, in the pre-trip phase, are naturally diverse and are dependent on the purpose of the trip. Of course, one of the key characteristics of tourism is that so much of the preliminary decision-making is based on intangibles. This underscores the pre-eminence of information in the tourism decision process.

A central theme of this text is the place of sustainability in this process; the role of ICT in making a positive contribution to sustainable tourism and the consideration of sustainability elements of a trip may feature early in the process, with the tourist as a central player. Tourists have many needs and uses for information during a trip, which are as extensive and diverse as are types of tourists; even subsequent to a trip, many will choose to use technologies to gain or further share information. In reflecting upon tourists' use of ICT for sustainability purposes it is clear that inherent in this is a consideration of what may drive tourist adoption (or otherwise) of any ICT *per se*, and *awareness of* and *engagement with* sustainability issues. This awareness and engagement are assumed pre-requisites for use of ICT by the tourist in support of sustainability. This chapter therefore takes us on a journey through these motivational issues and related education and awareness matters, before exploring examples of technologies potentially available to the tourist, thus providing a context with which to illustrate at each stage of the trip ways in which tourists are using the technologies in practice. The principal focus is the leisure traveller, but most points are more generally applicable.

Motivation

Underpinning much of the thinking in this book is the reasonable, perhaps optimistic assumption that given the right set of circumstances, information awareness, sensitivity and access to technologies, tourists would be positively motivated towards choosing sustainable routes to their experience. However it has been noted by some authors that tourists are, alas, not all necessarily displaying behavioural change, even in the face of high-profile environmental concerns (Hall and Gössling 2009; McKercher *et al.* 2010). Others, including the authors of this text, hold the view that new technologies offer an unprecedented opportunity to positively shift behaviour, and in particular to change consumption patterns and encourage approaches to sustainable destination management (Liburd 2005; Ali 2009).

Anecdotally we know that technology today is ubiquitous; we see everyone, from pre-school children to our most senior citizens, engaging in one way or another with technology. Whilst this is perhaps done with varying levels of skill and enthusiasm, nevertheless, technology is everywhere. This leads us to reasonable questions about the extent to which tourists are adopting and using the new technologies, and also prompts enquiries about their mode of use, their purposes – and how we measure these things.

One of the most widely applied approaches to assessing technology uptake is Davis' (1989) Technology Acceptance Model (TAM), although this is primarily applied in the broader organisational domain. Additionally there has been an admittedly much smaller range of more consumer-oriented pieces of work, examples of which include that by Höpken *et al.* (2008), Garcia *et al.* (2009) and Edwards *et al.* (2010). Although there is as yet no significant body of work on mobile use of ICT, it is emergent (see for example Barnes 2003; Rasinger 2007; Yang and Jolly 2008; Oh *et al.* 2009). Tourist use of mobile application prototypes has been researched to some extent for in-trip tourists (Hinze 2009; Tumas and Ricci 2009; Buhalis and Pistidda 2008; Garcia *et al.* 2009; Edwards *et al.* 2010). No substantive studies have made linkages between in-trip tourists' actual use of ICT and sustainable tourism; however, there is current research in progress (Scott 2011) seeking to answer just these sorts of questions. It may be argued that motivation to adopt new technologies and motivation towards sustainability issues are key to understanding current and projected tourist behaviour.

It would be useful to consider to what extent the big tourism players are focused on consumer choice and sustainability, and how this manifests itself from a tourist perspective. For example, TUI's Director of Communications, Christian Cull, stated in April 2011 that 'TUI is committed to raising awareness and converting that into actions, by making it easy for our customers to make sustainable choices when holidaying abroad' (TUI 2011).

Education

Raising awareness of sustainability issues and providing good, relevant information and education are recognised as universally important. There appears to be only limited evidence to date that such awareness of sustainability issues has in fact significantly altered any tourist behaviours (Miller *et al.* 2010). Education and training in this field may encompass many routes, both formal and informal, and a good starting point to place this educational need in context is perhaps to consider the importance of these issues through the United Nations' Millennium Development Goals (UN 2000) pledged by 189 member states in 2000. These are to:

1 eradicate extreme poverty and hunger;
2 ensure environmental sustainability;
3 promote gender equality and empower women;
4 improve maternal health;
5 reduce child mortality;
6 combat HIV/AIDS, malaria and other diseases;
7 achieve universal primary education; and
8 develop a global partnership for development.

These eight principles are framed in a manner that widely connects them to business and government tourism and tourism development. Given the economic centrality of tourism in an increasing number of countries, they must be taken into serious consideration by all tourism stakeholders. A progress update on these goals has been published (see United Nations 2010).

Education on sustainability issues varies widely in type and content in many countries. In the UK, for example, The Environmental Association for Universities and Colleges (http://www.eauc.org.uk/) seeks to integrate education for sustainability across the further and higher education curriculum, thus aiming to tackle macro-level issues for those likely to enter management positions. A further global example is the BEST Education Network (http://www.besteducationnetwork.org/), which focuses on sustainable tourism education and offers free downloadable case studies (entitled Innovation for Sustainable Tourism).

Bhawani (2009), in considering education for sustainable development, encouragingly reported that recent efforts have gone beyond simple integration of sustainable development into curricula, worthy though that is; in fact, many curricula are now being designed with the principles of sustainable development in mind. An interesting piece of work in higher education by Shephard (2007) investigated the world of attitudes, perceptions and behaviours in relation to how they could impact upon education for sustainability.

Furthermore, in the educational domain, whilst not specifically sustainability-oriented, INNOTOUR (www.INNOTOUR.com) – operated by the University of Southern Denmark – offers an open platform for 'educators, researchers, students and businesses committed to the development and dissemination of knowledge in the field of tourism innovation'. This platform again offers a range of case studies and other learning materials, a typical example being a sustainable development project in Puntacana in the Dominican Republic. ICT is utilised on the INNOTOUR site as the education medium permitting upload and download of material related to sustainable tourism development and encouraging tourist engagement.

Case studies are an excellent means of providing concrete examples of and real substance for some of the abstract concepts of sustainable development.

A more industry-focused education perspective is illustrated by the travel industry charity The Travel Foundation (http://www.thetravelfoundation.org.uk), which was set up to

> respond to concerns over the sustainability of travel and tourism. An independent UK charity which helps the travel industry, understand, manage and take effective action on sustainable tourism . . . to protect and enhance the environment and improve the well-being of destination communities as well as the holiday experience for visitors.
>
> (http://www.thetravelfoundation.org.uk, 2012)

Whilst focused through a group of industry stakeholders, this initiative has a well-developed web presence which clearly illustrates active projects and news, but also offers dynamic means of engagement such as its 'Green Business Tools' application and a section for the prospective tourist to delve into the reasoning behind such initiatives – and indeed be quizzed on their understanding!

Sustaining Tourism (http://www.sustainabletourism.net) approaches education through technology at a more individual level. This is an initiative driven by an underlying assumption that there is a demand for sustainable tourism, recognising that whilst most consumers will not specifically ask for sustainable options, there is an increasing expectation that the provider will offer them.

The role of education can therefore be seen to be complex, with some positive steps being taken at business and organisational levels, at an informal level and through formal courses and curricula at both a global and a local level. However, whilst the scale and penetration of these approaches looks to be on the increase, it will undoubtedly take time for them to have widespread impact.

Certification, labelling and branding

This topic was discussed in Chapter 3, but we encounter it here from the perspective of the tourist and its use in sustainable tourism. This is again an area primarily led by business and destination stakeholders; however, the central purpose of these initiatives is ultimately to persuade tourists that those offering what is sometimes referred to as green labelling are supporting lofty sustainability objectives. These approaches are envisaged as playing an increasingly important role in consumer choice, particularly through, for example, eco-certification and eco-labelling programmes. ICT is being used more and more to raise the visibility of sustainability issues and to support increased awareness and demand among consumers.

Eco-labelling

Eco-labels and eco-labelling are widely used terms, alas without agreed definition or application. They range from very general terms such as 'organic' through to rather more precise descriptions falling within the scope of consumer legislation. Eco-labels are often general claims; sometimes they may be verified and sometimes not. There are a number of sources of eco-label information available, including websites such as www.ecolabelindex.com, and this fast-moving area has recently seen the launch of iPhone and Android apps to assist the consumer. For example, a recent app made available from iTunes deciphers eco-labels, giving vital data regarding the soundness of the claims made. In effect this app is a mobile application from www.greenerchoices.org and puts a powerful tool in the hands of the consumer; its impact, of course, will be connected to the issues described above in terms of consumer awareness and predisposition. Of course consumers have to be alert to the sins of 'greenwashing', where purported green claims are in fact largely or entirely bogus and unsupported by evidence.

Tourists appear to show an increasing awareness of sustainability issues in relation to developing economies, and whilst more developed destinations have a longer history of offering eco-labelled products, it is felt that developing countries will progressively adopt eco-labelling as a contribution to environment management (Sasidharana *et al.* 2002).

Eco-certification

This term differs from eco-labelling, as it is usually used where there is some kind of third-party or independent agent which attests that some sustainable practice has been adopted in relation to the generation of goods or services. Like eco-labelling, there is no universally adopted standard or set of benchmarks in this emergent field, although it is worth drawing attention to the Global Sustainable Tourism Council (GSTC), which claims to be

> a global initiative dedicated to promoting sustainable tourism practices around the world. Momentum around this movement is growing. The GSTC is currently active in all UNWTO regions including Africa, The Americas, East Asia and The Pacific, South Asia, Europe and Middle East... The GSTC fosters sustainable tourism through the adoption of universal sustainable tourism principles; compiling, adapting and creating the tools and training to engage in sustainable tourism practices; and increasing the demand for sustainable tourism products and services.
>
> (http://new.gstcouncil.org/ 2012)

A good example of a well-developed eco-certification program which a consumer might encounter is Florida's, as seen in the case study below.

Case study: The case of Florida's voluntary hotel eco-certification programme

As of 2010 there were 39,6372 available rooms in Florida's 4,696 hotels, bed and breakfasts and timeshares (Florida Department of Business and Professional Regulation 2010). These properties serve the 35–40 million guests that annually visit the peninsula state and contribute more than $14 billion dollars to its economy, making tourism the top industry of the state (Visit Florida 2006). Although the lodging industry offers substantial financial contributions, its biological impact annually uses billions of gallons of water, more than 625 million kilowatt hours of electricity and contributes 4% of the state's overall solid waste disposal (Yon 2005).

The Florida Green Lodging Program (FGLP) was launched in 2004 as a voluntary initiative under the Florida Department of Environmental Protection (FDEP) that encourages lodging establishments to 'make a commitment to conserve and protect Florida's natural resources' (Florida Green Lodging Program 2011a). The FLGP was also developed to help improve occupancy rates and drive down costs by reducing waste water and energy use. In return the 680 certified properties (Florida Green Lodging Program 2011a) 'receive marketing and technical assistance benefits through the Florida Green Lodging Web site' (Florida Green Lodging Program 2011a), the ability to display the FGLP logo (see Figure 6.1) and to be featured on the FGLP Web site (Florida Green Lodging Program 2011a).

All certified properties must perform an evaluation, complete an application (Florida Green Lodging Program 2011b) and commit to six areas of sustainable business practices in the following areas: communication and education (customers, employees and public), waste reduction, reuse and recycling, water conservation, energy efficiency, indoor air quality and transportation.

Figure 6.1 Florida Green Lodging Program logo.

This government-sponsored initiative is organised primarily online but does conduct 'spot sight assessments ... in order to uphold the integrity of the program' (Florida Green Lodging Program 2011a). Certification is valid for three years but properties must complete an annual assessment that measures wastewater and energy usage. In addition, each certified property must implement a minimum of two new

Continued

business practices from the original FGLP six sustainable areas every fourth year. The state legislature, Florida's elected governing body expressed its commitment to the FGLP in 2008 when it passed HB 7135 which established Florida statute 286.29 that 'recognises the importance of leadership by state government in the area of energy efficiency and in reducing the greenhouse gas emissions of state government operations' (Florida Legislature 2008). This government endorsement is an added incentive that FGLP properties are eligible for as the state spent $19.6 million in 2009 and $15.8 million in 2010 on lodging expenses for state government employees because it requires all state agencies to use FGLP facilities for all official state travel meetings and conferences (Florida Legislature 2008).

We would like to acknowledge the Florida Green Lodging Program as the source of this information and thank them kindly for allowing us to use this material.

Tools, applications and journeys

Context

The use of ICT comprises a number of elements for the tourist at any stage of a trip. There is a degree of tangible access to information, very often in the form of brochures, catalogues or newspaper articles. Increasingly the medium of access is electronic, in the form of television travel programming, documentaries, dedicated commercial travel channels and perhaps even indirect information through movies, but very often today this information is accessed via the Internet. Information may be retrieved at a specific location, such as home or work, and increasingly it is being sought on the move. An array of devices (such as smartphones, laptops, tablets and eReaders) can be engaged with which allow the user to retrieve, store, process and transmit information. However, whether local or more remote; whether the tourist is static or mobile; regardless of trip stage, it is information that the tourist is after. The specific means of communication is secondary, only becoming important when this device becomes erratic, slow or in some other way a barrier to access. We are familiar with the strengths and weaknesses of many of the devices available and the inevitable compromises which ensure there is no 'one-size-fits all' device for all occasions. The smartphone is excellent for checking emails on the move but has issues of screen size and battery life. Tablet computers such as the iPad have larger screens but are not particularly pocket-friendly and are not the easiest to use for any significant amount of keyboard work. Tourists may find that they are operating a variety of devices at various times; they may also drop into an Internet café – or indeed, these days, almost any café with Wi-Fi access – or use the in-room entertainment system in a hotel to browse the Internet.

In Chapter 3 we introduced a number of the main ICT tools/applications which may be considered for use by those directly involved at the destination – primarily destination managers. Many of the tools and applications which the tourist may make use of at any trip stage will be the same, and they may be either directly or indirectly used. In addition to the tools mentioned earlier, this chapter introduces some others, such as augmented reality, mashups and social media and networks. Here we will be looking at tourist use of the technologies; given the space constraints, comprehensive coverage will not be possible. However, we shall take a look at examples of use and projected use, this time from the tourist perspective, selecting primarily pre- and in-trip stages.

Tourists may buy a ready-made holiday package ‘off the shelf’: this is the traditional domain of the tour operator and the travel agent. Not so very long ago, the only way in which a tourist would encounter technology would be watching a travel agent accessing cumbersome videotex screens and presenting the customer with proposed solutions, such as a three-week cruise or something more prosaic like an inter-city flight with a couple of nights in a chain hotel. Actually, this approach is still often seen. The former business models whereby airlines gave agents access to their inventory through computer reservations systems were the backbone of travel agency work for many years. The evolution of this model towards global distribution systems (GDS) saw the addition of car rental and accommodation, and larger independent hotels continued, along with tour operator packages, to provide the mainstay of the leisure travel agency business. Thus for many years the travel agent could rely on customers perusing attractive, glossy brochures filled with seductive holiday offers nicely packaged up for them by tour operators. The advent of the web and its inexpensive, ubiquitous use has been a game-changer for the travel agency business, and it is now much less common to see prospective tourists huddled around screens in a high street travel agency surrounded by brochures or in animated conversation with a (to some extent) knowledgeable agent. In fact it is much less common to see a high street travel agency. Travel agents still play a large part in the tourism business, of course, but their key pre-trip role has changed substantially, with many more of us now doing our own background information searches on a wide variety of destinations, modes of travel and other pertinent information related to this trip. These travel agents still have their place, but the role they play is evolving; they now act much more like a consultancy, and more and more of their functions are being promoted through their own websites, as they transact less tour operator business and fewer personal travel transactions in their branches.

Tour operators too have seen a transformation in their way of doing business. With the growth of technology, the traditional process of combining accommodation, food and beverages, transit trips and sites and attractions into holiday offers and presenting them in hard copy to be sold mainly through travel agencies is less common. This fact offers them the opportunity to be less reliant on travel agent intermediation, and they can now sell directly to their customers through their own websites. The information presented in holiday brochures is often out of date even before it is distributed, with prices and availability changing much more rapidly and dynamically today. This kind of information provision is ideally suited to easy online updating, and thus the web has strongly facilitated its change from relatively static to very dynamic. Perhaps the first question potential tourists should ask their travel agent or tour operator should relate to their sustainability awareness.

Of course, the individual tourist now has more access to information than ever before. Indeed, information on each and every element of a trip which a tour operator may seek to offer is now more or less available to the tourist through the web, such that they can now all play at being amateur tour operators and travel agents and dynamically package their own trips. Perhaps the most useful way to consider some of the technologies is to look at them through the stages of a tourist journey.

Pre-trip

At the pre-trip stage, our potential tourists are in information-seeking mode. They would more than likely be using a desktop computer or laptop mainly for web browsing, probably focusing more on destination and hotel information and review sites. They are less likely to be using social media to any significant extent in the pre-trip phase.

The predisposition to support sustainable tourism was discussed earlier in relation to consumer education, awareness and readiness to participate in this process. It is at the pre-trip stage that messages to the prospective tourist about sustainable tourism development should kick in. If the pre-trip tourist is strongly minded in favour of sustainable tourism, they should be provided with opportunities to filter their searches and encourage this sort of behaviour.

It is difficult at present to customise web searches to restrict results suitably, so the user has to do a fair bit of work in advance to reduce information overload. Perhaps increased use of eco-labels and eco-certification would help to 'bookmark' an independent search and social media could assist in flagging up options which are more sustainable tourism-friendly. There may be other clues for the pre-trip tourist to follow, such as use of carbon calculators, which were discussed earlier. There is a general understanding of the link between carbon dioxide emissions and climate change – indeed, inter-governmental agreements such as the Kyoto protocol have provided a formal framework for carbon offsetting.

Earlier we discussed how destinations may demonstrate the use of such tools to tourists to show their benefits and display their 'green' credentials; hence, environmentally aware tourists may more strongly support such destinations. Carbon calculators may be accessed by tourists at all stages of a trip and destinations in particular may seek to put these tools in the hands of both prospective and actual tourists. A number of companies are offsetting their emissions. Expedia and Travelocity also offer offsetting through Terrapass (www.terrapass.com), and here is a route for responsible tourists to make sustainable choices. Let us now put these considerations in the form of a conceptual tourist journey.

It is likely that in the early search stage, before narrowing down specifics such as hotels and transport, the prospective tourist will encounter a DMS. These systems have evolved to provide an ICT-based means for those with destination management responsibilities, such as national and regional tourist organisations, to communicate with their stakeholders. Some DMS are entirely or almost entirely information-based systems with no transaction component, whilst others are unashamedly both shop-window and sale room for the destination. In the cyberworld of today's tourist, where information is pushed and pulled from a bewildering array of sources, the DMS can usually claim to be the 'official' site of a destination. So, from a tourist perspective, this is often a major source of reliable information, and is invested with significant trust. It is here that the tourist can make judgements about sustainability issues; this is the connection point between the understanding of sustainable tourism imperatives at the destination level, the way these are represented by a web presence and the awareness and understanding already present in the tourist as they approach the DMS. An important characteristic of DMS generally is the degree of trust conferred by users, since the systems often represent national or regional tourist organisations and have an 'official' status. This trust matters; thus, if the DMS is projected as a platform to support sustainable tourism development, this will have an increased impact on the users. In that sense DMS could be regarded as a gatekeeper to sustainable tourism choices, as they are ideally positioned between supply and demand.

An example situation in which a DMS can perhaps have an influencing effect pre-trip can be seen on VisitScotland's website, where the tourist sees a direct means of exploring the site from a 'green' perspective, with a direct link through to a detailed explanation of the Green Tourism Business Scheme (GTBS). More information on this can be found at www.visitscotland.com.

Traditionally, DMS were straightforward websites which provided good, rich information concerning a destination, such as accommodation offers, events and attractions. However, they have evolved into multi-platform entities with multiple channels of communication, driven by Web 2.0, user-generated content and the culture of collaboration. The digital face of a destination today is presented not only through its 'official' website, but also through other routes such as Facebook (see for example http://www.facebook.com/visitscotland), YouTube (see for example http://www.youtube.com/watch?v=3ygqCYfeRhI), Twitter (see for example tag #visitscotland) and a variety of other social media forums. It is vital that tourism managers today understand the importance of presenting a holistic understanding of each of their channels and ensure that all messages, including those of sustainable tourism development, are appropriately configured for these channels.

In our interconnected online world, the pre-trip tourist may (virtually) arrive at the DMS directly, for example by searching for 'Scotland' and finding VisitScotland.com as described above, or may perhaps alight there after a TripAdvisor search or via a referring site such as VisitEurope or VisitBritain, or even a blog post. It may very well be the case that the first encounter the tourist has with a destination is an unofficial YouTube video. Perhaps they have seen the latest Tourism Victoria posting which has gone viral and are thus stimulated to explore further, or they may have encountered one of the thousands of spoof destination videos – many of which are distinctly off-message. Any and all of these potential information channels may be more or less supportive of sustainable tourism. Elsewhere we note that there are destination business and other stakeholder choices to be made regarding how such information crosses the prospective tourist's radar. Here we are considering the tourist's perspective and how they encounter sustainable choices. In any event, the tonnage of pulped brochures is beginning to shrink and far more information is being presented in an accessible and useful digital form. For example, it may be that interest in a destination such as Canada was generated through proximity marketing, by seeing a well-designed poster of the Rockies with an embedded near field communication (NFC) tag (see later discussion) whose rich information was gleaned through the simple swipe of an NFC-enabled smartphone (see later discussion).

Yet another possibility pre-trip is computer simulation. In this instance, unlike the earlier, destination-focused perspective, the tourist may engage with virtual reality to take a cyber tour of a potential destination. Of course, if the cyber-trip were to replace a physical trip, that would be the ultimate in sustainable tourism. The range of potential virtual trips may go from the relatively mundane, such as a slideshow or a virtual travel guide (see for example http://www.virtualtourist.com/), through tools such as Panoramio (see http://www.panoramio.com) which hook up geolocation with photo-sharing or even Google maps, to a virtual-reality fly-though. Whilst some destinations offer what they term 'virtual destinations' they are not all immersive in virtual reality, but still offer a virtual representation. Examples include Virtual Tallinn (see http://www.tallinn.info) and Virtual Malaysia (see http://www.virtualmalaysia.com).

There is no shortage of information available to our prospective sustainability-aware tourists. For example, they can peruse companies with formal sustainability policies and practices by visiting the National Geographic Center for Sustainable Destinations (see http://travel.nationalgeographic.com). They can also engage with green maps (see http://www.greenmap.org). Green maps are usually maps created by or for a local community, reflecting environmental elements of a local area. The elements contained in such maps may vary widely from one community to the next. They will usually contain information on recycling centres, visitor attractions such as heritage centres, community centres, green/socially aware businesses, and basically anything which assists communities to understand their immediate environment and make greener choices.

Ultimately, the broad destination search will narrow in focus to some specific choices. In the case of a tourist seeking a package holiday, maybe this will be a choice among a range of destinations, narrowing to a preferred choice, hopefully with a decision process influenced by sustainable tourism messages actively communicated by the destination. Further narrowing of choice from among competing tour operators again influenced by their sustainability credentials and ultimately to a single combination of travel and accommodation. At each and every stage the consumer has the ability to make informed choices that factor in sustainability alongside the traditional variables of location, cost, quality and other determining factors, whilst the supply side has endless opportunities to demonstrate their stance on sustainable tourism.

Perhaps the process does not involve a travel agent or tour operator but, as is more commonly the case these days, is an independent search seeking to dynamically package a trip from individually sourced components. In essence, the same process is undertaken; in fact, many prospective tourists will run parallel search procedures independently whilst also considering the agency and/or operator alternatives. Independent travellers may proactively seek out accommodation at the destination by looking for indicators such as eco-labels; perhaps if visiting the USA they could go to Energy Star (http://www.energystar.gov) for Hospitality, for example, to see if potential accommodation has earned the Energy Star label. Indeed, they may go further and entirely reduce the demand on dedicated tourist accommodation by making use of couchsurfing sites, which encourage tourists to connect in advance and either offer or seek accommodation from each other.

Thus we see a diverse range of activities possible at the pre-trip stage, with broad information searches filtered and funnelled into specific options and an increasing array of tools to improve decision-making in support of sustainable choices. An initially globe-spanning search can lead to highly specific localised choices, with ICT offering faster and richer support at every stage.

Transit

The increasingly sophisticated virtual representations of destinations do perhaps have a small role to play in replacing some demand, but for the most part it is safe to assume that most tourists really want to be at a destination and would not be satisfied with a virtual substitute. This brings our attention to the transit options between tourist origin and destination.

A very evident technology introduced not so very long ago and now familiar to travellers everywhere, from airlines to trains, is the electronic ticket or eTicket. The traditional method of getting paper tickets from a travel agent was consigned to history as soon as business-to-consumer (B2C) took off, and eTicketing is part of the end game in this process of empowering travellers and reducing clutter. eTickets have largely replaced paper tickets. They are often simply emailed to the recipient, who then has the comfort of knowing that another copy is always available and easily accessible and that, if need be, any alterations or amendments can be done electronically – reducing labour and wasted paper. The process naturally leads to electronic or online check-in, which is a familiar part of the travel process today. Even the process of communicating delays or other issues related to transit has been simplified by services such as SMS travel alerts, which are now offered by most airlines and a variety of third-party services offering this. For example, British Airways offer a range of mobile apps which bring together many services that were formerly the domain of paper applications.

QR codes like the one in Figure 6.2 may be used in many ways in tourism – integrated into posters and brochures, for example – and all that is required for their use is a QR code reader, which scans and interprets the contents of the code and often links to a website. There are a variety of free, easy-to-install smartphone apps that will do this job. Some airlines are beginning to capitalise on this technology. For example, to save customers printing boarding passes a QR code can be attached to the eTicket, which then generates the boarding details on demand.

Figure 6.2 QR code.

The customer then has a fully paperless route to their airline seat. If the QR code is linked to mapping information and GPS (global positioning systems) tracking, it can provide a highly convenient direction-finding tool. At an airport QR codes may be used simply for advertising, service provision and transport location.

Radio frequency identification (RFID) is an interesting way of linking a unique identifying code to objects or people. A well-established example of RFID for travellers is the Oyster card used on public transport in London. This card reduces a significant amount of labour and paperwork and offers the user an RFID solution which can be used on the underground, buses and rail services.

NFC is similar to RFID but is more relevant for shorter ranges, requiring proximity of the communicating devices. It is another technology suited to many stages of the tourist travel journeys. It is not a new technology, having been around for just under a decade, but it has recently been backed by big players such as Apple and Google; the next logical stage in development for this kind of service is to move to implementation on smartphones. A limited but increasing number of smartphones, such as the Google Nexus, have NFC capability built in, and Google Wallet is being rapidly adopted in many areas. For example in the New Jersey Transit, a wireless wave of the smartphone at the payment terminals is all that is needed to gain access. Related to QR codes and air travel, passengers could generate boarding passes or pay for purchases in-flight using NFC smart tags, which could be attached to almost anything directing travellers to further information. They could perhaps even be added to the end of the in-flight magazine.

So our sustainability-aware traveller has gone from home to destination making use of an array of technologies which improve efficiency and reduce the environmental cost of the trip, whilst providing a much richer sphere of information than has been hitherto possible. We will now look now at the possibilities awaiting the tourist at the destination.

In-trip

The tourist at the destination can avail themselves of many of the technologies referred to earlier, but may make use of them in additional ways, drawing upon services specific to the destination/location of the tourist, such as location-based services (LBS). As with many of the technologies, they have not necessarily been implemented with sustainable tourism in mind; it is more the case that their adoption may have positive benefits for sustainability. In-trip we are at the threshold of convergence technologies such as GPS, geographic information systems (GIS) and LBS which are having a transformational effect on tourism.

The sophisticated and extensive applications of GPS and GIS have enjoyed a dramatic upsurge in interest through the development of the smartphone, as consumers now carry formidable processing and display capability in their pocket. Mobile devices offer a vast array of LBS. The logical extension of this from a tourism perspective is the development of a GIS-enabled tourist guide: such guides may be real-time interactive or may be downloadable in advance. The key attribute here is relevance in real time. The user may query their immediate environment – that is, the query may be location-specific. Mobile devices such as smartphones permit geospatial information transfer, and hence offer the opportunity for value-added service provision such as journey planning and navigation and the generation of sophisticated tour guides. Such guides may of course be used either pre- or in-trip, but their most useful application is as a location-based service in-trip.

The tourist information voice system (TIVS) developed by Sharma *et al.* (2009) was a prototype LBS supporting a range of tourist modalities, in particular tour groups at the destination, on foot or on a tour bus. The LBS was enabled through a combination of GPS, GIS and wireless technology and offered a mobile commentary system, thus reducing the need for guidebooks, maps and other documents. It also reduced the level of demand places on the tourist information centre at the destination. The LBS meant, for example, that the user location (identified via GPS) could be connected to geo-tagged information on attractions, enabling customisation and flexibility of any route.

If we think back to QR codes, in San Antonio the famous River Walk Tour can be accessed through a convenient QR code with excellent location-based information, offering a self-guided tour with mobile support (see http://www.visitsanantonio.com/visitors/play/history-heritage/index.aspx). Not only is the rich audio-visual support helpful to the tourist; it also allows them to dispense with maps and general clutter and provides for a higher quality experience. Furthermore, appropriate tracking can provide those involved with local tourism with a utilisation pattern, highlighting walking routes, traffic, volumes and patterns.

Once back in their hotel, the tourist may find that this trip experience can be taken to another level, with QR-coded menus offering links to the way in which the restaurant's dishes have been prepared and perhaps video of the chefs in action. This service can be found at the Radisson Edwardian (see http://www.radissonedwardian.com/feature.do?feature=press_qrcodes2011). Visit England is now testing QR codes in Leicester, Shrewsbury, Chester, Rochester and Rutland. The tourist, via their smartphone app, connects directly to online text, audio and video about specific locations. In Leicester, the codes promote the cultural quarter and National Space Centre, whilst in Chester they focus on the city's Roman past. Shropshire Council's business development manager, Dominic Wallis, commented that the QR codes could be changed far more easily than traditional plaques and offer much richer content. In Shrewsbury the technology is being used to reveal more about one of the town's most famous residents, Charles Darwin. People visiting the library and other key locations around the town can find out more about each building's link with Darwin by scanning codes printed on small plastic signs.

There are some useful examples of NFC beyond QR codes. In Caceres (a UNESCO world heritage city), for example, tourist information centres are lending out NFC-enabled Google Nexus smartphones to facilitate the tourist experience. They can be used to access city museums, for example, as well as to obtain visitor attraction information, rich online content and multimedia guides. The plan is to take this further to incorporate purchase of goods and vouchers. The approach is intended to not only improve the visitor experience, but also reduce resource use.

The use of devices such as smartphones in-trip will increasingly stimulate demand for online access, although tourists are conscious of high roaming charges and data download cost when overseas. This in-trip demand will obviously encourage greater use of such LBS if there are low or no connection and data transfer costs. Whole businesses, such as JiWire (www.jiwire.com), have now developed around informing the public where they can find the nearest (ideally free) access to the Internet. Thus, apart from consideration of an array of possible devices that the tourist may be contemplating at any phase of the trip, the question of how one accesses the information goes beyond the communication medium and device: it goes to the software environment, the application and the interface they plan to use and the services they wish to use.

One example of such innovative software is Monument Tracker (see http://monument-tracker.co.uk). This app can be downloaded by users of Android and iPhones, and alerts tourists when they are close to a monument or cultural attraction. Once the tourists receive an alert, they can gain more information on the attraction, see pictures, find its exact location and get directions. As the information for the app is currently provided by tourist organisations, here sustainability can be built. Once the tourist request more information on the attraction, the tourist bodies can use this as an opportunity to educate the tourist and make them a more sustainable consumer. Information can be provided regarding sustainable travel routes to the attraction, expected behaviour, conservation and how the tourist can become more environmentally friendly and aware.

Out and about in-trip there are new applications on the horizon. We may begin by looking at what promises to be one of the most exciting developments in tourism: AR, which is closely related to what is known as ambient tourism. In a way, the QR codes discussed earlier are a form of simple AR, connecting as they do the physical environment with enhanced information – but there is much more which can be done. AR – as opposed to virtual reality (VR), which replaces real-world environments with simulated environments – refers to a real-time view of a real-world physical environment, which is enhanced using computer-generated input. It is a subset of a field known as mediated reality, in which realities may be either enhanced or simplified. The computer-generated input in AR may come from many sources, and take many forms and may present itself typically in graphic video or sound form. Through AR, information about the surrounding real world of the user becomes interactive and digitally manipulated. Artificial information about the environment and its objects can be overlaid on the real world.

AR is not by any means a new concept – it has been around for many years – but only in very recent times has there been the right convergence of processing power, screen display and sufficient mobile Internet access to begin to put these technologies in the hands of the consumer. Smartphones have catalysed a dramatic rise in the tourist potential for AR. Perhaps one of the best-known applications of AR beginning to enter consumer use is produced by Layar. Layar's model is to provide an AR platform into which third parties may also write applications, which enable the user to filter their augmented environment in selected ways. Using their smartphone's compass and GPS functionality, users can generate an enhanced map of their view, including such items as Wikipedia information, Flickr photos, Google searches and YouTube videos all superimposed onto a picture of the scene. One especially useful application for the in-trip tourist is Yelp (www.yelp.com), an AR application that rates/reviews restaurants.

The Spanish Transit Authority and the mobile network provider Orange have teamed up to provide bus riders with a 'layer' featuring the location of bus stops in the city of Málaga. This layer application is available for iPhone and Android. Residents and visitors to the Spanish city can easily find the nearest bus stop and, as an added bonus, can view the estimated wait time for the next bus. The layer is part of a commitment to sustainability and innovation on the part of the Spanish Transit Authority and they hope it will attract more users to the bus system. Digital travel guides are another example of AR travel guiding, as is the app from Geotravel, which displays online and offline modes.

Where a destination has embraced the principles of sustainable tourism, visitors will often have the option of a technology-facilitated experience. Broads Authority, UK is national park authority and a navigation authority responsible for a large (1,000 square kilometres) area of wetland, which includes protected areas; sustainability is very much to the fore in its strategic planning. A tourist visiting this area will thus encounter a plethora of activities considered from a sustainability perspective, with augmented-reality touchscreen programmes and eBooks amongst the innovative interpretation techniques.

Google of course offers a bewildering choice of tools accessible via computer or mobile device, some of which may be used to significant effect to make well-informed choices at the destination –even if this is simply through using Google Books travel guides as a digital resource or consulting Google Maps. Most of us would recognise the now familiar Google Map interface, which is a pretty intuitive means of accessing accurate mapping information and is especially useful as a location-based resource. These maps can also provide up-to-the-minute information on traffic conditions, again location-based, which may offer a means of avoiding congested routes. They offer, via the satellite icon, photographic detail, and there is even the option to explore streamed real-time webcam information to give an even more up-to-date perspective on travel attractions and events. Referring back to the mapping approach discussed above, Green Maps systems (www.greenmap.org) have been developed collaboratively since 1995, and the movement has spread to over 775 cities, towns and villages in sixty countries. The in-trip tourist may opt to make use of the Green Map app to discover places locally that are supportive of sustainability principles.

Post-trip

Perhaps the most widespread technologies used following a trip are review sites, social networking sites, photo and video sharing sites and personal blogs. Hopefully the accommodation provider has offered electronic feedback in-trip, but certainly post-trip many tourists give such electronic feedback directly to the provider, and many post reviews on travel review sites such as TripAdvisor. These are powerful opportunities for the tourist to highlight their good and bad experiences in terms of sustainability issues, offering such electronic feedback directly to the provider. A considered and reflective assessment of their experiences and sharing this with wider communities through the plethora of social media tools available is part of the awareness and education process discussed at the start of the chapter. Informed tourists generating considered commentary on the sustainability credentials of the destination by picking up on the positives and negatives throughout their trip make a real, affirmative contribution to sustainable tourism.

Conclusion

This chapter has offered an indication of some of the technologies available to the tourist. It could never provide comprehensive coverage and, given the nature of the field, could never be complete. However, a number of critical issues have emerged: among them, that the issue of ICT-mediated sustainable tourism has to be seen from a holistic perspective and is in itself an ecosystem. With this in mind, destination stakeholders of all types and, centrally, the tourists themselves may have their awareness raised and become increasingly better informed not only about what sustainability actually means and why motivation is important, but also about how to do something positive in support of it. There is the potential for positive synergy between the informed tourist demanding more sustainable offers and the supply side considering how to make offers more supportive of sustainability goals, and how best to communicate this to the tourist. As we have seen, technology has a growing role to play in support of these outcomes, and many of the technologies discussed in the chapter are already playing a part; however, there is much undeveloped potential and the extent to which the technologies will be employed specifically to support sustainable choices remains to be seen. What is clear is that our future tourist will have the option of constant connectivity and intelligent interaction with an environment in which all objects are effectively online and offering information about themselves. We shall explore this Internet of Things (IoT) and intelligent environments in Chapter 9, as we see tourists faced with a multitude of communication channels and technology formats and an increasing dependence on the Semantic Web. It is to be hoped that our tourist of today will use these technologies to make greater demands on the sustainability credentials of suppliers at every stage.

Chapter 6 questions

1 Do you think education on sustainability issues is improving? Provide evidence and examples.
2 Should destination managers or destination management systems be directly proactive in promoting sustainable tourism issues, or leave this to other organisations and businesses within the destination?
3 Will QR codes be with us for the next five years or so or will they be superseded – if so, by what technologies?
4 There is increasing convergence of technologies and applications with smartphones as they become ever more capable. Discuss some technologies which do not lend themselves to smartphone implementation.
5 Why is GPS accuracy of particular importance for AR applications?
6 Travel review sites are frequently used pre- and post-trip. Argue the case for increasing use of such sites in real time, in-trip.

7 The value of social media to sustainable tourism

Learning outcomes

In this chapter the reader will learn about Web 2.0, explore some of these applications and examples and gain an understanding of social media and networks, their uses and how they can be supportive of sustainable tourism development. After reading this chapter you should be able to understand:

- the ways in which social networks may be fostered, supported and managed to enhance sustainability; and
- how the tourist, tourist organisations and host communities have different perspectives on sustainability.

Introduction

Socially mediated sustainability may first be considered by reflecting on what we mean by social media, sometimes referred to as new media. Of particular relevance is social media's capacity to configure information in ways which can have the power to very quickly precipitate mass engagement. From viral marketing campaigns to the individual download and/or viewing of a video by millions within the space of a few days, we are in an unprecedented information age where social connectedness is increasingly centre stage. Sustainability is a global challenge and the power of social media places in the hands of individuals real possibilities for effecting positive change.

There are many pessimistic predictions for the future of our planet, and this book's premise is that among the array of ICT tools available to stakeholders, ranging from destinations to those all along the supply chain, none are more important than those which are in the hands of the individual, the consumer, the tourist. This chapter therefore offers examples of current and potential roles for social media as a vehicle for positive change in sustainable tourism. Perhaps social media will ultimately empower individuals to come together and achieve critical mass to effect the change which is vital for the continuance of the tourism industry. 'Critical mass' originally refers to the coming together of the components necessary to create a nuclear reaction. Separately these components have powerful potential but brought together in the right way they can produce a dramatic change through criticality – the minimum amount of material necessary for a fission to result in an additional fission. Some would argue that this is what is now needed in sustainable tourism: a chain reaction of informed decisions in sustainable directions.

In this chapter we explore the possibilities of this latent potential coming together. It focuses on the power of social media as an agent of change for sustainable tourism development. We stand at an interesting and important crossroads where criticality is possible, and this chapter will concentrate on what this is and what may be. Leiner and Stoll-Kleemann (2009) argue that Web 2.0's potential for sustainability could be progressed through sustainability participation, particularly focused on wikis, blogs and podcast. We shall look at these in the broader context in this chapter.

Social media and Web 2.0

It is all about sharing. Park and Oh (2012: 94) commented that social media is founded on 'openness, connectedness and participation'. It is barely two decades since we were first able to use the web. Individually and globally, our world of information has expanded dramatically. In these past twenty years, the rate of change has been so rapid that people now talk about the 'Internet Years' in the same way that we refer to 'Light Years': the latter is the inconceivable distance travelled by light in an Earth year, whilst the former is a reflection of the astonishing time compression within the Internet. The adoption and diffusion of technology *per se* is a well-researched field; a common theme is the 'take-off' point, or the point at which a critical mass of adopters will drive what sometimes becomes ubiquitous adoption. There is a slow, gradual building process and then a sudden inflexion occurs. For example, the Internet existed for around twenty years and was primarily the elite domain of the military and research communities, until it was packaged nicely as the world wide web and became accessible and affordable by all. Here we have lift-off, with the Internet becoming mainstream.

Most organisations were generally slow to adopt the web in the early years. This was however followed by a decade of accelerated development, with huge numbers of domain registrations by public, private and third-sector organisations as well as individuals. Everyone wanted a web presence and this included hotel chains, tourist boards, airlines, travel agents and tour operators. This initial web presence took the form of little more than electronic versions of printed documents, such as marketing material and travel brochures. As technologies improved, alongside advances in bandwidth and increases in supplier and consumer demand, these sites became more graphically driven and engaging – for example, offering integral newsletters and loyalty programmes. Commerce was also being embraced, with these businesses offering full online transaction capability. These developments were welcomed as they still followed an early mindset regarding how business-to-consumer (B2C) communication and transactions would work.

The real revolution was still waiting in the wings. This was driven by the growth of spaces where consumers could interact with one another, customer to customer (C2C). There was a natural path from consumer sharing, to consumer collaboration, to co-creation: the world of Web 2.0 was then at its inflexion point. Web 2.0 was defined in Chapter 2. Hence, social media can be expressed as online tools/applications/networks/platforms/media which provide anyone with the ability to interact, collaborate, create and share content which they or someone else has created. However it is rather difficult to demarcate a precise boundary or enshrine an unambiguous narrative definition for Web 2.0. One gets a better sense of it through immersion in examples of Web 2.0 in action. O'Reilly (2005) produced what was referred to as a 'meme map' to illustrate the principles of Web 2.0; this can be seen in Figure 7.1.

Memes borrowed from Richard Dawkins' concept of a meme as the social equivalent of a gene. Dawkins (1976: 206) stated:

> Examples of memes are tunes, ideas, catch-phrases, clothes, fashions, ways of making pots or of building arches. Just as genes propagate themselves in the gene pool by leaping from body to body via sperms or eggs so memes propagate themselves in the meme pool by leaping from brain to brain via a process which in the broad sense can be called imitation.

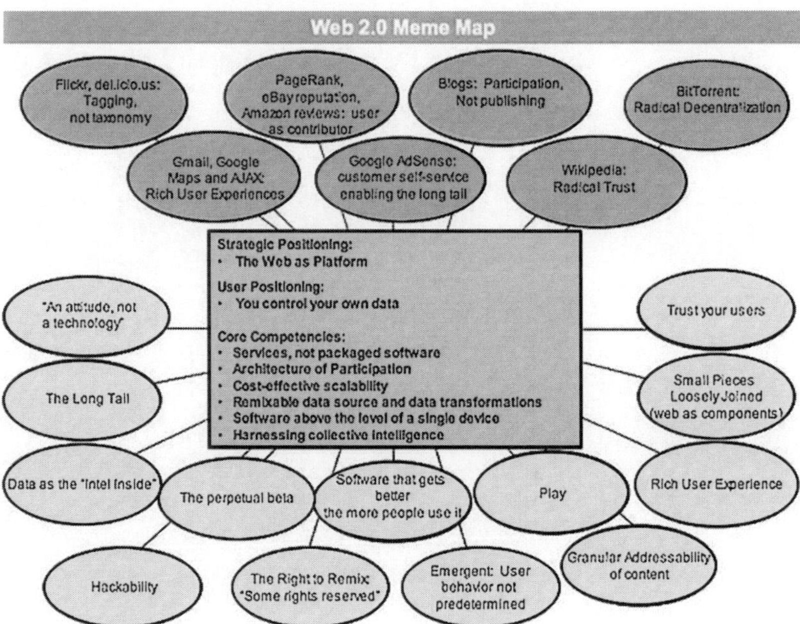

Figure 7.1 A meme view of Web 2.0.

Source: O'Reilly 2005.

In many ways this captures the spirit of the new media. This 'meme' map is useful, but is of course only one way of viewing Web 2.0 applications. It does, however, give a sense of the dynamic, social nature of Web 2.0 in a way that simple narrative definitions cannot. Web 2.0 technologies offer users interactivity in unprecedented ways, with web platforms increasingly generating 'online communities' and facilitating information and opinion sharing. One unarguable driver for the rapid adoption and diffusion of these technologies is of course that there have been some remarkable free services with astonishing functionality and some well-known examples are Facebook, YouTube and Wikipedia. Another alternative perspective placing some of these applications in a different context may be seen in Solis' and JESS3's (2008) often-referenced image of The Conversation Prism, as seen in Figure 7.2.

Users have flocked in their millions, indeed billions, to share the benefits of online collaboration and what has become known as user-generated content (UGC). This peer-to-peer sharing of content is perhaps the most recognisable characteristic of this array of networks called Web 2.0. It is interesting to do, for

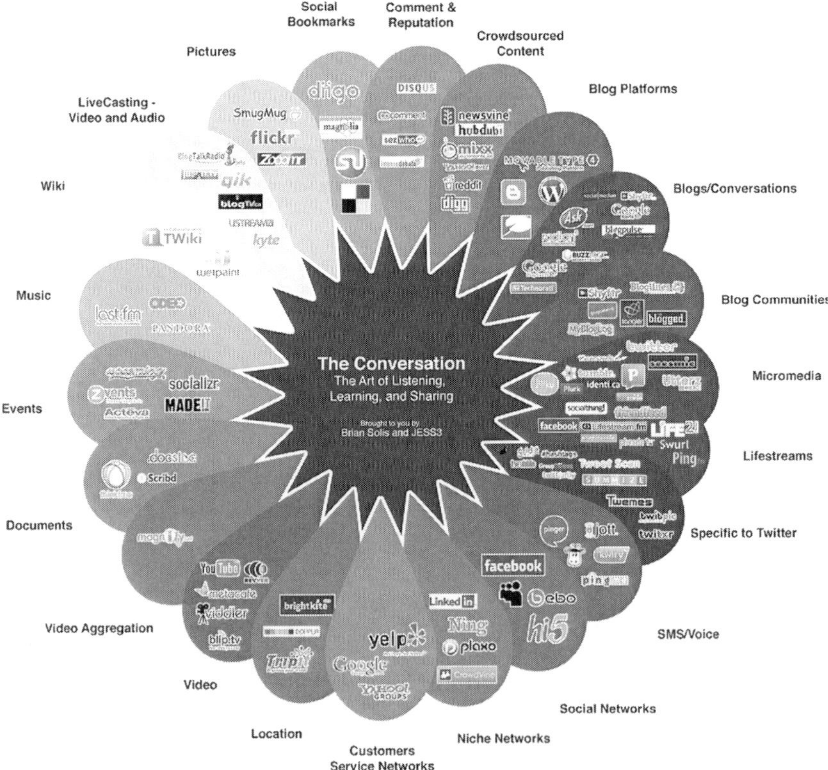

Figure 7.2 Web 2.0 conversation prism.

Source: Solis and JESS3, 2008.

example, a Google Images search for Web 2.0 to see the variety of responses. Table 7.1 gives an indication of the overwhelming volume of users.

The above contains a range of Web 2.0 sites; however it is by no means intended as a comprehensive listing of the most important sites. By the time this text goes to print this fast-moving area will have generated some significant new entrants, and may have seen the demise of others.

Web 2.0 characteristics, functions and applications

Web 2.0 applications almost universally use the Internet as their platform and this means that although there may be a very diverse collection of devices available, with either wired or wireless access, ultimately this universality depends upon the Internet for hosting and for transmission. Web 2.0 applications are global applications or services where the defining characteristic is the general utility of the application or service. They are usually completely open and general, although some may be targeted at a more limited and well-defined user community. They typically entail large-scale collaboration or mass peer-to-peer or user-generated content and tend to be interactive rather than static, as user engagement is placed at the core: hence, they have a distinct social component. These applications are mostly hosted or cloud-based services and importantly, at least at entry level, they are usually entirely free of cost for the user. Further characteristics of Web 2.0 applications include the way they facilitate potential impact and engagement for business. They can radically alter business outlooks and ways of thinking and forms of business intelligence are enhanced, as are opportunities for consumer interaction (Ayeh *et al.* 2012).

The following section tries to give a flavour of the types of tool we associate with Web 2.0 and examples of their use in support of sustainable tourism. Many of these tools may be used in combination, and indeed the whole essence of Web 2.0 will be seen in the multitude of prompts on many sites to click on a link such as the unassuming little 'share this' icon (www.sharethis.com). This indication of Web 2.0 in action often prompts sharing of information and links either through an e-mail or by selecting some or all of a range of social networks.

Typically, the minimum number of social media connections offered on websites today is likely to include Facebook, Twitter and YouTube. However many sites offer a much greater number of onward links – often into the hundreds – by accessing the share icon or similar. Just as it is difficult to pin down a clear, unambiguous definition for Web 2.0, so it is impossible to formulate an exact nomenclature or taxonomy for Web 2.0 tools. However, the next sections offer some of the terminology currently used to group these examples and provide some instances of their applications within the sphere of sustainable tourism.

Blogs

Weblogs, commonly known as blogs, are a form of personal web page carrying the opinions of the blogger, background material, suggested relevant links and other

Table 7.1 Web 2.0 sites and users

Site	*URL*	*Use*	*Users*
Facebook	http://www.facebook.com/	General use	800000000
Youtube	http://www.youtube.com/	Video sharing	800000000
Qzone	http://qzone.qq.com/	General Chinese	480000000
Twitter	http://twitter.com/	General micro-blogging etc.	300000000
Renren	http://www.renren.com/	General Chinese	160000000
LinkedIn	http://www.linkedin.com/	Professional networking	120000000
Vkontakte	http://vk.com/	Russian-speaking network	111000000
Orkut	http://orkut.com/	General popular in India/Brazil	100000000
Google+	https://plus.google.com/	General	100000000
Myspace	http://www.myspace.com/	General	100000000
Friendster	http://www.friendster.com/	General Southeast Asia	100000000
Flixster	http://www.flixster.com/	Movies	63000000
Flickr	http://www.flickr.com/	General global photosharing	32000000
Mixi	http://mixi.jp/	Japan	24000000
Skyrock	http://www.skyrock.com/	French-speaking social network	22000000
Friends reunited	http://www.friendsreunited.com/	UK work school college etc.	19000000
Care2	http://www.care2.com/	Green health social activist	18000000
Plaxo	http://www.plaxo.com/	Aggregator business address book site	15000000
StumbleUpon	http://www.stumbleupon.com/	Interests-linked networks	11000000
WAYN	http://www.wayn.com/	Travel and lifestyle	10000000
Foursquare	https://foursquare.com/	Location Based Mobile	10000000
Delicious	http://delicious.com/	Social bookmarking	9000000
Couchsurfing	http://www.couchsurfing.org/	Traveller-Community interaction site	2900000
Travelbuddy	http://www.travbuddy.com/	Linking travel	1600000
Zoo.gr	http://www.zoo.gr/	Greek web meeting place	900000
Hospitalityclub	http://www.hospitalityclub.org/	Free hospitality exchange network	330000
Travellerspoint	http://www.travellerspoint.com	Travel community blogsite etc.	300000
Academia.edu	http://academia.edu/	Academic and research network site	1000000
Wiserearth	http://www.wiserearth.org/	Social network for sustainability	45000

information this person wishes to share. There are many free tools for bloggers to use; two of the most common are blogger.com and wordpress.com. These tools enable the creation of sharable content and are replete with clever methods to track traffic and even generate advertising income. They also come with a meta-level community of online support forums and user groups. Early blogs concentrated on text, rather akin to a personal news column, but they have evolved such that today one can see the full gamut of sophisticated technology tools being used on many of the popular blog sites.

There are many examples of blogs which focus on sustainability issues and there is no shortage of good commentary out there for those interested in becoming more environmentally aware. Blogs vary from individual, amateurish sites with limited or poor content to very sophisticated individual sites with rich, well-structured content and high levels of user engagement. It is common to encounter blogs which are subsets of much larger organisational sites, and increasing numbers of tourism stakeholders are beginning to see the value of developing blog sites as they generally carry with them a more 'human' element which organisational websites usually lack.

There is a full spectrum of peer sharing of user-created or co-created content (C2C), stakeholder interactions with one another, business networking (B2B), the natural extension of a business website to include the organisational blog (B2C), and finally, for the formal entities associated with destinations, there is the possibility of DMS-driven blogs, a variant of government-to-citizen (G2C). Indeed, in the sustainable tourism domain we see blog contributions from generic sustainability entities such as Forum for the Future (http://www.forumforthefuture.org/), as well as travel-specific blogs such as that of Sustainable Travel International (http://www.sustainabletravelinternational.org/). There are many individual blogs with a focus on tourism sustainability, and this again is a growing channel of communication on the issues. For example Robin Tauck (see http://www.robintauck.com/blog), a sustainable tourism consultant, connects us to specific initiatives such the World Travel and Tourism Council (WTTC) Innovative Award and Tourism for Tomorrow's Destination Stewardship Award in her blog, in true social media style.

Another interesting site is the National Geographic Intelligent Travel blog, which states:

> Cultural Authentic & Sustainable: This is your brain on travel. We showcase the essence of place what's unique and original and what locals cherish most about where they live. And we highlight places, practices and people that are on the front lines of sustainable travel–travel that preserves places' essential uniqueness for future generations (http://intelligenttravel.nationalgeographic.com/ 2012).

There are many sites such as these, providing relevant, dynamically updated content which both informs and provides positive encouragement for destinations and awareness-raising for other stakeholders and tourists in general.

The Global Sustainable Tourism Council also has a blog (http://new.gstcouncil.org/blog), which forms part of their larger web presence and their wider communication strategy. This includes a Twitter feed at @GSTCouncil and an active presence on Facebook (http://www.facebook.com/GlobalSustainableTourismCouncil).

Destination blogging, whilst not yet the norm, is increasingly becoming a feature of a destination's engagement strategy; more enlightened destinations have an integrated approach across all their channels, leading to enhanced efficiency and effectiveness. Blogs have also spawned a range of sub-categories, such as microblogging, where tools are used to provide news or updates in a limited format. This is the case for Twitter, with its 140-character constraint. A message sent in this format through Twitter is called a tweet. Social media connectedness has reached the stage where even products themselves have a Facebook page or a Twitter feed. There are many instances of active participants in the sustainable tourism domain offering a Twitter channel, such as that of the University of East Carolina (see http://twitter.com/#!/c4suto_ecu).

Sharda and Ponnada (2008) adopt a different perspective by connecting blogs with the virtual world. This work seeks to dynamically bring blog information to life by generating for the user an 'audio-visual interactive presentation' from shareable content objects (SCOs), to be replayed on a variety of devices. It is envisaged that this kind of information packaging will offer tourists a sort of virtual trip experience. Again, one imagines the informed tourist seeking to build such presentations from relevant sites supporting sustainable tourism principles.

Mashups

Another Web 2.0 phenomenon is the mashup. In our digital 2.0 world, a mashup is recognised as an interaction between one or more digital information sources, usually with collaborative content. There are many types of mashups in existence – for example, mapping mashups. These take account of the fact that a lot of the information that is accumulated may be 'tagged' with a location and, if these sets of data are represented on a map, it can create a useful application. Mapping mashups received a huge boost when Google brought out Google Maps and the Google Maps Application Programming Interface (API), which allowed a cascade of developers, whether professional or amateur, to utilise the interface to produce useful mashups with software such as Microsoft's Virtual Earth or Yahoo's Yahoo Maps.

Some mashups take news feeds from a single recognised source such as the BBC or Reuters. These may be pulled through really simple syndication (RSS) feeds personalised by the user, with several sources brought together to produce a news mashup. There are also video and photo mashups. Another example is Flickr, which opened an API for photosharing and took a leap forward into the world of mashups, as clearly one of the defining characteristics of a photograph is where it was taken. Therefore tagging has produced a variety of interesting mashups, as metadata associated with the images permits association with other information. For example, a mashup might show social networking graphs based upon photo metadata. Shopping mashups such as Amazon and eBay are examples of online retail platforms which have now offered APIs to connect to their content.

At Mashupaustralia (http://mashupaustralia.org) you can see the results of an innovative exercise whereby a wide range of government datasets were released to encourage open competition to produce mashups based on the data. Of note was the Earth:Australia mashup, which transformed a number of the datasets to provide a interactive map-based tool for accessible query. An illustration of a simple but effective contribution that mashups may make to the sustainability agenda can be seen in connecting location to restaurants. Thus the variables involved in any menu can be reduced to the location of the restaurant, the location(s) of suppliers and the location(s) of ingredients. A tourist may browse for a restaurant in the normal manner through using the web to identify the restaurant's address, contact details and directions (perhaps via Google Maps). They can then drill down to more detailed information on menus, dishes and other relevant information. This is where the supplier may offer information beyond the usual narrative or visual descriptions of menus, providing dish ingredients, suppliers and sourcing information. These values may even be weighted to provide an indication of information such as degree of local supply. From the informed tourist perspective it might then be possible to search for restaurants and filter not only by the usual attributes, but also by sustainability. With food tourism an increasingly important niche, there is a growing demand for information sources which will permit choice based on sustainability.

Another way of looking at the potential role of mashups is to consider our traveller looking for hotel accommodation using a mashup tool such as BedMap (see http://www.bedmap.com/) and in future seeking to filter by not only existing criteria, such as free Wi-Fi, but also by eco-label or eco-certification. Having arrived at the destination there are often a multitude of available mashups incorporating connections to many new media approaches. A great example of this is TorontoTrending (http://trending.seetorontonow.com), which incorporates Google Maps, Twitter and Foursquare to allow visitors to tweet about things to do or places to visit. As we shall see in Chapter 9, the Internet of Things offers the prospect of taking mashups to a new level.

Photo sharing

With the advent of digital photography the traditional scenario of post-holiday snaps being passed around at a family reunion has changed and gone global, and the family has become larger. Digital cameras and recorders have made the taking and sharing of photos and videos simpler and cheaper. These photos can be attached to an e-mail, posted on a personal website, added to a slideshow in a digital photo-frame and submitted to a range of mashup sites. Tales of travel and the shared experiences of tourists have a long history; they are now vastly enhanced by enriching these stories with pictures and can be distributed most powerfully using Web 2.0 tools. There are now a great many tools, such as Picasa and Flickr, which help in storing and organising photo galleries and sharing photos with a global public or a private group. These technologies are increasingly, in both direct and indirect ways, enhancing our understanding of the realities of tourism. Many individuals and organisations are now using shared visual information in support of sustainability goals – for example, the International Institute for Environment and Development has projects which look at how the local community and the environment can be placed at the fore of tourism development. On its website, its narrative is strongly supported with an array of visual material and a shared gallery publicly available through Flickr.

It is of course very easy, whichever tool you choose, to upload and then tag to provide an extra information layer. They say a picture is worth a thousand words, and we should not underestimate the power of tagging and sharing images. Many web albums are being developed specifically to share and promote the cause of sustainable tourism. An example of a small group using this method can be found at http://www.flickr.com/groups/sustour/, where visitors can neatly explore the images through a map tool. The Cluster site (http://www.cluster.eu) uses photo and video sharing alongside blogs and a host of other Web 2.0 tools to promote sustainable tourism by disseminating the outcomes of a focused workshop.

Podcasts

The ubiquity of the iPod produced the term 'podcast' by combining the concept of a 'pod' with broadcast media such as audio or video that is able to be played on a mobile media player. Podcasts are usually available through a distribution server and received through a podcast client prior to playback. They are primarily audio files but may also be RSS feeds. Podcasts very much conform to the notion of Web 2.0 characteristics, especially in the fact that it is easy to create content and to use them, so consumers may produce and producers may consume.

An example of relevant podcasting can be heard in the *Guardian* newspaper's podcast located on its Guardian Focus website and entitled 'What role can tourism play in development?' (http://www.guardian.co.uk/world/audio/2011/apr/28/focus-podcast-tourism-development). The central context of the podcast is the UNWTO contention for the role of responsible tourism enshrined in the Millennium Development Goals identified earlier in this book, and it offers a range of stakeholder perspectives. Another example is the podcast strategy adopted by the Broads Authority (referred to in Chapter 5), which supports its portfolio of sustainable tourism initiatives with a selection of podcast materials (see http://www.broads-authority.gov.uk). The Broads Authority's multi-channel and rich social media approach, underpinned by central goals of sustainable tourism, may be contrasted with the Glasgow Merchant City 'Creating the Buzz' approach outlined by Hamill and Stevenson (2012). In this example, a formerly neglected area of the city had benefitted from sustained investment to redevelop its infrastructure and ultimately brand it 'Merchant City'. Near to the city centre and directly identified in the main tourism strategy for Glasgow, much is expected from this 'destination'. The central goals of those involved were clearly articulated; there was an emphasis on sustained growth in volumes and values, with some very ambitious numbers attached to each. However, there is no underlying recognition or apparent reference to the sustainability of tourism itself, despite the aggressive growth targets.

Social bookmarking

Social bookmarking works in a similar fashion to the personal favourites lists in browser options, entailing lists of links on networks. If one can connect to that network one can link to the lists, usually through a keyword search tool. Users define their own taxonomy (or folksonomy) in effect, bookmarking pages by tagging them. Tagged pages are then stored on the web and may be categorised and shared. Both businesses and consumers increasingly use social bookmarks. Interesting links are usually submitted to sites through tagging, and many tourism businesses today are using social bookmarks to solicit visitors and build traffic. Perhaps among the best-known social bookmarking sites are deli.cio.us and Technorati. In the latter case, as an illustration, users may alight on the social bookmark site, search – for instance – 'green', and be directed to a plethora of relevant (admittedly rather North American-centric) blogs and links: (http://technorati.com/lifestyle/green), or may alternatively seek 'travel' links and be directed to an equally diverse selection of travel-related links. A tourist seeking information sources for sustainable tourism may simply search such social bookmarking sites for relevant keywords. In the former case a search for 'Sustainable Tourism' via deli.cio.us revealed thirty-four relevant stacks, providing 743 relevant links. The real power of these bookmarks lies of course in the sheer width and depth of content shared by users, combined with the keyword tagging systems, which enable an almost thesaurus-like search process to hone in on material of real relevance. Notable among other social bookmarking sites are Digg, Stumbleupon and Reddit.

Social networking and community applications

Social networking essentially entails using the web and/or mobile technologies to expand the number of social connections one has. Today in reality this also encompasses business connections. Sometimes such groupings are general; at other times they are specific to user groups with a special interest, such as a conference site or an action group. As has been said before, the categorisation of these tools is an imprecise science as there is so much overlap in function and use, so the many interconnections these media have with others must be considered.

Facebook

With over one billion accounts, Facebook really needs no introduction. It is the dominant social network site in the English language and has been around for about eight years, although there has been significant development and evolution in that time. Today Facebook is used for many different purposes, from simple individual profile pages to highly active group and corporate sites. Individuals, organisations and products are increasingly represented through a Facebook presence along with utilisation of the spectrum of other Web 2.0 tools which have been discussed. Its users regularly access it, with statistics showing that almost half of all users log in daily. This login is increasingly via smartphone and on the move, so for the tourist it is clearly becoming an important and ever-present technology.

Twitter

Originally conceived as a social networking tool to keep friends or colleagues connected through short tweets, Twitter is now used widely by businesses, celebrities, political parties and almost anyone in the general public. Once an account is set up messages can be initiated or received by SMS or the Twitter website, and increasingly by third-party tools such as Tweetdeck by Twitter. Forwarding tweets or retweeting is similar in function to e-mail forwarding and is a potential viral channel. A tourist wishing to keep abreast of issues in sustainability may, in addition or as an alternative to other technologies described here, choose to sign up to or 'follow' relevant Twitter channels such as Sustainable Tourism (@C4SUTO_ECU).

LinkedIn

LinkedIn is also a social networking application, although this is not its exclusive function. It is much more specifically targeted towards the corporate and professional world, with users creating a mini resume in their profile and linking this to friends and colleagues. LinkedIn can be a useful tool in that it connects to special interest or sector groups and users may connect with others sharing a common interest. LinkedIn users connect in many ways, sometimes offering professional services, sometimes seeking advice, often just sharing information. The structure of LinkedIn facilitates the development of focused groupings: thus, for example, we can see a dedicated group formed under the skills and services section as Sustainable Tourism (http://www.linkedin.com/skills/skill/Sustainable_Tourism).

There are a number of active sustainable tourism groups within the LinkedIn network – for example, VISION and the Global Sustainable Tourism Council discussed earlier. At times a conference group might be established, such as the Ecotourism and Sustainable Tourism Conference, hence offering more of a variety of ways to use Web 2.0 tools to cascade messages of sustainable tourism.

Tagging

Tagging has a wide variety of meanings but basically means providing a label which links in some way to further information (metadata). It has become immensely popular since the advent of Web 2.0 and is illustrated through, for example, tagging individuals in photos pasted onto a social network site. Tagging may also refer to hashtagging in Twitter, where a word or phrase may be preceded by the hash symbol (#) to indicate that the recipient can link to other tweets on that subject. Further geo-tagging is increasingly common; in this last case it refers to providing geographical/geospatial metadata which can be linked

Figure 7.3 Sample word cloud for Chapter 7 (created at Wordle.net).

to a wide variety of location specific uses. In social media the process of tagging is a very powerful means of distributing targeted content (in effect keyword labelled) across platforms and applications. Tag clouds are a way of visually indicating the relative frequency of usage of terms: a tag cloud for this chapter (generated by Wordle.net) would look like Figure 7.3.

Video hosting

There are a great many instances of video-sharing opportunities available today, some of which are even as simple and direct as a smartphone broadcast. However, again, Web 2.0 comes into its own in the enormous range of ways in which videos can be shared – from being attached to blog posts to their use as part of a podcast. The possibilities of geo-tagging video have already been discussed, whereby a simple but powerful mashup such as Google Maps enables the tourist to search by location, and selecting a video collects together all relevant geotagged video from YouTube and layers it on to the map. YouTube is easily the most prominent video hosting service, and has become so powerful and rich in channel content and opportunities that it is already being compared to large international television networks. Many social network sites permit the posting of user-generated videos – although it is not their main function, it enriches the site and enhances network interaction – however, there are a great many sites dedicated specifically to video hosting services. Grossman (2012) comments that ‘For every minute that passes in real time 60 hours of video are uploaded to YouTube’.

Whether the tourist is searching for specific destination information, hotels or restaurants, there is an ample supply of YouTube material to meet most needs.

Additionally, the user may search for wider terms related to sustainable tourism. Of course, as with any online search, relevance is difficult to judge at times – frequency of download indicates popularity only. For example, here are some outcomes for a basic YouTube search conducted in early March 2012 on relevant terms:

Sustainable Tourism	4,110 results
Sustainable Travel	4,480 results
Sustainable Tourism Development	4,030 results

An indicative example might be the VisitScotland offer on Sustainable Tourism Businesses (see http://www.youtube.com/watch?v=8oKm3E63Z4k), which uses YouTube videos to covers a range of approaches to sustainability from a number of tourism stakeholders.

Virtual realities

Since the board game Dungeons and Dragons migrated to become the first online multiplayer game inhabiting virtual worlds, often collectively known as multi user dungeons/dimensions (MUDs), Internet users have virtually collaborated and competed in fictional worlds. Brought up to date, this world has witnessed vast strides forward in technology and huge growth in player numbers. Today these massively multiplayer online role-playing games (MMORPGs) have become fully 3D meta-verses which are highly graphical and interactive, with many added dimensions beyond the original 'hack–and-slay' games. All of the characteristics of Web 2.0 are to be found in modern MMORPGs, whether in the adventure genre of World of Warcraft or Runescape or in the more socially oriented Second Life. In most of these applications the user is represented by a graphical image or an avatar and interacts with other avatars in co-created space. These environments, especially Second Life, have been strongly embraced by the tourism world, where we have seen the creation of virtual representations of many destinations and attractions. With user numbers in the many millions, it is unsurprising that we see enormous diversity in the approach taken to representation in Second Life, ranging from individual efforts to more formal and structured official tourism efforts. One sustainable tourism effort within Second Life is the Massai Tourism Project; one could also visit a Facebook group such as http://www.facebook.com/virtual.travellers and bounce through the links to wander an array of virtual worlds. For example if a potential tourist wants to visit Dublin but wants first to check it out virtually, he/she can explore Dublin's representation in Second Life.

Sigala (2010), writing on the politics of sustainable tourism, notes that many stakeholders have already established a Second Life presence, including embassies, tourism boards and companies. She cites the well-known example of Starwood using Second Life residents' intelligence and knowledge to help construct the Aloft hotel concept. Sigala also makes reference to the Michigan

University project which created a Second Life island to examine sustainable behaviours. Virtual tourists can test simulations of proposed tourism services and hopefully improve sustainable service and destination design prior to any implementation. This would be of benefit all round.

VOIP

VOIP stands for voice over Internet protocol and is a collection of technologies that permit the Internet to be used as the transmission medium for telephony. Sometimes it is in fact called Internet telephony. If we reflect for a moment on the characteristics outlined earlier for Web 2.0, this technology surely conforms to many of them. The basic service is in most cases completely free, only invoking a premium if additional services outwith the basic Internet telephony are used, such as calls to landlines and mobiles. In terms of global connectedness this could be regarded as a building block for many additional services and is often associated with other social media. Perhaps the best-known programs are Skype, Google Voice and FaceTime. The term 'VOIP' does not really do justice to the sophistication these services now offer, which go well beyond simple voice. Tourists today take for granted voice, chat, file sharing and live video links, with the applications being used between a pair of users or indeed to facilitate multiple communication.

These services are just one more way in which today's tourists are in much more sophisticated real-time communication with each other and their wider communities. This communication potential is enormously powerful in offering immediacy for the sharing of experiences within destinations and to these much larger audiences. This potential underlines the power available to the sustainability-aware tourist (or business) to highlight and share experiences of both good and bad practice. There are many proprietary systems available in the marketplace offering very full functionality to operate, for example, desktop sharing, presentation software, educational webinars and much more, and the tourist is highly likely to be using one of the free applications such as Skype or Google Talk.

Gamification

Gamification, as discussed in Chapter 2, is another Web 2.0 application which can be used to assist in sustainability. One of the best known among these is Foursquare (www.foursquare.com). As with most gamification, Foursquare takes the well-known human predisposition to engage with games and satisfies it by awarding badges for positive behaviours. Foursquare is a social network tool distributed primarily as a free app for smartphones, which enables you to interact within your environment with friends or people with similar interests and is location-oriented, using the inbuilt GPS technology in the mobile device. Users 'check in' to a venue and are rewarded for increasing loyalty with badges and other treats on an increasing scale. Businesses may offer discounts, so the users can get insider tips from those with expert local knowledge and can also create their own lists. In terms of sustainability, this social media tool can be used by businesses to put themselves on the Foursquare radar by permitting check-in and tagging with sustainability tags. For example, one could check in to the University of New Hampshire's sustainability academy at http://www.sustainableunh.unh.edu/ and experience gamified persuasion in support of sustainability.

Another example of a similar tool is SCVNGR (see http://www.scvngr.com/), an app designed as a game allowing the user to discover new places to go and fun things to do there, and then allow this to be shared with friends. The game has challenges built in where the user is allowed to earn points for successful completion. Therefore sustainability can be included here to increase users' awareness of their impacts on the environment as they venture to a new place, with the hope that the prospective tourist will be motivated and educated to become more sustainable.

Wikis

A wiki is basically web-hosted content which is generally (collaboratively) created by and edited by users. Users may edit any page or create new pages using only a basic web browser. Page links encourage topic association and there is an organic and continuous process that constantly changes the site. Single wiki pages interconnect by hyperlinking to create a database. Depending on the nature of the wiki (personal, public or enterprise) and its scale, there may be no editorial restrictions or there may be a hierarchy of editorial controls. The best-known wiki is Wkipedia; in the tourism domain, http://en.wikipedia.org/wiki/Travel is probably the most commonly used area. There are many other travel and tourism wikis, of which http://wikitravel.org/en/Main_Page is a popular example. If we look to sustainable tourism wikis, we can see on the Good Travel and Tourism Wiki how wikis can be co-created and shared. In fact, the 'share' tool on this site offers several hundred direct links for sharing. The relevance of this kind of wiki is illustrated by the shared opinion piece from Beary (2009), in which this author outlined his views on technology and sustainable tourism:

> Thus a responsible tourism model filtered through Web 2.0-enabled CGF that reflects a growing social conscience is therefore the best solution to the problems the tourism industry is facing today. The survivors of the present economic crisis will be those who are quick enough to adapt during this period when the 'responsible model' replaces the 'slash and burn model' at the mainstream of tourism. All tourism business operators and destinations regardless of their financial resources or skill levels can participate. Those who are slow to adapt will be swiftly swept away.

Beary (2009) recognised that in an ever challenging marketplace, responsible tourism – through attending to a range of issues, from reducing energy costs to waste reduction and recycling, inherently all ultimately cost saving practices – would provide a competitive advantage. Further, the opportunities – especially through social media – to engage host communities with activities related to sustainable tourism (such as Green Maps) would be beneficial. Web 2.0 empowers both host communities and tourists, with its many rich and immediate channels enabling shared experiences to build an increasingly trusted environment.

Conclusion

Web 2.0 and social media have grown at a phenomenal rate in recent years, and this trend will undoubtedly continue. These media, tools and applications are capable of supporting dramatic and apparently sudden inflexions in social behaviours, as has been seen in the geopolitical sphere. It is to be hoped that the early signs of use of these media in support of sustainable tourism goals may follow a similar path towards critical mass. We have seen a broad collection of technologies characterised not only by their power to connect individuals, groups and organisations but also by their strong interconnectedness to one another. This truly is a remarkable web, permitting rapid exploration of relevant topics, and these media – in combination with increasingly sophisticated devices, both static and, more often, mobile – equip today's tourist with unparalleled levels of information and choice.

We have considered the tourist's awareness of sustainability issues and motivations to use technology and have also looked at a variety of technologies and stakeholder approaches, but is travel planning actually being facilitated and supported in any significant way by social media, and are tourists actually changing behaviours? Litvin *et al.* (2007) examined the importance of sharing personal experiences and electronic word of mouth (eWOM) in emphasising the value of social media to travellers, whilst Xiang and Gretzel (2009) offer evidence of the growing importance of such socially mediated content to travel product search. Fotis *et al.* (2012) offer an interesting empirical insight into the role and impact of social media on holiday planning by studying travellers from the former Soviet Union Republics. Here they found strong influencing links between social media and travel planning decisions. Again, as was seen throughout the text, decisions informed by good (and increasingly real-time) information about destination choices, travel arrangements and other related factors – which incorporate a growing awareness of sustainability issues – aligned with user-generated evidence and an ability to filter in meaningful ways, will make a substantial contribution.

From a destination perspective, we see for example in the destination outreach that Tourism Australia's Facebook page (facebook.com/seeaustralia) has recently passed two million fans, making this now the largest Facebook page in Australia and the world's most popular destination page. This is evidence of a concerted social media strategy which not only facilitates the sharing of experiences and media, but also pays attention to the feedback loop. There is integration with Tourism Australia's overall social media presence, including Twitter, a YouTube channel, Google+, Instagram and more such media.

The central question is: if social media is influencing our activities, then which media channels are doing so, and how? Kumar (2011) found that friends and family attached importance to status updates, picture, videos and other social media postings. In their own destination decision-making, Twitter was ranked highest, with Facebook a close second. This research also stated that seventeen per cent of respondents had been to a sustainable tourism destination; when questioned further regarding the reasons behind their choice, twenty-seven per cent understood the positive environmental benefits and twenty-two per cent considered it to have a positive impact on the local economy.

Tourists are at an interesting junction in time socially, technologically, economically and indeed politically, as many forces and interests position themselves within the sustainability debate that is gaining traction worldwide. Never before has so much potential power been at the disposal of the tourist, and it remains to be seen how this latent influence will play out. In Chapter 9 we will examine some future scenarios.

Chapter 7 questions

1 Argue the case for or against the use of replication as an appropriate concept characterising social media.
2 Why are individual blogs often regarded as among the most powerful kinds of social media application? Give some recent examples of influential blogging in sustainable tourism.
3 Identify some key advantages of Web 2.0 in trip planning and indicate how sustainable preferences might be included in the process.

8 Influencing factors for technology uptake for sustainable tourism

Learning outcomes

This chapter provides a discussion of the factors that can affect the uptake of technology for sustainable tourism development. After reading this chapter you should be able to understand:

- the influencing factors for the use of technology for sustainable tourism development; and
- the support stakeholders require to be able to effectively use such technologies.

Introduction

For technology use to become an effective concept, stakeholders must have knowledge and understanding of the factors that can have a bearing on the successful implementation of these technologies, as this has strategic implications for destination competiveness. Awareness of these factors is vital to developing an understanding to ensuring that these limitations form part of tourism stakeholders' strategic planning. The purpose of this chapter is to contribute to a greater understanding of the elements that will influence the use of technologies for sustainable tourism and the necessary conditions that will facilitate such uptake. The first section of this chapter discusses what are termed 'influencing' factors, whilst the second part focuses on the settings needed to facilitate uptake and use of these technologies.

Influencing factors

Influencing factors hold sway over whether these technologies are used for sustainable tourism development. In the literature they are commonly referred to as critical success factors and barriers. We have chosen to use the expression 'influencing factor', as one person's critical success factor is another's barrier. This term better reflects what can shape the uptake of technologies by destinations, tourist businesses and tourists. These factors are discussed below.

Cost

Funding is always an overriding concern in the uptake of any new technology, and adoption of ICT for sustainable tourism is no exception to this. Cost has to be considered from both a hardware and a software perspective. If destinations and businesses do not have the finances to support the implementation of these tools, there will be little or no use of technology (Nodder *et al.* 2003) for sustainable tourism development. In making a case to secure funding to support the adoption of these technologies, stakeholders need to be assured that the benefits of using these technologies outweigh the costs, and that they would have a long-term impact on how sustainable tourism is managed. It is critical to determine what business processes will be supported by these technologies and understand the cost involved.

Moreover, linked to the point above, if governments provided support in the form for funding, this would afford stakeholders a greater opportunity in securing these technologies. If destination management organisations (DMO) were accountable to their members for financing, or if they were commercially based, then their focus would be on revenue generation. This would make it more difficult for them to invest in these technologies compared with government-funded organisations, which would have a greater responsibility to the community. HVS (2012) commented that hoteliers are more willing to undertake large projects when third-party funding is available, and therefore there is a need for innovative funding mechanisms. The government can lead this initiative.

It might be feared that in times of economic uncertainty, investment in the technologies needed to maintain the sustainability of the tourism industry will be low or non-existent. Bramwell and Lane (2009), however, commented that the future cost savings to be realised from such investment might be more appealing to organisations during this period of economic recession. Technology is usually associated with the intrinsic notion of costliness, but rapid advancements indicate that these technologies are becoming more powerful and complex and, in turn, cost-effective and user-friendly, which provides advantageous opportunities for organisations (Buhalis and Law 2008). For example, a first-generation geographical information system (GIS) would have cost an organisation tens of thousands of dollars, but now sophisticated GIS can be obtained for under US$500. Therefore one should not be quick to judge technology use for sustainable tourism based on cost, as this can be deceptive.

For the tourist, cost will be influential in determining the types of devices and the software they purchase to allow them to engage in sustainability. Many of the tools discussed in Chapter 6 require the tourists to be connected to the Internet and this comes from having a personal computer, laptop and/or smartphone (particularly useful in the in-transit stage). Costs are associated with purchasing these devices; however, they are becoming price friendlier. Additionally, when travelling out of country, the use of these devices – particularly smartphones – have associated roaming charges if free Wi-Fi is unavailable, which can be quite costly depending on the mobile provider.

The meaning and management of sustainable tourism

Many tourists, professionals who manage destinations and tourism businesses possess a limited outlook on what is actually meant by 'sustainable tourism'. They do not have a clear understanding of the key ideologies of the concept, and furthermore they do not know how to go about translating the principles of sustainable tourism into affirmative action. Moreover, there seems to be a preoccupation with associating sustainable tourism with primarily the natural environment; often little thought is given to socio-cultural aspects. This lack of understanding of the concept's fundamental nature is a perilous deterrent in using technology for managing sustainable tourism. Before any technology can be considered, the users must develop their knowledge of the meanings of sustainable tourism.

Destination managers need to possess a sound understanding of which aspects of destination development require management and control, as destinations are dynamic entities which grow and advance as a result of varying factors such as popularity, marketing and promotion and investment. Destinations are in sundry stages of development and will have different sustainability concerns at any given period of time. Comprehending this is strategic to selecting the right technologies for use in destination management. At the destination level there also appears to be confusion about where the responsibility for sustainable tourism lies. Is it with the government, the destination management organisation, the local businesses, the host communities or the tourists? It can be argued that sustainable tourism is indeed the responsibility of all these stakeholders; however, direction is required from a responsible party, and in many of these destinations this lead is evidently absent. Sustainable tourism is hardly managed; rather, individual organisations or groups consider it from their own vantage point instead of taking a coordinated and collected approach. There tend to be many quick fixes suggested for addressing the negative impacts of tourism, without looking at the bigger picture and trying to determine how it all fits together, from the local to the regional and national levels. This will undoubtedly lead to conflict and duplication of efforts. It can be argued that destinations are not serious about pursuing a sustainability agenda, but rather use this as more of an awareness and branding mechanism. Many destination organisations, which are charged with responsibility for holistic planning and management of a destination, evolved from marketing organisations, and still see this as the core of their business. Sustainability is discussed but not actively pursued, as priorities lie elsewhere. If destinations do not have a coordinated approach to the management of sustainable tourism and are only paying it lip service, then the use of technology as a workable reality for solving some of the problems of tourism will be ineffective.

Tourist businesses are also in this precarious position and are pursuing sustainability policies because of government pressures, customer demand and the need to keep up with competitors. Many – especially the smaller businesses – do not possess a clear understanding of the various facets of sustainability; they have difficulty comprehending the value added and how it can be linked to their businesses objectives. This is probably increased by a lack of direction from the main tourism organisation at the destination. Ayuso (2006) supports this, finding that Spanish hoteliers were unclear about the meaning of sustainable tourism and the impacts of their businesses beyond the economic sphere of sustainability. This lack of knowledge is indeed an impediment in fostering technology uptake for sustainable tourism. Additionally, as part of technology uptake for sustainable tourism, tourists need to be educated on the implications of their actions when visiting a destination. Education alone is not sufficient: they must also be motivated to pursue sustainable activities at all stages of their trip, as discussed in Chapter 6.

Achieving sustainability goals

The technologies being used must be fit for purpose, in that they fulfil the goals that the destinations and businesses at the destinations are trying to achieve. Destination stakeholders will select the technologies for use based on the sustainability goals of their destinations. If both a local attraction destination management organisation and a continental tourism organisation were experiencing problems in selecting areas for tourism development in order to ensure sustainability principles are reached, they would both consider the use of a GIS. If they were experiencing difficulties with the host community and wanted to engage them more in the tourism development process, they might use the output from the GIS to explain proposed developments. They may also want to consider the use of community informatics. Likewise, if they wanted to track the movement of tourists at the destination so they can more efficiently plan tourist routes or identify areas of tourist concentration, they may employ a GIS or a global positioning system (GPS). This same principle applies for businesses' and tourists' use of these technologies. However, these stakeholders must also be convinced of the value being added by using these tools and of the actual effort to implement versus the expected benefits. Their understanding of the technology would directly impact this and what it can accomplish for them, as discussed earlier.

The table below provides a snapshot of some of the technologies that can be used by destination stakeholders to achieve different aspects of sustainable tourism development.

Stages of tourism development

Butler's (1980) life cycle of a destination hypothesised that over time, destinations develop through a series of stages, determined by the number of visitors and the destination's infrastructure. The stages that a destination progresses through are exploration, involvement, development, consolidation, stagnation and rejuvenation or decline, as depicted in Figure 8.1. This model has been criticised (see for example Haywood 1986 and Prosser 1994) and modifications have been proposed (see for example Agarwal 1994; Russell and Faulkner 1999); despite this, Hovinen (2002) argues that this model is still of value in understanding a destination's conditions and is a useful framework for academic research focused on destination development.

Table 8.1 Indicative technologies for aiding sustainable tourism development

Sustainability goal	*ICT-based tools/applications*
Inventorying tourism resource	Geographical information system
Identifying suitable locations for tourism development	Computer simulation Geographical information system
Identifying damaged areas at the destination	Geographical information system
Managing the destination's resources	Destination management system Environment management information system Geographical information system Location-based services
Managing sites and attractions	Geographical information system Location based service Tourism information system Virtual tourism
Managing tourist flows	Geographical information system Location-based services Tourism information system Virtual tourism
Tracking tourist movements	Computer simulation Geographical information system Global positioning system
Producing realistic images of what a proposed development would look like	Computer simulation Geographical information system
Influencing tourist behaviour	Carbon calculator Community informatics Destination management system Location-based services Virtual tourism
Involving the community in the tourism development process	Community informatics Computer simulation Geographical information system
Collaboration with local businesses at the destination	Destination management system

Using Butler's life cycle analysis it was determined that the stage of tourism development is important to the uptake of technologies for sustainable destination management. There tends to be a greater use of technology at the development and consolidation stages of destination development. Whilst it is better for destinations to use these technologies during the early stages, it was during the development and/or consolidation stages that difficulties due to improper tourism planning and over-development were realised (Martin and Uysal 1990). This provided greater justification for its use in the earlier phases, as tourism's negative impacts become more advanced in the later stages of a destination's tourism development. Moreover, in the early stages of development, destinations may have problems in taking up technology due to funding. Their priority would be

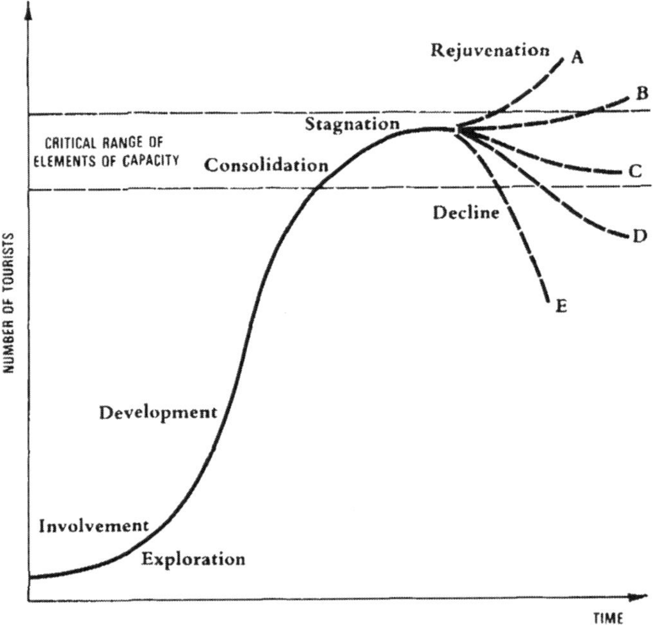

Figure 8.1 Butler's life cycle of a tourist destination.

Source: Butler 1980.

marketing, promoting and getting the destination known, rather than sustainable tourism development. If destinations plan and grow their industry in a sustainable manner at the beginning of their tourism development, they can prevent many of the problems which occur later on in the destination's life cycle (Manning and Dougherty 2000).

The users

Not only are destination stakeholders unsure of the meanings of sustainable tourism; also, they have limited cognisance of technologies and how they can be of benefit to them. They need to become aware and educated with regard to what technology means and what it can accomplish for their destination management before they can start using it to support sustainable tourism. Tourism stakeholders should also have a staff member who has developed expertise in using these technologies, as this person would be able to provide guidance on the right technologies to employ the data required for input and how to make sense of the output. Lack of knowledge about what technology can do for a destination prevents operational conversations with the suppliers of the technology with regard to what they require. This leads to the challenge of finding the right technologies to help alleviate their tourism development problems. Therefore the users, and their appreciation of technology for sustainability, are a critical success factor. Many stakeholders in tourism have yet to embrace technology to its fullest level in terms of benefiting their businesses and from a sustainability perspective.

Moreover, when new technologies are introduced, organisations can encounter the challenge of user acceptance. Difficulties in acceptance may result from a deficiency in training, lack of confidence, fear of improper usage or having to continuously update their knowledge on technologies that may change rapidly. Some of these impediments may be avoided if the technologies were user-friendly and easy to understand and use. This in itself is a critical success factor. Several theories have been proposed to explain employee resistance to technology acceptance – for example, Davis' (1989) Technology Acceptance Model and Schein's (1993) theory of Career Anchors. The researchers will not expand on these here, as they are beyond the scope of this book. Destination stakeholders need to be aware of users' opposition to these technologies and should ensure before implementation that these employees are sufficiently trained, so as to minimise any resistance to and improper usage of the said technology (Nodder *et al.* 2003).

Employees are viewed as organisational assets rather than costs, as they play a large role in generating continuously improving quality and productivity (Mefford 2011). In implementing technology for sustainable tourism development, destination organisations need to have the right employees, who are innovative, have the required skills and vision, understand the nature of the business and continuously develop efficiency gains and quality improvement. Staff training and an appropriate working environment is important in developing employees of this calibre, who will be able to execute the technologies necessary to make sustainable tourism a fruitful reality. It would also foster increases in business quality and productivity.

The consumers

Tourism consumers are becoming more aware of the impacts of their behaviours on the environment, and this has heightened with the increasing awareness of climate change. As consumers begin to adopt more environmentally friendly practices in day-to-day living, they will seek out holiday destinations which are operating in a sustainable fashion, as it is expected that these travellers will not abandon their responsible daily practices whilst on vacation. Green Travel News (2011) reports that baby boomers, Gen-Xers and millennials are pursuing authentic green experiences as they continue to search for richer meaning in their vacations. Sustainability is becoming a key consideration in consumer culture. The future trend may well be that consumers will visit only those destinations which they consider to be operating according to the principles of sustainability. This increasing pressure from consumers may be the momentum that destination stakeholders require to adopt and adapt technologies for sustainable tourism.

The technologies

There are some challenges present in the actual use of the identified technologies. For example, mobile technologies present issues with usability, accessing information over different devices, tourist confidence and interactivity. These difficulties can however be surpassed with the development of sophisticated user models for tourism (Werthner and Ricci 2003). There are questions relating to security and privacy issues, for example, with RFIDs. For location-based services to be successful, complementary factors such as bandwidth, positioning, availability, user interface, security issues, availability of accurate and timely information, localised data, end user costs and trust must be taken into consideration (Zipf 2002).

Buhalis and Law (2008) observed that the popularity of Internet applications has caused many tourism stakeholders to embrace these technologies as part of their marketing and communication strategies. The popularity of these technologies for sustainable tourism development can be a critical success factor in their utilisation. Many tourism destinations are followers rather than leaders and tend to manage based on what competitors are doing. If destinations found that competitors were using these technologies for sustainable tourism, they would be more inclined to adopt and adapt, as they would feel this necessary to keep abreast with the competition. Tourists and their use and adoption of technology also project the behaviour described above.

Conditions required for implementation

Several factors important to the implementation of technology for sustainable tourism are beyond the control of destination stakeholders. Further support is needed to make these technologies a workable reality for destinations, tourism businesses and tourists. This is discussed below.

Government support

Governments at the state and local levels have an integral role to play in formulating tourism policy and planning, and a noteworthy part of this is executing sustainable tourism development. Some of the key roles that concern governments in tourism planning and development are: providing tourism legislation and regulation, economic support for tourism initiatives, developing and maintaining the infrastructure and attractions of the destination, marketing and promotion and overseeing the growth and development of the industry and its impacts on the environment. Baum and Szivas (2008) commented that the level of a government's involvement and engagement with tourism at a destination is contingent upon the planned models of economic development that are predominant at a given point in time. The same can be said for a government's approach to sustainable tourism development.

A strong stance from the government is necessary for destinations to develop in a sustainable fashion. This is because the tourism industry is dependent on the environment, since the human and physical environment is tourism's core product (Murphy 1985; Poon 1993; Murphy and Price 2005). Tourism's existence and its continued penetration of many countries is validated by its contribution to the economy. However, tourism's rapid growth has produced several negative impacts, largely due to unplanned and unregulated tourism development (Holloway 2002). Therefore what is required is guidance and support from government, to ensure that whatever tourism development occurs is done in a sustainable manner.

Government support is therefore integral to destinations' uptake of technology for sustainable tourism development. As discussed in the introductory chapter of this text, many of the current approaches to the management of sustainable tourism have not performed as predicted, and the use of technology can alleviate some of the challenges currently experienced by destinations with regard to minimising the negative impacts of tourism and maximising the positive ones. If governments engage in a policy that supports technology use and invest the time, effort and training that allows destinations to take up the technology necessary for them, there would be a stronger momentum towards using this technology. Destinations would feel more comfortable and confident in using this technology as the impetus will be coming from government, and therefore they would have greater motivation for adoption.

Partnerships

In Chapter 2 we discussed how partnerships can lead to cultivation of sustainable tourism development and this can be enhanced through the use of technology. Budeanu (2009) commented that the development of clear, sustainable tourism strategies is hampered by the disjointed nature of the tourism industry. The creation of partnerships is also critical for the uptake of technology for sustainable tourism, as these associations enable stakeholder consultation and information transfer. This can be a strategic tool for building and strengthening relationships, networks and communities, which can transform the tourism planning process and enhance economic development at the destination level. Many of the technologies discussed in Chapter 2 have multiple applications and can benefit more than one stakeholder group. For technology to be successful in sustainable destination management it is integral that these delegations co-operate, as they can share technology applications for mutual benefit. Creating an environment which facilitates partnerships and co-operation may stimulate greater buy-in for adopting these technologies. Stakeholders would no longer feel pressured to bear the full cost of purchasing the technologies, hiring the necessary expertise and training staff. If stakeholders become champions of applying technology to the management of sustainable tourism then they will work towards greater implementation.

An example of this is the use of intelligent transport systems (ITS) by destinations to provide a better ground transport system, which allows tourists to be more aware of their exact travelling times at the destination. This leads to wider usage of public transport rather than hiring private cars at the destination and, in turn, energy savings and protection of the environment. A better transport system also benefits the local community, as it reduces traffic congestion at the destination. Host–tourist antagonism can decrease, since locals may no longer be resentful of tourists crowding the roads with their rentals or not understanding the driving rules and regulations of the destinations. People will feel more at ease since transport is relatively hassle-free. ITS also provide information about accidents and the safest routes to take, thus increasing the safety of both the visitor and the host community.

ITS therefore have implications in facilitating policy objectives beyond the individual tourism stakeholder. They are making a difference in the way traffic is managed both in rural and in urban areas and have wide-ranging advantages beyond those offered to transport users. Tourism stakeholders working together can make the use of this technology a fruitful reality for destinations in the management of sustainable tourism. The case study below focuses on how a partnership can make traffic management a success by using ITS.

Case study: Partnerships with intelligent transport systems Stockport UK Parking Guidance Information (PGI) System

Site description

Stockport identified a need for a PGI system to be installed around the Stockport Town Centre area. This is in part due to the large volume of parking available (with approximately 2000 spaces in the immediate vicinity of the town centre and a further 3000 spaces within reasonable distance from the town centre). Potentially 10 Full Function Variable Message Signs (FFVMS) will be installed at locations on the periphery of Stockport Town Centre which will convey parking information and/or other traffic advisory information.

Site problems

It was considered that some of the car parks were not being fully utilised whereas others were suffering from congestion due to over demand. In addition Stockport Council was keen to explore the benefits that technology may offer them in assisting traffic flows around the town centre.

Scheme description

Initially it was planned to install a stand alone system that would be controlled from Stockport Council offices. However discussions were then held with Greater Manchester UTC (GMUTC) about GMUTC providing a centralised car park guidance control function for the PGI system. It was considered that this would maximise the utilisation of existing control room operations staff already based at GMUTC and allow future expansion of the system to include other local authorities within the Greater Manchester area. At the same time this system offered Stockport Council the flexibility to remotely monitor the operation of the PGI system. The system implemented was UTMC compliant. The software used in other urban ITS systems

Continued

has been remodelled to make it suitable for Stockport PGI and the main controls located in the GMUTC control room. The system offers the potential for controlling broader ITS services to the Greater Manchester district in the future, fitting well with the aspirations of Stockport Council to develop full function VMS to notify drivers of road disruption events and providing safety information.

The equipment includes monitoring loops sited at all 13 car park entrances/exits and on street VMS units. The system communicates via a GPRS network. This method was chosen due to the significant savings in communications costs that GPRS offers over such a large system. Initially the communications costs were estimated to be £70K per annum using a conventional telecom network but have been reduced to £20K per annum due to the GPRS communications.

Due to the extensive coverage of the system within Stockport an approach has been adopted to group car parks into key zones e.g. Historic Market Areas, Shopping Areas, Leisure/Rail. This allows information about availability of spaces in a parking zone (which will include a number of car parks), allowing drivers to head towards that area of Stockport. As they approach the area including those coming from the approaches from the adjacent motorway network M60 the signs will show the availability of specific car parks and guide them to the desired areas of Stockport. This approach has allowed maximum information dissemination without over provision of information.

Scheme objectives

The key objectives of the system were to:
Provide a base ITS provision on which to build further ITS applications providing a greater level of information to drivers entering the Stockport area and helping manage traffic in the urban area. This would include full function VMS on the approaches into Stockport which could display information about events happening in the town and accident/road safety information.

Improvements

It is anticipated that the system will:

- Reduce the search times for parking spaces around Stockport and hence reduce the circulating traffic around the town centre.
- Improve utilisation and turnover of car parks, spreading and balancing demand between available provision.
- Improve the image of the town centre.
- Offer safety benefits by guiding drivers to an available parking space.

Integrated systems

With the system being controlled by GMUTC, it is possible for other local authorities to install ITS systems that can also be controlled from the same location. There would be in station development costs.

Continued

Costs

Capital costs: £660k including provision of [unclear amount] per year for maintenance and communications

Benefits

Benefits are shown in the table below.

Actual benefits reported		
Impact assessment	Environment	Reduced vehicle emissions. The reduction in circulating traffic (see below under Efficiency and Economy) and excessive queues at car parks should reduce vehicle emissions within the town centre
	Accessibility	Improved utilisation of the off-street long stay car parks may improve the accessibility to short stay on-street parking areas
	Safety	Improved parking information could lead to safer driving behaviour within the town centre as drivers are guided straight to an available space
	Efficiency and Economy	Reduction in the search time for off-street parking which could have significant time savings for road users. Case studies have shown up to a 30% reduction in search time in major cities Case studies have shown a 10 to 15 percent increase in patronage of underutilised car parks with the introduction of a PGI system. This improved utilisation of off-street car parks could also free up existing road space used for on-street parking at present.
	Integration	No benefits expected or reported.
Technical performance		Following system set up and addressing the initial issues no technical problems reported.
User acceptance		Improved parking information could improve the public's image of shopping within the town centre which would lead to improved revenue generation within the town centre
Working relationships and potential future development		The close partnership working of the two bodies Stockport Council and GMUTC working together to deliver the system providing greater opportunities for future development achieving significant value for money improvements and effective utilisation of resources within the Greater Manchester area. This partnership also included AECOM Mott MacDonald VMS Limited and IDT all working together to deliver

Continued

the system. The end result offers a real chance for the system to grow and for other local authority areas to tie in allowing shared costs more coherent data collection and a common approach to parking guidance provision. Support was also obtained from the local businesses, some who contributed to the funding of the scheme, recognising the higher profile PGI systems can produce in an urban environment. Installing a UTMC compliant system also allows for greater potential expansion and links to other ITS systems operating in the area, again offering the chance to maximise benefits.

No attempt has been made to validate the results reported. Users of the guidance are encouraged to assess the robustness of the results presented and the likely transferability of the case study to their own local environment.

This case study was taken from the UK Department of Transport's website. This information was last updated in June 2010. It can be accessed at http://www.dft.gov.uk/itstoolkit/CaseStudies/stockport-pgi-system.html

Accurate data

To engage with these technologies, data is required in order to generate the required information for decision-making. However, many destinations have not collected data on the sustainability aspects of their destination. Where data have been collected, destinations – especially the smaller ones – lack confidence in their knowledge and the quality of data they have to build their capacity to make use of these technologies. The vital element in using these technologies would be to collect the appropriate data and mature this data over time for the production of measurable, easy, accurate and timely results, which can be easily interpreted for destination decision-making. Many destinations do not possess enough data to engage in activities like scenario modelling and forecasting.

The suppliers

The suppliers of these technologies can be a deterrent to their adoption for sustainable tourism. Suppliers of tourism technologies do exist with regard to website design, booking systems, destination management systems and development on intranets and extranets. However, when it comes to more sophisticated technologies, such as an environmental management information system (EMIS) or a GIS to be used by sustainable tourism management destinations, many encounter difficulties in sourcing suppliers. The reasons for this are twofold. Destinations and businesses have not been demanding these technologies from suppliers; therefore, the market has not been developed and suppliers have not engaged with these technologies. This limits destinations' awareness of their existence and value for sustainable tourism. As sustainability becomes prioritised in destination development, technology will indeed be used as a mechanism for managing and mitigating tourism's negative impacts, and therefore it is important that destinations have access to these technologies. There is no doubt that once demand for these products increases, suppliers will begin to increase the range of technologies offered to destinations.

Conclusion

This chapter has brought to the fore a number of factors involved in making technology use a reality for destinations. These issues are by no means unique to any particular destinations or businesses; rather, any stakeholder may experience one, several or all of these factors. From the above discussion it is evident that these factors are wide-ranging in their implications, as tourism is a complex system. Thinking about tourism in this way helps to understand the phenomena in light of the larger whole and assists in explaining the complex interactions that take place (Hall 2000). Due to this intricacy the solutions proposed for sustainable tourism development will indeed have influencing factors that will affect its uptake, and necessary systems are required to gain commitment. Greater use of these technologies would be seen once their uses and benefits have been confirmed to be economical and contextually suitable for tourism stakeholders. Benchmarking and auditing can support this process. The encouraging news is that many of the factors discussed earlier can be overcome once destination stakeholders are committed to technology and its uses and applications for sustainable tourism.

Chapter 8 questions

1 Using a transport-related example, identify key business processes which are being transformed through the use of ICT.
2 What is your view of the opinion that sustainable tourism cannot be managed in any meaningful way?
3 Give an illustration of how real-time geo-tagging of tourists at a destination could assist sustainability research.
4 In your view, which is the bigger barrier to ICT-mediated sustainable tourism development: stakeholder education on sustainability or stakeholder understanding of available technologies?
5 What is your opinion of the benefits assessment offered in the case study? Should intelligent transport systems be rolled out more widely?

9 The way forward

Learning outcomes

This final chapter explores some of the ways in which we may see the interplay of technology, tourism and sustainability develop in the short to medium term (longer-term predictions are more the domain of science fiction). After reading this chapter you should appreciate:

- examples of technological development likely to impact tourism;
- some of the themes and trends shaping the development of ICT-mediated sustainable tourism development; and
- the significant levels of uncertainty in forecasting in this area.

Introduction

The earlier chapters explored different perspectives on the ways in which technologies may act in support of a sustainable tourism development agenda. The consumer, the tourist, destinations, businesses and other organisations at the destination will all look rather different in the years ahead and it is pertinent to consider some of these futures. Here we look ahead whilst accepting at the outset that any attempt to glimpse the future is beset with challenges and uncertainties, which amplify the further forward one seeks to forecast. Tourist movements, volumes and values will be influenced by many factors in the years to come. Inevitably, political and social forces and the economic context and influence of technology will play a significant part. The nature and shape of the evolving ICT world is perhaps the most difficult of all to predict, but for sure it will be faster, more powerful, more widespread and more influential than ever. There is no simple or single solution to the challenges of making tourism sustainable and there will undoubtedly be a wide array of developments and a diverse level of uptake and implementation. There is no reference roadmap to the future – indeed, textbooks could be written about alternative scenarios, and thus all we can reasonably aspire to in this brief chapter is to highlight some of the forces at play, some likely technologies and strong candidates for emergent adoption and some indicative prospective examples drawn from across the industry, and seek to place them in a meaningful context.

We have already seen just how transformational ICT has been – now more than at any other time in history – and how profoundly it has impacted all walks of life and penetrated every corner of business and social life. Tourists are also better prepared today than in previous generations to anticipate and accept a continuing and dramatic rate of change. Ponder for a moment that the first talking film arrived barely eighty years ago, the first satellite was created fifty years ago, the web is only just celebrating its twentieth birthday and, with Web 2.0 hardly five years old, we have already begun envisaging the shape of Web 3.0 and beyond.

Paradoxically, there is at times a danger of complacency in our anticipation of ever accelerating rates of change – but here this complacency would be misplaced, and these bewilderingly rapid changes are already straining political, legal and social systems. Governments struggle to understand and manage issues such as the tax implications of Internet trading and the scope of legal jurisdiction. There have been many well-publicised cyber attacks on military and industrial systems through cyber espionage or malicious interference, or indeed the leaking of documents through 'whistle-blowing' and release of confidential data through sites such as www.wkileaks.org. Then there are the challenges in the areas of copyright and patent protection, perhaps the most regularly visible being the widespread challenges in the areas of music and film copyright infringement through peer-to-peer file sharing. This darker side of the web, often nurtured by what is known as the Dark Net, will be discussed a little later.

Not only are government and industry finding it difficult to keep up with the pace of change; individuals are also facing unprecedented challenges. The 'digital divide' which highlighted the gulf between the information-rich and the information-poor, i.e. those who did or did not have access to ICT, is diminishing as more and more of the world becomes connected and the entry costs of access and use of computer-based systems continue to fall. It is, however, becoming replaced by a much more subtle spectrum, ranging from those who fully engage with and use the new technologies to those who are overwhelmed by their complexity. There is no obvious brake likely to be applied to this speeding ICT juggernaut in the foreseeable future, so the real challenge becomes how to make the new technologies relevant, simple to access and intuitive to use.

In order to narrow the scope to more manageable proportions, this chapter will not seek to attempt to quantify in any way just how attention to sustainability issues will expand in importance in the coming years; rather, we will hope that there will be an increase in attention and it will be significant. This throws the spotlight more clearly on questions relating to how both our natural and built environments will transform, how the technological environment and tools may develop and how these may be of assistance.

To offer a little structure, two simple, related perspectives will be adopted in approaching consideration of these futures: the technology environment, and access devices and interfaces. In short, the technological environment in which we live, the physical means we have to access and use this 'grid' and how we directly engage with ICT. Let us start by looking at how our technological environment may change.

The technological environment

We have already seen that we are dealing with a massively interconnected world, with huge growth in computer and smartphone ownership, improved bandwidth and reduced costs of Internet access. Bandwidth, you will recall, indicates the amount of data one can send/receive through a connection. The usual analogy is to think of traffic flow, with our vehicles representing data in transit. Greater bandwidth means a greater number of vehicles may travel at any one time, thus producing faster information flow between Internet addresses. There will ultimately be a question around how much bandwidth or how many addresses will be sufficient for all our needs, which leads to further questions over whom or indeed what might need an Internet address, and for what purposes.

When the Internet Protocol (IP) addressing system was first seriously revised a couple of decades ago, it was felt that 232 addresses otherwise known as IPv4 would be more than enough for all forecast widespread use. This is the IP system most of us are familiar with. For example, the computer on which these words are being written is happily residing at 192.168.186.205. However, IPv4 in fact probably reached its exhaustion point in 2011, due to enormous and unanticipated (to the original designers) growth in Internet users. Vast numbers of 'always-on' devices such as your friendly ADSL modem, not to mention the astonishing growth in smartphones which all required IP addressing, all conspired to pressure the system. A variety of clever techniques were used to prolong the life of IPv4, but essentially in the past few years IPv6 has slowly begun to be implemented, and this permits 2,128 addresses. Try multiplying two by two 128 times and you will see just how mind-boggling the increase in available addresses actually is! However, this will take time and will require widespread replacement of IPv4 hardware; nevertheless it will be interesting to see the changes in the wake of IPv6.

The importance of IPv6 should not be underestimated. The future we are swiftly moving towards is one where it is forecast that almost every single object in our world might benefit from being connected to our 'grid' and if, as is likely, we do move in this direction – towards the Internet of Things (IoT), as it is known – then even 2,128 addresses might begin to fall short. Any future is certain to contain an increasing number of smart objects. These objects will be everywhere in our environment – to a larger and larger extent they will actually *be* our environment, in homes and offices, in buildings and streets, in public and in private transport. Let us look a little more closely at the Internet of Things.

Originally this was associated with technologies such as RFID tags; however, the concept has evolved very rapidly and there are today many different definitions of what is understood as the Internet of Things. Basically, there is general agreement that in our future all unique objects will have information pertaining to their attributes, such as location, connected to a virtual representation of the object. These so-called cyber objects may be passive/static objects or, as is increasingly likely, active participants in future value chains. If active they may adopt the role of agent in many functions, including for example acting as autonomous or semi-autonomous decision-making agents for personal or business travel organisation.

Conceptually one must imagine a probable future where there is considerably increased blurring of boundaries between the physical and virtual world, where most physical entities have a virtual representation and where not all virtual representations have a physical counterpart. By the way, that future is already present.

IPv6, as noted above, is a key enabler allowing communication with devices attached to virtually all human-made objects. So, our future holds the likelihood that effectively every significant object in our environment will be connected to the Internet, have its own ID and IP address and be machine-addressable, with perhaps even a degree of autonomous action. Some observers think this future is closer than you may think:

> Imagine Googling your home to find your child's lost toy. Or remotely turning on the tumble dryer for yet another cycle – after it has texted you that the clothes were still damp. Or your plant tweeting you to be watered. It might have been sci-fi just a decade ago, but with the Internet forcing its way into every aspect of our lives, cyberspace is leaking out into the real world.
>
> (Moskvitch 2011)

The 'things' or objects referred to so far are, in the main, likely to be static objects, but in fact may be of any size – from buildings such as museums and galleries, for example, which themselves will contain myriads of further objects, down to small and indeed very small or 'nano' objects. They equally well may be moving objects; they may be real, but increasingly they will have virtual representations and the distinction between real and virtual, for many practical purposes, will become meaningless. To give a sense of the seismic shift in what will constitute tomorrow's realities, consider the world of small-scale futures. For a number of years research has gathered pace around an area of microscale computing called, variously, smart dust, pixie dust or mote computing. 'Smart dust' may be broadly defined as tiny electronic particles with the ability to sense, compute and wirelessly communicate, with their own on-board power and unique ID. Typically today these particles are about the size of grains of rice, but they are capable of significant size reduction. So, in an echo of the way in which the PC became a global computing commodity, these truly micro – indeed, nano – computers will be sufficiently inexpensive and low-powered that they can be everywhere.

Military applications of smart dust have been obliquely referenced for almost a decade and it is clear that this work is now about to go mainstream in a raft of everyday applications. An interesting video entitled Dust Networks: Helping Build Smart Cities of the Future (http://www.youtube.com/watch?v=OE4aZ7i-jK4), explores this phenomenon. Examples here include the use of smart dust to create intelligent environments, from monitoring traffic flow to individual recognition throughout the environment. It is probable that these ubiquitous dust networks will assist in areas of human activity from agriculture (e.g. micro-management of irrigation needs) to physical infrastructure maintenance monitoring. Obviously, among a number of practical challenges to be overcome in implementing these networks is power consumption, but much research is already being applied to this area – such as the example below from Hewlett Packard:

> HP's nano-crossbar memory is designed to enable these distributed devices to operate in the most efficient way – they will wake up, take a measurement, make a decision, communicate if necessary, store the result, and go back to a zero-power sleep. Power requirements will be small enough to enable on-chip batteries to last a lifetime. Even more exciting, keeping power requirements low may make it possible to harvest the needed energy from the sensor surroundings such as solar light, heat cycles or vibrations – eliminating the need for any batteries at all. HP Labs is applying its nano-crossbar memory to developing nanosensor technologies designed to allow instant identification and analysis of a biological or environmental hazard or change...
>
> (http://www.hpl.hp.com/environment/nanotechnology.html, 2012)

Sustainable sewers and radiation counters

One firm making software for the Internet of Things is Pachube (pronounced 'Patch-Bay') (https://pachube.com), which connects developers, people and objects to the Internet. An example project, which seeks to manage water pollution in New York, is dontflush.me. Leif Percifield, founder of dontflush.me, explains that New York City has 'a mostly combined sewer system, where sanitary wastewater and storm water share the same pipes. This causes a problem when it rains, as the system is not designed to handle the excess flow – at these times the system overflows into the nearest waterway'.

Sensors are put in place at sewer overflows which relay regular updates to Pachube, who may then instruct a further device to alert members of the public that they could take some water-saving action until the level drops. To generalise, if you have any kind of data collecting device and you connect it to Pachube, their servers will produce output usable by a wide range of open source software, providing potential mashups, e.g. Google Maps mashups, limited only by our imagination. Another example is seen in the Japan Geigermap, where radiation readings, which may be fed into the servers by official sensors, or individual readings are then presented on a single map. The pace of change is remarkable in this area and even the innovative start-up Pachube has rapidly evolved into a new shape in the form of COSM (http://www.cosm.com), where the concept is expanding from connected devices to connected devices and people: this is known as the Internet of Social Things, with shared devices and communities.

An initiative in a similar vein which brings together thinking on how the rapid advances in information, gathering, processing and dissemination might work for sustainability is Wickichains (http://www.oii.ox.ac.uk/research/projects/?id=75). This website provides an environment to support open and ethical consumption through encouraging users to upload information in a wide variety of forms, to enrich consumer understanding of the commodity chain.

This combination of superfast broadband, ubiquitous sensors, shared servers and databases will undoubtedly catalyse a future technology environment that is both qualitatively and quantitatively different to that of today. The concept of IoT – and, indeed, likely future scenarios – are different to, but (as we shall see) intimately connected with, the concept of Web 3.0 and the Semantic Web. It is also part of the world known as pervasive or ubiquitous sensing, computing and communication.

Pervasive or ubiquitous computing brings a new way of thinking about how we compute. Earlier discussions of information and communication technology paradigms emerged from developments in fixed and wireless systems, revolutions in tagging, sensing and devices and it is clear that where we are now with, for example, mobile computing will give way to pervasive computing platforms, whereby ambient intelligence almost subliminally emerges from always-on cyberobjects in a ubiquitously connected network. In other words, an increasing proportion of our daily use of computer-based devices should be conducted without explicit human action and machine-to-machine (M2M) communications will be a commonplace background.

Extra lanes on the superhighway?

It is exciting to many to imagine a future with this level of connectivity, but what if these digital superhighways, with an almost infinite number of 'vehicles', are limited to crawling speed as they approach gridlock bumper to bumper? IPv6 ensures we have enough destinations; IoT means there will be no shortage of vehicles, but the traffic needs to keep moving at an acceptable speed. This brings us to bandwidth. Already today we see ISPs imposing 'fair usage' policies to seek to limit and control the almost insatiable consumer demand for more and more bandwidth, as usage has migrated from simple web browsing and email exchange to music and video download/streaming, with their far greater hunger for bits. In recent years we have seen, for example, hotels having to introduce load-balancing software in an effort to try to mitigate peak fluctuations, causing problems for some guests. Twenty years ago a simple modem would be happily working away with 56 kbps transfer limits; today, in the era of cable and ADSL modems, we are ever more attentive to our upload and (usually more important) download transmission rates. Available bandwidth of course very much depends on your network. Accessing the world at large through an ADSL modem may (on a good day) offer speeds of up to 1.5 Mbps, whereas if your needs are more local – perhaps across a work ethernet – you find your data cruising along happily at up to 100 Mbps. Sitting comfortably with your laptop accessing your home network via Wi-Fi (under e.g. 802.11g) may offer up to 54 Mbps; of course, once your data ventures out onto the world stage it will ultimately join the traffic at the speed of the slowest choke point! It is worth noting that there is a gulf between advertised broadband speeds and the averages actually achieved. In the UK, the telecom watchdog (OFCOM 2010) identified an average speed of 'only' 6.2 Mbps.

Turning to mobile bandwidth, the Internet connection speeds available to users of 3G are typically described as being up to 28 Mbs. The newly emergent 4G networks will take this to a different level: for example, in trials, speeds of up to 150 Mbps were achieved in the UK (http://www.digitalspy.co.uk/tech/news/2012). The UK government report (BIS 2010) on the development of superfast broadband specifically identifies next-generation mobile being encouraged by the release of the 800 MHz and 2.6 GHz spectrum. Long-term evolution (LTE) is envisaged as the technology most likely to deliver mobile services with high potential bandwidth. It is likely that sooner rather than later, the third-generation universal mobile telecommunications system (UMTS) and second-generation Global Standards for Mobile Telephony (GSM) will be replaced by LTE, although alas there will not be a common global frequency for implementation.

In any event, developed economies are already demanding ever more bandwidth, and this strategic challenge is being faced by many countries. Again, using the UK as an example of a developed economy facing potential bandwidth challenges, a good reference point is the UK government's own publication, 'Britain's Superfast Broadband Future', published in December 2010. This report examined many aspects of moving to ever faster infrastructure speeds over the coming years. The importance of a fast, robust and accessible communications infrastructure was emphasised in terms that most countries would recognise, along with a clear identification of the need to ensure equivalence of development and access for both rural and urban environments. Central to the thrust of that document is the economic imperative of superfast broadband. Table 9.1 shows some current comparative broadband statistics.

This report makes clear that there is no single solution to the many types of demand for access and use of any future broadband in the UK and envisages a mix of fixed, wireless and satellite solutions. The report also makes play of the importance of access to broadband, encouraging

> greater innovation activity by: helping to spread new ideas and knowledge more quickly and widely, bringing about the transformation of business models and organisation structures as well as greater collaboration between firms and academia through virtual networks and new ways of working (e.g. teleworking, cloud computing), development of new applications, such as services and content including new business products and applications (e.g. software as a service), on-line services (e.g. Internet banking) and entertainment applications. . . . the development of components and software needed to support this revolution is important to the creation of jobs.
>
> (BIS 2010: 10)

Web 3.0 and the Semantic Web

A fact we should keep in mind is that the web is not necessarily restricted to content and use designed only around humans. Providing that information can be appropriately presented, software robots or agents may in fact be well placed to search, retrieve and process information from the Internet. At present, most

Table 9.1 UK broadband statistics

Percentage of UK Households with broadband access	71%	EU average = 56% OECD Average = 53.5%
Percentage of UK households with fixed broadband access	65%	
Percentage of UK households with mobile broadband access	15%	
Average UK broadband speed	5.2 Mbps	
Percentage of UK business with 10 or more employees with broadband access	87%	(EU average = 81%)
Percentage of UK business with 10 or more employees selling online	32%	(2nd in OECD)
Percentage of UK business with 10 or more employees purchasing online	47%	(8th in OECD)

Source: Adapted from: Ofcom Communications Market Report 2010; OECD ICT Outlook 2010; Ofcom Communications Market Report 2010.

content is obviously designed to be 'human-readable', but more and more information needs to be presented in machine-readable form. New web languages and technologies are being constructed to make it simpler for us all to generate such content. These are Web 3.0 technologies. Without becoming overly technical, Web 3.0 utilises the Resource Description Framework (RDF) to link data from multiple sources, and whilst no doubt the marketers will be touting its presence long before the reality, it may take a number of years for Web 3.0 to become widely implemented. It is inevitable, but we can only speculate on what it might look like. Web 3.0 is often associated with the concept of a Semantic Web. We will ultimately have all information stored in a form which can be read and understood by humans and machines alike, and which will be much more useful. The Semantic Web is essentially about sharing and collaboration and is championed by the World Wide Web Consortium (W3C). Organisations such as Mondeca (www.mondeca.com) are actively working in the tourism sector, using Semantic Web concepts to work with tourist stakeholders to help build semantic knowledge bases which may generate rich contextual information. One may anticipate such knowledge bases in future being interrogated by intelligent software agents to respond to responsible tourism filter requests.

Access devices and interfaces

Once upon a time how we accessed the Internet was relatively simple. We sat down at a computer and then keyed in commands; and in the early days, these were pretty abstract commands. This process improved markedly with increases in computer power and the evolution of increasingly powerful devices, but even today a technology, which has been around for 150 years, the keyboard, is still a central part of most people's computing experience. The human–computer interface (HCI) – or, more simply, user interfaces – and the way we engage with technology have changed a lot from these early days. Graphical user interfaces (GUIs) are now up against new user interfaces which may raise the game to an entirely different level. A single, repetitive means of interacting with our computing devices may lead to a range of problems, such as repetitive strain injury (RSI), back and neck ache, and so on, but we are in transition towards a much richer interface environment, from speech to gesture to multi-touch. Some of these are briefly outlined below. We have already explored some new and emerging technologies in this book and earlier in the chapter we outlined a picture of a future with an increasingly ambient intelligence. In what ways are we likely to interact with this very fast, intelligent environment? Broadly speaking, we are about to enter the era of natural user interfaces (NUI), where our engagement utilises interactions much closer to our natural senses.

It is important, in considering the following indicative developments, to think not so much about any one potential application area being a 'killer app' for sustainable tourism, but rather to more holistically reflect on the combined impacts. These technologies are developing with different trajectories – all of them are rapid, however, and undoubtedly many of them will, sooner rather than later, significantly impact upon and permeate our sector. Software and hardware developers alike will seek competitive advantage by incorporating such technologies in applications and systems. For those involved in destination management, as has been seen earlier in the book, there is a large and indeed at times bewildering range of applications already available, but uptake and deployment seems to be relatively low at present. Much of this seems to be less about cost and more about appreciation of potentially relatively high learning curves. With the advent of the emerging systems, technologies in support of sustainable tourism will offer much more capability, be more highly integrated, be able to deal with rapidly changing complex variables and will do so with a much more intuitive suite of interface options. These systems will have embedded intelligence. Taken together, these developments will undoubtedly lead to more widespread adoption of relevant support technologies by destination managers in pursuit of enhancing the sustainability of their destination. It is almost a given that there will be a very significant upswing in responsible tourist demand for appropriate offers from the supply side.

From the tourist perspective, of course, whilst there is an anticipated growth in informed responsible demand from tourists who are looking for evidence of suppliers' active engagement with the challenge of sustainability, human nature inevitably produces a trade-off. It can be time-consuming, particularly in the pre-trip search phase, to fully investigate offers and optimise choice. Yes, of course the more proactive responsible tourist will invest more time – but on average, at present, despite initiatives such as eco-certification, tourists generally find it fairly laborious to identify the ideal range of offers. However, many of the developments outlined below will support for tourists, as for destination managers, much more easy-to-use, comprehensive and rapid-response systems. If the effort involved in identifying products and services which incorporate tourist requirements in respect of sustainability is reduced, it will undoubtedly become a much more common feature and this set of variables will become an increasingly central component of search processes, whether human or machine initiated.

The supply side will thus be directly affected by these interface developments, as those involved will now see an elevated demand for sustainability credentials and a demand which is very highly informed and eager for satisfactory and rapid response. All stakeholders will have two primary considerations in seeking to address this demand: first, they will look for continual improvement in the sustainability of their offers, and second, they will look to the dramatically changing tools and applications landscape.

Artificial intelligence

Artificial intelligence (AI), or machine intelligence, essentially refers to computer-based systems capable of perceiving and learning from their environment. At a very basic level in tourism we are already familiar with software robots which, to some extent, will do our bidding in the form of searching and retrieving information from the web; the technologies described above make it clear that the way will soon be open for bots or virtual assistants capable of much greater autonomous action on our behalf. One can imagine a (potentially very large) set of such personal intelligent agents or autonomous avatars interacting with the vast databases on the Internet in the realms of travel, accommodation, visitor attractions and so forth and refining their queries through a set of sustainability filters before reporting back to their user. The work of researchers such as Batet *et al.* (2012) on intelligent software agents in tourism has shown some of the breadth of potential applications. Some examples of application areas include mobile agent applications, proactive recommendation systems and tourist activity planning, where intelligent agent planning systems may support tourist choice and optimise trip time by providing suggested temporal itineraries.

The Turist@ multi-agent system referred to by Batet *et al.* (2012) is identified as a working prototype for a cultural recommender system. As we will see in the Epilogue, it is envisaged that such systems will in future gain rapid acceptance and be used to make proactive recommendations incorporating a responsible tourism agenda on behalf of the prospective tourist.

Brain–computer interfaces

We are already aware of the blurring of the boundaries between computer-based systems and the body. We can readily accept that our interfaces with the Internet have become mobile and increasingly virtual, and also that embedded processor-based bio-sensors are a reality in some areas of medical monitoring, so it is not such a stretch to think about our brains being directly in control of system instruction. Current research is investigating a number of ways to offer a brain-to-computer interface, whereby the computer-based device is directly under the control of brain waves, ranging from headbands to directly implanting sensors into the brain. It is fair to say that at the time of writing, the software is more fully developed than the mechanical implants.

Nevertheless, if this seems far-fetched, the progress is remarkable – as research at Brown University, USA showed researchers were able, via a brain implant, to offer a tetraplegic subject independent control of a remote robotic arm (http://crave.cnet.co.uk/gadgets/paralysed-woman-controls-robot-arm-using-tiny-brain-implant-50007992/).

The potential for this kind of technology is mind-boggling. It may well be that the first significant numbers of tourists adopting these new and enabling technologies will emerge from among those with disabilities limiting fine motor control, but as the technologies are increasingly refined it will be interesting to see how common they become, especially as they become less invasive. In the short term there may be limited evident contribution to responsible tourism; however, one may envisage these technologies permitting sophisticated control of the external world, converging with the ever improving worlds of augmented and virtual realities and perhaps also combining with gesture technologies to offer tourism substitution opportunities.

Biometric and cybernetic interfaces

These devices are already becoming much more common and utilise the fact that biological systems, such as ourselves, may be uniquely identified. We are already familiar with retina scanning at airports and fingerprint recognition as security, for example on laptops. Cybernetic interfaces have been under development for a long time and may, as we shall see, take the form of sensors embedded into or woven throughout clothing and be used to monitor and communicate data such as physiological status or health monitoring, for example. The ability to uniquely identify a wide range of attributes of individuals (or groups for that matter) from location, consumer preferences, health status and other parameters will in future offer extensive opportunities and challenges – not the least of which will be privacy issues, which are already a concern for many us.

In terms of sustainability issues, on a positive note, one may imagine this kind of technology being linked to monitoring and management of, for example, personal carbon accounting. A refined ability to micro-manage personal carbon utilisation may be seen as integral to the future of responsible tourism, as in this scenario tourists will be filtering choices by carbon costs and all stakeholders in the tourism supply chain will ultimately be required to factor carbon costs into offers. Some potential applications are indicated in the Epilogue.

Gesture interfaces

A gesture is a movement or expression which conveys information. In gesture recognition the computer identifies and interprets body movements, and some early entrant companies such as Panasonic have offered remote control of TV sets through such an interface. However, the most substantial area in which gesture interfaces have rapidly progressed and gained early acceptance is the video gaming world. The Nintendo Wii's gesture-recognising control system, which still required a hand-held physical device, was followed by the genuinely pioneering Kinect from Microsoft Xbox 360. This is a fully motion-sensing and voice-recognising input system; a fully-fledged NUI which has prompted development and application beyond the gaming world. One of the latest gesture interface developments is the recent addition of a very fine-grained USB-based sensor from Leap Motion (http://www.leapmotion.com). The device has a claimed accuracy of 1/100th of a millimetre with low latency (almost no lag) and can track even at fingertip level. This kind of quantum improvement in gesture recognition offers all kinds of potential applications and may provide a much more intuitive interface to support easier engagement with the sometimes complex systems supporting sustainable destination development.

Multi-touch interfaces

In many ways, multi-touch interfaces are like gesture recognition interfaces, but a touch screen is needed and the historical mode of single touch using a stylus or a finger is nowadays being supplemented or replaced by the ability to accept multiple input points. Users of many smartphones are familiar with the option to pull images around or access menus with one finger, pinch and zoom with two or select a variety of options with several fingers. An interesting extension of multi-touch in a larger scale is shown by the Microsoft surface, which can take input from more than one user simultaneously and also incorporates object recognition. The New York City Visitor Center in Manhattan is a good illustration of how a variety of interfaces, but especially multi-touch, can be used to enhance visitor experience. Tourists use the technology to plan itineraries around the city (http://www.youtube.com/watch?v=RO4ymFBpW8k). In-trip it is easy to foresee this technology incorporating options which flag, for example, carbon cost, eco-certified suppliers and sustainable travel options, thus offering the responsible tourist a highly effective trip-planning tool.

Skin-based interfaces

This interface produces a touchscreen on the skin and uses a tiny projector, usually in an armband to beam keyboards and other graphics on to the user's forearm, for example. It is usually coupled to a detector capable of picking up finger pressure, and may even be used wirelessly to connect to other devices. This type of interface device can detect gestures when the user is moving and can support wireless connectivity. At present it is difficult to imagine truly practical and effective uses of the technology, but once it is fully developed it should have low power demands and have the advantage of reducing hardware overheads; as with many technology developments, it may well complement other technologies rather than substituting them.

Telepresence

This literally means 'to be present at a distance' and might be illustrated through remote control of robots of various kinds, from military to industrial. Indeed nowadays there are examples of surgical procedures being carried out remotely using this technology, with real-time feedback through a wide range of sensor types. In tourism terms, telepresence could be a feasible way for many more humans to gain some more direct experience of challenging environments which involve high-risk, fragile ecosystems or are very remote – perhaps even space or other planets – from the comfort of our homes. Telepresence technologies combined with AR (augmented reality), VR and nano technologies can lead to some surprising potential outcomes, as indicated in the Epilogue.

Voice control

Voice commands and voice control of systems have become relatively common. Whether you are using Google Voice Search on an Android or other smartphone or commanding Siri on your iPhone, nowadays it is pretty straightforward to use voice for many functions in place of typing. Voice command is particularly useful when in hands-free mode, such as driving, or perhaps more commonly in 'hands-full' mode as a tourist. More and more search is being conducted by voice, with outcomes communicated in a range of modes, such as audio and visual, with a choice of display options. A particularly useful application is the area of speech-to-speech translation, where not only is the quality of voice recognition software enormously improved, but so too is the accuracy and relevance of translation applications. Again, as with a number of the interface developments, there is no single specific area in which one may say that this will be a vital interface to enhance the activities of the responsible tourist, or to support the work of those charged with sustainable tourism development. However, taken alongside other interface developments, voice recognition and voice command will undoubtedly improve the usability of systems.

Wearable computing – augmented reality

Again, the path towards acceptance of wearable computers has already been progressed by, for example, the widespread use of digital hearing aids; there is no doubt, especially with the ubiquity of mobile computing devices, that most of us would find it a short and reasonable journey towards more powerful, networked, wearable computer systems. A key challenge of course lies in making such systems intuitive and non-intrusive. As we have seen already in an earlier chapter, AR combines real-time images with relevant localised data and commercial applications are currently in the marketplace, albeit with some limitations. The contributing technologies will almost certainly catalyse significant growth in the area in the immediate future, and some of these technologies are quite remarkable. For example, one technology supporting AR developments is the development of a contact lens-based display where information may be placed directly in front of the eye. Closely related developments include the much-heralded Google Glass project which would, if implemented as envisaged, truly be a quantum leap in AR and what is known as wearable computing.

There has been considerable publicity recently relating to the practicality or indeed feasibility of the Google Glass project (or indeed the touted iGlasses or similar projects). This features full mobile computing and a head-mounted display. In this case the computing and signalling system is an Android smartphone. We have already seen AR earlier in the book, utilising a smartphone, its on-board camera and Internet connection; similarly, Google's glasses also utilise the Internet, but the possibilities of additionally interacting with a smart environment where Wi-Fi, RFID, NFC and other technologies are commonplace – not to mention with the pixie dust of the future – are boundless. Not for the first or last time will we need to consider the future fusion of virtual and physical realities.

SixthSense (http://www.pranavmistry.com/projects/sixthsense/) is an MIT project presented by Pranav Mistry that comprises a worn gesture interface and seeks to bridge the gap between the smartphone and how we naturally interact with our environment. An on-board projector sends visual information to any surface that can then be used as an interface, whilst the on-board camera tracks gestures and objects. The SixthSense system can additionally function as an augmented reality environment by providing real-time information to supplement a viewed object: for example, in true Harry Potter style, newspapers can be used to display a context-relevant video feed.

Reflections

Perhaps all we can do is point towards changes which are more rather than less likely to occur, as this is all still a game of guesswork and probability. In this section, therefore, we briefly outline some possible ways in which a future technological environment, with its new array of interfaces and devices, may be used by tomorrow's tourist, by destinations and by other tourism stakeholders. When it comes to predicting technology use it is best to keep an open mind, but in light of the foregoing excursion through some potential technologies of the future, we can at least speculate on some possibilities.

Any tourist experience will usually begin long before arrival at a destination, and many would argue that the first real experience of the destination is the initial stimulus which prompts interest and an initial information search. Our personal, intelligent electronic space will progressively be populated by marketing messages, promotions, offers, friend and social space updates and the results from our portfolio of software agents, including feeds from the Internet of Things and the Internet of Social Things. These messages will arrive using the full audio-visual spectrum of media and be presented though a very wide array of device and interface options.

It is clear that from a supply-side perspective, much greater attention will need to be paid to the proliferation of sophisticated channels available for distribution and the growing array of modes though which the prospective tourist may be connected. Whether it is communication of destination messages from a DMO or more specific offers from others in the supply chains, they will all need to be aware of and to effectively utilise this changing technological environment. This will require recognition of how to bundle messages in an appropriate way for each intended channel and, more importantly, a recognition that the control of destination information will in future be mainly in the hands of others: the user-generated content communities. The historical models of wrapping factual information in persuasive words and imagery will still be necessary but will form a much smaller proportion of the tourist information-scape.

Push information channels will be increasingly patrolled by intelligent agents or software robots searching the Semantic Web for relevant information on behalf of their masters (you and I). Such soft machines will be only too delighted to encounter suitably dressed information for a little M2M communication, but of course will be unimpressed by visits to sites which do not know how to respond properly – that is, which are not appropriately configured for Web 3.0 machine-readability. An early challenge for suppliers will therefore be to ensure that their information offers are machine-ready. These intelligent agents will travel with a substantial amount of information on board, such as relevant profiles of the individual who instructed them and a wide range of filters, which will be search-dependent but, for example, will include criteria on price, dates, etc. – and which for our purposes will more than likely also challenge receiving sites on their green credentials. So from both the supply and the demand side there will be an opportunity to present and to demand information which supports a sustainable tourism agenda.

However unlikely it may seem today, there is no doubt that in the near future we will see computer-based representations of tourism offers seeking to be highly personalised and persuasive to virtual representatives of our future tourist. Thus, with very little effort, the tourist will be able to set and implement sustainability-driven information search and subsequent decision-making actions that would today be tedious and time-consuming. From the demand side, we will thus see a shift from today's e-mailed airline, tour operator, hotel offer, or Facebook update prompting us to consider a potential trip towards much richer, current, immediate information. But let's rewind a little. back to the destination. If the destination is of primary importance to the prospective tourist, then we need to consider how the new technologies will come into play even before thought is given to their promotional use. It is important to bear in mind that the traditional use of these technologies saw an emphasis on controlled distribution – that is, the key destination messages were bound up with any destination management system (DMO) with glossy print material, carefully constructed persuasive text, images and other promotional material all extolling the good points on offer about the destination. This is already being complemented, or indeed supplanted, by user-generated content (UGC) about all aspects of a destination, which gives a much more accurate and up-to-the-minute representation. This trend, which empowers the tourist and reduces the impact of the controlled messages, is set to continue and to become even more central to tourist decision-making, as UGC is generally accorded a higher trust status than more official content. The challenge for those at the destination will be to ensure that the information provided through the official channels of DMOs, businesses and other tourism stakeholders matches the information generated by UGC. This leads to transparency challenges, as any discrepancies between the marketing rhetoric and reality will be very rapidly revealed and publicised.

This will be true for all principals and all those involved in the supply chains. If one assumes a heightened awareness of and a desire to conform to the principles of good sustainability practice among the stakeholders, it follows that they will wish to be seen by all (real or virtual) prospective or actual customers as implementing good practices. They will need to use attractors and evidence such as eco-labels, certificates and awards, in all channels and in all connections – and, on the ground, they will need extensive use of ICT to implement their green credentials. All of the technologies referred to in earlier chapters are likely to play a part to some degree, but what we can be sure of is that our prospective tourist of the future will have very powerful, easy-to-use tools at their disposal. They will use these technologies to drill down into supplier information and reject all offers failing to meet the minimum sustainability threshold deemed appropriate to them as individuals. This interface between the tourist and the destination will become ever more important. As destination managers begin to appreciate that their degree of message control is reduced, perhaps they will focus on what many would regard as the more central aspect of their work: stewardship. This would lead to more detailed consideration of the use of ICT for sustainability. This will require a significant re-think for many destinations, as recent political steering has been towards increasing emphasis on sales and marketing and being commercially driven and industry-led. As real-world models are increasingly fed with up-to-date information courtesy of the IoT and faster management information systems, destination managers will increasingly be dealing with what are in effect real-time models. As an example, one can imagine employing the above technologies to link to EMIS, green maps and other mashups to monitor and direct waste management, traffic handling, visitor flows, emission measurement and other sustainability concerns. Ultimately, of course, if one continues this mode of action far enough, the vast quantity of real-time data and the need for ultra-rapid decision-making will lead to the decision-making process being embedded in routines and algorithms and the entire process left to M2M interaction, with a decreasing level of human intervention – eventually only in exceptional cases.

Conclusion

It is certain that tourism is here to stay and is likely to be of growing importance to many economies. It is equally certain that without strong legislation, irrevocable damage to many areas dependent on tourism is likely. Destinations – the key focus of most tourism – will be degraded unless there is action to address sustainability, and central to this will be tourism stakeholders adopting and implementing practical, cost-effective solutions. It has been the thesis of this text that ICT and the new technologies offer significant opportunity to address sustainability concerns. Tourists, like all consumers today, have a rapidly changing, diverse and increasingly personalised range of requirements. We have seen the revolutionary transformation of the industry in the past decade or so through the application of new technologies, although this is primarily seen in distribution, marketing and basic operational support and back-office functions; however, ICT continues to become cheaper, faster, more mobile and more widespread, and the growth of UGC and crowd-sourced information will be a part of any future. An array of technologies, mainly Internet-based, have been introduced and already it is clear that the rate of change being precipitated in the industry is accelerating, given the rapid growth in mobile computing use by tourists and the development of LBS.

Destination sustainability will be vital to stable economic wellbeing in a very large number of countries, and the beneficial synergy between technology and tourism is identified as key to this future. Tourism destinations have undergone radical change in the past fifty years, with a vast increase in tourism numbers and ever-increasing and better-informed tourist demands. At the same time there has been a progressive, if slow, raising of awareness of sustainability issues, especially in the wake of the Brundtland Report. The issues of sustainable tourism development have been widely researched for over twenty years so there is a relatively robust evidence base; however, implementation and practice are a different matter. Destination professionals have lacked the means to effectively change things and to gain a wider understanding of the interconnected elements of sustainable development. The literature, and indeed practice, has to date failed to fully recognise the potential of ICT as a means of mitigating tourism's negative impacts. It is envisaged that this will have to change. We have seen some of the kinds of management approaches employed at the destination, from visitor management techniques to tourist taxation, so we know there are methods already in use for managing sustainable tourism development. However, as has been said – and DMOs are no exception to this – to date, technology has been primarily used for marketing and promotion and simple back-office functions. The next phase of improving business processes is really only just getting underway, and the technologies are beginning to be used more for gaining a deeper insight into the motivations and needs of the tourist and for tracking behaviour and activity. There is undoubtedly a deep need for enhanced education for destination managers on how the new technologies may aid tourism management for sustainable development.

Thinking about destination management-related use of ICT is one thing; a broader and ultimately more fundamental challenge lies in how tourism businesses will engage with the technologies in a way which meets the needs of their customers but also addresses environmental, economic, social, cultural and technological changes. Once again, we have seen in earlier chapters that a range of technologies are available and emerging, and managers must recognise how applying technology to the nature of their business can make their businesses more sustainable.

Exploration of supply chains has demonstrated that they are often complex networks of small businesses combining to create tourism products, interconnected and working within the tourism system. There is an ecosystem, in which technologies may have an impact, but there needs to be an understanding of the interdependence of business functions throughout supply chains. Pressures will be placed on these supply chains from all sides – from tourists, other stakeholders and government – and ICT can play an integral part in how sustainability may be incorporated into supply chains' formation, development and management. Tourist use of technology has also been seen to be dramatically changing, with even the more recent technologies such as high-end smartphones and applications such as AR beginning to move towards the mainstream. There is still a long way to go in deepening tourist understanding of sustainability issues and connecting this education to motivation and buyer behaviour. Tourists have more technology, more access and more information, and we are beginning to see the interface between what tourists will demand and what is on offer through destinations and other tourism suppliers.

Social networks perhaps hold the prospect of being the biggest driver of change in the direction of increased sustainable tourism development. We have all seen the power of social networks in supporting political change, and it seems likely that if a mass shift in approach to real sustainability is to come, this will probably be a major channel of contribution. Web 2.0 and social media have grown at a phenomenal rate in recent years and this trend will undoubtedly continue. These media tools and applications, as has been seen in the geopolitical sphere, are capable of supporting dramatic and apparently sudden inflexions in social behaviours. It is to be hoped that the early signs of these media being used in support of sustainable tourism goals may follow a similar path towards critical mass. We have seen a broad collection of technologies characterised not only by their power to connect individuals, groups and organisations but also by their strong interconnectedness to one another.

For technology use to become effective in sustainable tourism, stakeholders must have knowledge and understanding of the factors that can have a bearing on the successful implementation of these technologies. Effective deployment of these technologies is critically important in ensuring tourism stakeholders have the necessary tools and mechanisms available to manage their sustainability concerns, as this has strategic implications for destination competiveness.

So where, you might ask, will we go from here? Technology is galloping ahead, economic contexts are changing at the greatest rate in decades, there are major shifts ahead in geopolitical power relationships and there is the inevitability of increased legislation. However, at the end of the day, people will still have a fundamental desire to see more of their world – so will the pressures on limited resources ultimately be the death of tourism, or is there light at the end of the tunnel? Perhaps it will be best to leave the reader with a future scenario based not on science fiction, but on some possible and, indeed, probable paths that current and emerging technologies may take.

Chapter 9 questions

1 If you were designing a hotel of the future with sustainability in mind, to what types of technology would you give priority?
2 Accessing ICT continues to be of increasing importance to tourists at all trip stages. Giving reasons, explain what you see as the ideal mobile technology format for use in-trip.
3 Imagine ten years into the future and describe a short city-break from the perspective of your intelligent mobile device. Include all trip stages.
4 Indicate some ways in which you think 'cloud computing' may further impact upon travel and tourism.
5 It has been argued that in future virtualisation will be a major contributor to sustainable IT infrastructure in air travel. Discuss this from an airline or airport perspective.
6 Can space tourism ever be sustainable?

Epilogue

The large multi-touch smart table had efficiently taken their drinks order and displayed item cost, source, carbon debit and nutritional profile. As Zoe sipped her local beer and reflected on how good life was in the French Alps at 2,500 m on this crisp, clear February day, she smiled at the rest of her group, excitedly placing their various devices on the table to share and compare their vertical drop, distance and speed data for the morning's ski-runs. They were a nice friendly group and this was their eighth year together, although this time they had a new member. Zoe cast her mind back to that dismal London evening that triggered this latest instalment of their annual trip. At 28, Zoe had done well to become the youngest partner in her Internet law firm, and the fact she had travelled home on the top deck of the bus that particular November evening rather than using either her personal transport or the ubiquitous London Bicycles was due to the inclement weather and a desire to build up her Personal Carbon Credits. Still, it was only a minor hassle, as her firm now employed a fully cloud-based electronic document and case management approach – staff simply hot-desked in shared office space as and when really being there mattered, and really being there seemed to matter less with each passing month. The carbon cost of permanent offices and staffing was an unnecessary luxury these days and Zoe found herself commuting perhaps only five or six days a month now: home really was the office these days for a very large proportion of the workforce. In fact, with the increasingly smooth functioning of their telepresence suite, a regular question on the agenda was whether there was a need for any physical shared space for the partnership. Telepresence had, surprisingly, also begun to change the face of the city, due to the shrinking demand for new office space and the reconfiguration of more and more of the existing office space into domestic property. This shift had brought with it a concomitant reduction in traffic flows into and out of the city and an increase in tourism to London, perhaps encouraged by its emergence as a quiet capital.

Having an affinity for law and having been a self-confessed 'geek' since school, it was in a way inevitable that her path through university would lead to Internet law. Constant technology growth and the general lethargy of legislation was productive territory for her profession. The 2020 global summit on sustainability had contained a lot of the usual political compromises, but among the positive outcomes – and perhaps one of the most practical – was, finally, the implementation of the Universal Personal Carbon Allowance scheme. Who would have thought the UK's Climate Change Act of 2008 would presage such sweeping change? A similar scheme had of course been operating for many years among businesses, and there was a mature and well understood and regulated carbon trading market, but the decision amongst the global powers to agree to allocate a PCA to every individual, within national carbon budgets, owed much to the ability of today's ICT to track personal activity, and even more to the widely recognised drive to create individual accountability. It had seemed a huge challenge, of course, but the Indian biometric unique ID project initiated way back in 2009 had shown that large-scale individualisation was indeed possible – and this global PCA scheme was proof positive. Yes, it did seem that every year carbon costs seemed to be rising, but at least there were still many ways to earn and buy credits. Almost every activity these days used up carbon credits, so it was nice to do things which made even a small contribution, and taking the bus home from work was an inexpensive way of incrementing her personal carbon account. The health of her carbon account was important to Zoe as, whilst she considered herself to be a responsible citizen doing her bit for the environment, she had to balance this with her desire to see the world and indulge in her favourite leisure activity, skiing. Both of these activities were exceptionally carbon-hungry activities, generating large carbon debits.

Comfortably settled into her seat, she called up a visual display on her brand new iGlasses, entered her IDspace (the retinal security check was imperceptibly fast) and noted that her carbon account was already in a pretty healthy state. She did not particularly enjoy wearing any kind of glasses, as she had excellent vision, but the contact lens alternative was even less appealing – not to mention very expensive. These glasses had themselves cost a fair bit more than the standard issue – it was nice to have the choice about whether or not to accept advertising, and she had also specified shatter-proof, light-reactive lenses to accommodate her summer and winter tourism indulgences. She was always conscious of a desire not to disturb her fellow travellers, so had toggled off voice command on her glasses but left the audio-response live through the glasses' ear buds. Despite the infrequency of her travels, the bus of course recognised Zoe immediately; it informed her that she was twenty-five minutes from her destination and envisaged no problems or delays. The bus also knew from experience not to intrude by recounting its many fine attributes: it was after all an intelligent eco-bus and would not only update any who would listen on all of its features, but would happily provide similar information on any bus in the fleet via a friendly mashmap with overlays of one's choice. If Zoe had only but asked, the bus could have told her that 876 tourists had been aboard that day, from twenty-three different countries, for an average trip of 1.8 kilometres; but of course passengers rarely asked the bus much about itself.

The transport manager, of course, was a different story. Her query bots were all over her area of London's Intelligent Transport Systems, reporting performance and making suggestions. The group of sixteen managers played a gamified model of the transport network, trying in real time to optimise the network's efficiency. The new GIS/GPS tools, combined with IoT, made the job highly interactive and there was a nice monthly performance bonus in both cash and carbon credits for the manager achieving the greatest resource efficiency and lowest environmental impact score. The local DMO regularly interrogated their data – and vice versa – and it was a very useful information symbiosis. The transport managers found it very helpful indeed to have highly accurate tourist traffic forecasts with which they could refine their scheduling; the DMO in return fed the information into their EMIS, shared in the carbon credit efficiency gains and were able to incorporate these into their visitor management techniques, for example in order to direct tourists to particular attractions; again, managing impact. Real-time computer simulation of destinations was now commonplace and, as her brother kept telling her, the technologies were making a real contribution to destination sustainability.

Zoe toggled her social network receiver on (keeping broadcast off) and immediately saw that of the twenty or so people on the upper deck, seven were 'live'. With a smile, she pulled up her personal agent suite (whilst trying not to give the appearance of winking) into her field of view and sent three social bots off in search of a little more information on the single male personas who were on open broadcast. As the likes of Facebook and Google – or indeed the world of apps – had done years before, there were still start-ups springing surprises and becoming household names and major business players apparently overnight. AxonBuddy was just such a company. It was barely five years since it had launched its first suite of friendly, easy-to-use and highly configurable intelligent software robots (to give them their proper name); the beautiful thing about them, she thought, was just how quickly they learned not only from their own tasked searches but from each other. No wonder they had become so popular so quickly. Of course, perhaps for obvious reasons, the quickest growth and hence the best bots emerged in the world of travel and tourism. Some of the early software glitches had presented fertile territory for her legal work. She was now the proud owner of quite a family of these bots; like an ever growing number of people, she found it hard to imagine life without them and in fact found it even harder to remember the days she used to directly conduct every one of her own web searches – life was too short.

A snowflake landed on the window, and inevitably this drew her thoughts to the ski slopes. Her annual one-week trip with friends was the highlight of the year for her and this time it was her turn to initiate the planning. Almost before the snowflake had melted, she called up her smart little brigade of bots, layered on her ski group notes, and sent the happy emissaries off to explore some ski holiday options for mid-February 2025. Every year since university, her group of eight had skied together, usually alternating between France and Austria; however, Austria had now become impractical, with too few remaining slopes due to climate change and too high a carbon cost. Each avatar already had her personal preferences loaded and only needed a little tweaking of relevant filters prior to action. Needless to say, each had already been informed of each of the group's relevant search constraints by their counterparts, and each was also instructed to ingest all appropriate factors from real-time reviews and archives.

'Twenty minutes to destination, on time', the bus cheerfully scrolled across the top of Zoe's left field of vision. Bot1 (flights) was despatched with a few dates, country and price filters. It was already configured to optimise and sort any 'hits' by lowest carbon debit. Bot2, a super little accommodation agent which was similarly optimised, was tweaked with some price and standard filters and linked to Bot1, whilst Bot3 was sent off scouring ground transfer options, again linked to 1 and 2. After a little thought she also sent Bot4 (trains) to explore rail alternatives (no pain, no gain), and a fifth was despatched to cross-compare any tour operator offers – although there were so few left these days that this was more in hope than anticipation. In fact, since the sweeping uptake of the Semantic Web, sometimes known as MachineSpace, it was hard to imagine how any real intermediary managed to make a living these days, although some patently did. As usual, she instructed that all reports be saved to her personal Cloudspace; she would peruse the outcomes in the comfort of her home.

'Fifteen minutes to destination, all well', scrolled the bus. Ignoring the few incoming mail, text, voice and video messages that had made it past her gatekeeper bot, she called up the digital programme guide for that evening's broadcast TV but was interrupted by a flashing icon indicating her social bots were ready with an update: Male 1 was a thirty per cent compatibility match, Male 3 was an interesting eighty per cent and, curiously, whilst Male 2 had apparently omitted being in a relationship from his primary profile, the busy, intelligent little piece of software had located more than enough background to suggest deletion of this persona. It appeared that some people just had not kept up with today's ubiquitous transparency! This looked promising, she thought. She toggled her broadcast persona to 'on' and paused only briefly as her display intruded enthusiastically to announce that there was a sale at the local ski store only a little distance from the bus route home. The store was being very persuasive, with some lovely video offers, and she did need a new ski jacket. There were at least two compelling offers, modelled of course directly onto biometric data and presented as persuasive holograms in her front field of vision. She paused the virtual shopping, pushed it to her personal Cloudspace and proceeded to scroll through the public media released by Gavin, Male 3. 'Likes travel, music, snow sports'; a few video clips confirmed him as a competent off-piste skier, and he had lots of interests in common with the group and an apparently wicked sense of humour. A potential person of interest, she mused.

With 'ten minutes to destination', Zoe decided to send Gavin an invitation to her personal social space, with limited access to her ski-group profiles and media. She was almost oblivious to the bus route, but she wondered how different the same trip was for a tourist, with so much rich media ready to pour out of the surroundings hoping to get into the devices and consciousness of the tourist. She knew that in that situation she would have already set her bots to optimise the personal interest and green filters, so the mediated reality tools could subtract everything boring, irrelevant or intrusive in her field of view. It was still odd to look at a less-than-real view of the surroundings, she thought; on the other hand, in tourist mode it made the job of the interpretation bots much easier.

'Five minutes to destination' and now her eager social bot alerted her to the fact that Gavin was exploring her recently released media space – interesting. Anyhow, to the main business in hand: she called up her home space, located her microwave, checked the temperature of the quiche (yes, she knew she was lazy) and switched it from chill mode to heat. A little more housekeeping revealed a larder in need of some supplies. Her shop bot displayed a suggested list which she approved only after adding a few more bottles of Kent red wine – after all, one never knew...

Oops! This was her stop, and she risked a careful glance in Gavin's direction (she might replay some of the camvid later) as she headed downstairs – so far, so good. The bus bade her farewell and she walked the short distance to her apartment building, where she was greeted by a pleasant surprise: a new AR beacon had popped into view. The building had just been eco-certified at ninety per cent and she was delighted. All the hard work with her fellow tenants had paid off – the insulation, the water management, the solar contributions to the grid, etc. This level of approval meant a ten per cent reduction in their collective carbon costs for the building, plus on-going microcredits for the infrequent but nonetheless useful grid contributions. Her door recognised her biometric signature, opened (it was so much more than a pendant!) and, home at last, she took off her glasses and was glad to be off the digital radar for a while. It was always relaxing to have some 'me-time' offline, she thought as she concocted a salad – but not too often!

Dinner over, Zoe stepped into her living room, with its stark, minimalist furnishings and plain white walls on all four sides – although in fairness, the walls were rarely plain, as there was always something on display. All over the world living rooms like hers were being converted into immersive bubbles. She recalled sitting at a desk with a screen and keyboard as a teenager and wondered if one day soon her bubble would seem equally quaint and outmoded. Activate BotSpace! The room automatically reduced illumination and all four walls offered competing 3D options. She recalled reading about the early VR pioneers and the clunky kit they used to wear: the full helmets, the data gloves, and so on. With hindsight it should have been obvious that with the gamers driving voice and gesture recognition on the one hand and the likes of Second Life and Google Earth coming ever closer together on the other, it would not be long before really immersive experiences would be both inexpensive and breathtakingly powerful!

She called up the results of the bot searches, pushing the social search – a.k.a. Gavin – onto the wall to her left and the ski searches onto the wall on her right as she limited each to a priority list of five and looked at the recommender bot proposals. They had been their usual thorough selves and, in addition to the regular search criteria, had interrogated OurSpace, the open review space. The first generation of review sites had never enjoyed universal trust, though they were widely used and served a useful purpose; however, ultimately a non-proprietary, bot-friendly, open system had come to dominate. So it looked like the ski trip would be straightforward. The social report was equally simple – strong recommendation to progress with Gavin – so, calling up her social space out of the wall in front of her, she figuratively dragged and dropped the bot search recommendations onto her ski group along with the camvid footage, and turned her full attention to the final stages of the ski-trip search. As she did so she recalled her brother's doctoral work on tourism models and their challenges, remembering his forecasts and dire predictions for the sustainability of most business models in intermediation space. Even he, however, would have been surprised at the rapid decline of the real intermediaries. She now tossed the five best ski options onto her ski-group space and it was not long before a flood of responses started filling that space, so she left her social bot to do its work filtering, categorising and summarising the waves of input from her friends. She de-activated her BotSpace, re-acquainted herself with her red wine and settled down to immerse herself in a documentary on coral reefs, taking advantage of the premium nano suit option: skiing was one thing, but a visit to a coral reef was a definite no-go for her.

A few days later she convened a ski-group meeting. Through the wonders of telepresence all eight sat round tables in seven living rooms across London and one in Sheffield and discussed the alternatives. They knew each other so well now that an agreed favourite was quickly identified: Courchevel had narrowly beaten Val D'Isere to top spot and, despite some minor protestations on price, what had made the difference was actually a very clever move by the destination, which had offered carbon discounts on the ski-lift passes. Once more she recalled her brother's work, which had been hugely critical of what he called the DMO charade. Of course, she had to ask what that meant and he had immensely enjoyed explaining that this was the heart of the problem! Mostly these often government-funded agencies called themselves destination management organisations and liked to project an image of global, or at least local, concern, but of course they were nothing of the kind. As the 2010s unfolded it was increasingly obvious that in the main political pressures pushed DMOs ever more down a road which most were already on – they were really destination marketing organisations, and were *de facto* becoming agents of commercial interests at the destination. This was a great pity, in his eyes, as more than ever what that decade needed was holistic stewardship of destinations, organisations with real power and resources to look at the destination as a sustainable whole, with an informed and engaged host community, and not a sales and marketing tool as an end in itself.

However, things changed astonishingly fast. First, around 2018 the Semantic Web achieved critical mass quicker than any had forecast; then, in a timely symbiosis, AxonBuddy made M2M communication easy-peasy, and almost overnight the need for intermediaries had all but vanished, or at best had metamorphosed into very smart avatars. Of course, it took a few more years to really sink in; DMOs were particularly slow to grasp the fact that the job specification they had created for themselves was no longer needed and their showcase DMS had become about as relevant as using salt as currency. Nevertheless, as it turned out, this was a blessing in disguise – with prospective tourists now able to massively and very rapidly interrogate, filter and sort destination offers, the real competitive advantage transpired to be co-operative development at the destination, and the more forward-thinking DMOs understood that tourists (or rather their bots) were increasingly prioritising carbon cost in holiday decisions. DMOs were now embracing ICT-mediated sustainability as never before; the speed and nature of the new communications space meant that for the first time, destination-wide integration and sustainability management was a real possibility. Anything that could offer a reduced carbon cost would be an attractor, but of course there were rules on what was allowable. Yes, DMOs knew that sustainability was a complex concept interweaving economic, political, social and cultural dimensions, but at the end of the day real influence was always about money and law – or perhaps money, law and carbon credits! As it turned out, and Courchevel was a good example, the DMO had proposed a carbon pooling initiative which, in short, meant that the carbon credits gained by local businesses' good work on reducing their own carbon costs could be aggregated. The DMO proposition was that this pooled carbon credit might be used for a number of things, such as donation to a pro-poor charity or a re-forestation programme, but one of the initiatives was to use this pool to reduce the carbon cost (the monetary cost was unchanged) of the area's ski-lift passes. Of course, when skiers' bots factored this benefit in, it automatically elevated that destination in the reported rankings – a smart move. It appeared DMOs were back in the game; now they could really begin to think of themselves as destination stewards. It was remarkable how many businesses and tourists had become carbon-literate in the space of a handful of years.

So in no time at all, the trip was booked. Zoe thought about the old days of eTickets and QR code boarding passes and smiled ruefully: it seemed obvious in hindsight that the connection of all relevant travel details should be securely connected with a personal ID Space. Each buy bot had already negotiated and finalised the trip details; all this information was now securely stored in eight sets of cloud-based data ready to be challenged and validated as needed, using whatever devices the users happened to be carrying. Before the group went offline, however, two – as it turned out, pertinent – facts emerged. The first was that Brian had been interviewed by hololink for a job in Melbourne and there was an outside possibility that he may have to miss this year's ski trip. The second was the unanimous approval of Gavin as a potential addition to the broader friend group. The meeting adjourned and Zoe found herself now immersed in Courchevel's vMirror. Again, with the convergence of technologies around the time of the Semantic Web, vMirrors had burst onto the scene – this was again obvious with hindsight, and the big clue was open geocoding standards. There was of course even five years ago fairly widespread acceptance that the virtual world had become a kind of symbiotic partner to the real world. Augmented reality had been the first real killer app, and the inevitability of the world of online gaming fusing ever more with virtual worlds produced a much deeper acceptance of the importance and usefulness of virtual worlds. Second Life and Habbo had been among the early harbingers of change; however, the concept of a mirror world existed only in theory and conjecture at that time. An easy way to look at this, she thought, was to think about the increasingly fine-grained Google Earth being populated not by imaginary objects but by real objects: in other words, the Internet of Things meets Google Earth. This produced the first practical mirror world, a virtual simulation of the real world but in fact populated by real data, dynamically shifting. vMirrors took this to a logical conclusion, a co-existing real world, virtual world and mirror world. The prospect of using a virtual world where one could rely on the accuracy and authenticity of objects represented there whilst at the same time being able to move among and manipulate them with illogical speed was just too seductive, and so vMirrors of course became must-have environments.

Yes, Zoe thought, what would I do without my little bots endlessly seeking and sorting data? On the other hand, there was something uniquely human about wanting to see, touch and move objects, even in cyberspace. With that thought she called up Courchevel on the wall in front of her and immersed herself in the amazingly lifelike 3D representations on offer. She virtually flew though the town centre and up the Bellecote Piste, and banked west as she saw the hotel that the group would be visiting in a few months' time. Going in through the front door, she was immediately welcomed by Jean the concierge – or, to be more accurate, his rather handsome avatar. She ignored this as she went straight up to the fourth floor and flew along the corridor and through the door of her spacious single room. There was a remarkable view of the mountain, even on this dark November evening. She was hailed by an eager minibar and took the time to configure its contents for her stay, though she left her media bot to sort out ambience preferences. It was fun to explore the resort this way. She knew that all the practical concerns – flights, transfers, luggage tracking, ski-lift passes – had all been automatically resolved, accounting for all group and individual constraints, so she flew over all the main pistes and had a quick look at the mountain restaurants. She noticed a bird flying alongside here, which was an odd flashing red colour – ahhh, an alert: time to relax and watch some mindless TV. As her immersive sphere receded to leave the volume occupied by the holoTV broadcast, she knew she had already selected the café for their first day's lunch-break and, as a teaser, sent the ski group a recording of her vMirror flight – although no doubt they were all doing very much the same thing.

Alas, as it turned out, Brian would be missing this year. Delighted as they were with his new job in Melbourne, the group knew that his absence from the winter pilgrimage was a signal of change – although to be fair, fate seemed to take a hand to soften the blow. Gavin's ready acceptance to join the group and to come on this year's trip was a surprise, and he had fitted right in with them – another social bot success!

Daydream over, Zoe finished her beer as they stretched and helmeted-up: next stop, the Grande Couloir. Like the others, Zoe toggled the video camera on her iGlasses to 'on' and selected group network mode. She knew her brother would love watching her steep, scary descent of the couloirs, and if he were to have the opportunity of watching in real-time, he would have the luxury of eight different perspectives! Back in his New Delhi living room, Tushar was alerted to Zoe's plans; within moments he was suited-up and off to Courchevel courtesy of his immersive space, and he immediately synched with Zoe's suit. These new, lightweight, state-of-the-art nano suits were expensive but worth it, especially now the nanotech was fast, seamless and smooth and the network of nanosensors in the suit gave an astoundingly accurate pressure sensation of the twists and turns of the ski run. He never had learned to ski, but he still shrieked in terror – boy, it really did feel like the real thing! Tushar wondered how long it would be before real ski trips were a memory and only suit playbacks would provide the experience. Perhaps he should write a paper on the subject.

Glossary

Term	Definition
Ambient tourism	Describes a tourism experience whereby the built or natural environment offers readily accessible information about objects' characteristics in real time and is sensitive to the presence of people. The concept derives from ambient intelligence.
Application programme interface	A set of functions, routines, resources, protocols and tools for developing software applications.
Augmented reality	Augmented reality takes real-world video imagery and enhances it with overlaid computer-generated information.
Avatar	Used by a computer user to represent himself/herself in an online environment. Can be personalised to the user's preferences.
Awards	Presented to tourism businesses by a recognised body as prizes of excellence in recognition of their efforts in becoming more sustainable. Examples include: Tourism for Tomorrow Awards organised by the World Travel and Tourism Council, Environmental Award organised by American Society of Travel Agents and Virgin Holidays Responsible Travel Awards organised by Responsible-Travel.com
Bandwidth	Indicates the amount of data one can send/receive through a connection.

Baseline issue	A main issue set as a benchmark to be used as a basis for comparison. In sustainable tourism development these issues are chosen based on their applicability to the issues of sustainability and the relative ease of measuring and understanding.
Blog	A personalised website which contains updated entries about events, commentaries and other items such as videos, music, sketches and photos. Blogs are usually arranged in chronological order and most allow the reader to leave comments.
Broadband	A high-bandwidth connection to the Internet, which allows large amounts of information to be transmitted at high speed to one's computer.
Carbon calculators	The impact of individuals or organisations on the climate can be calculated by measuring the amount of carbon emissions and other greenhouse gases produced, as a result of their choices and activities in consuming different products and services, by using a carbon calculator.
Carrying capacity	Refers to the number of visitors a destination can sustain without damage to the environment, community or visitor experience. Once this number is exceeded, negative impacts are thought to be felt at the destination.
Certification	A process that ensures there is some criteria by which organisations can conform in order to meet certain requirements or standards. When organisations or businesses become certified they are usually given an eco-label.
Climate change	Refers to variations in weather patterns over an extensive period of time.
Codes of conduct	Codes of conduct serve as guidelines outlining proper practices and responsibilities in relation to how the tourism industry should operate. These codes are not enforced, nor are they enforceable, but are adopted voluntarily by stakeholders in the tourism industry. Therefore, there are no statutory requirements for the adoption of these codes of conduct. There are different types of codes, ranging from general

tourism industry codes and codes that address specific sectors and activities to codes for tourists and codes directed to local communities. Some examples of codes of conduct in tourism include: United Nations World Tourism Organisation's Globe Code of Ethics for Tourism (2001) and World Travel and Tourism Council's Corporate Social Leadership in Tourism (2003).

Community informatics — An ICT-based tool/application focused on the design and delivery of technological applications for enhancing community participation and development through the use of e-mail, bulletin boards and networks based on the Internet.

Community participation — This refers to communities being involved in the decision-making process in matters of tourism that affect them. For example, if there is a proposal for the development of a hotel in a community, the community's views should be obtained, since this proposed development will have both positive and negative impacts on their lives.

Computer simulation — An ICT-based tool/application that is used to simulate real-world settings by demonstrating how a system operates over time. In sustainable tourism development, this can be used for simulation of issues which are too complex for direct observation, manipulation or statistical analysis.

Consolidation — This stage of tourism development at the destination is characterised by increases in tourist arrivals, with the total number of tourists to the destination being greater than the population of the destination. However, the rate of increase in tourist numbers will begin to decline. At this stage, the economy will be heavily dependent on tourism, with extensive marketing and promotion activities focusing on extending the tourist season. A large number of visitor facilities will be provided and major franchises and chains will be present. The local community may pose some opposition to tourism development.

Controlling use intensity	Refers to stresses placed on sites and systems at the destination relative to the desired level of use brought about by the increase in tourist numbers placed on the use of these sites and systems.
Critical success factors	Essential factors that must be in place or essential areas of activity that must be performed in order to achieve the desired result. For example, in sustainable tourism development, a critical success factor is community participation and involvement.
Customer relationship management	This term describes the strategies, processes, people and technologies used by organisations to manage their relationship with customers in an organised manner for profit maximisation and customer satisfaction. It usually involves the capturing, processing, storing and archiving of customer data. For example, an organisation can build a database of its customers so that members of the organisation or the customer themselves can access this information and match the customer's requirements with the product offerings.
Decline	This stage of tourism development at the destination is characterised by the destination facing a decline in tourist numbers due to losing its appeal and its inability to compete with newer destinations. Tourist facilities at the destination begin to disappear as the financial viability of tourist establishments are questioned, with the destination being mainly visited for weekend and day trips. Local involvement might increase at this stage, since locals may purchase declining tourist facilities and put them to other uses.
De-marketing	An aspect of marketing that relates to generally discouraging customers or discouraging a certain class of customers on a temporary or permanent basis from using a product/service. In sustainable tourism, de-marketing is focused on dissuading tourists from visiting a destination.
Destination	A physical space/geographical area which contains tourism products and services to be consumed by the tourists as part of the experience, and which is promoted and marketed by an organisation such as a DMO.

Destination management organisation (DMO)	An organisation responsible for the holistic management of tourism at the destination level, which encompasses a range of tourism development, planning and marketing activities.
Destination manager	The person responsible for the overall management of a DMO.
Destination management system (DMS)	A system that consolidates and distributes a comprehensive range of tourism products through a variety of channels and platforms, generally catering for a specific region. This is an internet protocol-based application, which supports the activities of a DMO in the region by marketing and selling the destination to customers.
Destination system provider (DSP)	Third-party business that distributes ICT-based tools/applications to a DMO across a network from a central data centre. DSPs distribute ICT-based tools/applications such as DMS. This type of business provides a way for a DMO to outsource its ICT requirements.
Development	This stage of tourism development at the destination is characterised by a well-defined tourist area that is marketed and promoted to tourists. Natural and artificial attractions will be developed and marketed to tourists; the physical appearance will be changed, with some local facilities disappearing and being replaced by larger and more modern facilities. Local involvement in and control of the tourism development process will lessen.
Digital divide	Refers to the gulf between the information-rich and the information-poor, i.e. those who do and those who do not have access to technology.
Development control	Measures put in place to guide the tourism development process towards achieving the desired outcomes of the destination and the host community. These measures should be aligned with the greater development plan of the destination. Includes placing controls on the location of a development and the type and size of the development.

Distribution channel selection	Refers to selection of the appropriate channel/s to get the tourism product/service to the customers. Organisations can choose to distribute directly to the customer or use direct mail, telemarketing, the Internet, travel agents, tour wholesalers or retailers.
Drinking water quality	Purity of the drinking water supply at the destination. This is important to tourists since a poor water quality at the destination may lead to negative effects on tourists' health. This may decrease tourist arrivals to the destination, since they will not want to travel to a destination that they perceive as putting their health at risk.
eCommerce	The buying and selling of products over the Internet.
Eco-labelling	A marketable logo or seal that a business receives after it has successfully completed the certification process. Some examples of eco-labels include Green Globe and Blue Flag.
Economic impact analysis software	Software used to measure and monitor the economic impacts of tourism by providing such information as the type and amount of tourist spending. Examples of this software include IMPLAN, RIMS II (Regional Input-Output Multipliers), REMI (Regional Economic Models Inc.) and the Fiscal Tool.
Economic benefit	Viability and competitiveness of tourism destinations and businesses so that they provide tangible benefits to the local community in the long term. Some examples of this are increasing employment opportunities, better standard of living and greater business opportunities for the local community.
Effect of tourism on host community	Refers to the positive and negative impacts of tourism development and tourist activities on the local community. This includes but is not limited to local community satisfaction with tourism, social costs and benefits associated with tourism and impacts on the lives of members of the community.
Energy consumption	This refers to the amount of energy consumed in undertaking activities associated with tourism, such as transportation to and from and at the destination, as well as the provision of facilities and services at the destination.

Energy management — This refers to strategies adopted in reducing the amount of energy consumed in undertaking tourism activities. Some of these strategies include: reducing energy use and encouraging conservation of resources by reducing consumption of natural resources, lowering carbon emissions and using renewable energy sources. Reducing energy consumption will reduce costs for the tourist business, reduce the pressures placed on utilities and have positive effects on the environment.

Environment — A broad perspective of the environment will be adopted which encompasses environmental, economic and socio-cultural aspects.

Environmental impact assessment (EIA) — A planning tool used in projects to determine the approach to sustainability by assessing whether the perceived economic benefits are aligned with the environmental, social and cultural costs.

Environmental management information system (EMIS) — A combination of computer hardware, software, and professional services that integrates disparate information about environmental issues in order to manage the environmental function within an organisation. EMIS systematically gathers, analyses and reports business information related to environmental management, such as waste tracking and emissions monitoring. This allows a company to track, refine and improve its environmental management practice.

eRating system — An Internet-based sustainable tourism rating expert system that provides a rating of a destination based on a common definition of sustainable tourism and considers different categories of sustainable tourism. This rating can be done by three types of expert: a person who has visited the site, the destination manager and a sustainable tourism auditor or sustainable tourism expert, based on a specific set of criteria.

It serves as a form of monitoring and compliance for destinations and can aid them in aligning themselves to the principles of sustainable tourism development. This approach can be useful due to the fact that the information is available through a variety of mediums, transparency of rating via different raters, accountability of a person who uses the system and incorporation of knowledge from experts and field data.

Exploration	This stage of tourism development at the destination is characterised by a small number of tourists visiting the destination, with these tourists being attracted to the destination because of its unique features. These tourists tend to make their own travel arrangements, use local facilities, interact with the local community and do not contribute much to the economic prosperity of the destination or affect the social life of the local community.
Extranet	A private network which utilises World Wide Web technologies, Internet protocol, connectivity and the public telecommunication system to securely share an organisation's information and enable communication with business partners. It is usually considered an extension of an organisation's Intranet.
Folksonomy	This is also referred to as tagging, where users categorise the content on web pages using their own words.
Fiscal incentives	Economic instruments such as financial support or commercial opportunities can be used to influence tourism organisations to align themselves to the principles of sustainable tourism development.
Forecasting	Refers to predicting or calculating in advance. For example, destination managers may want to forecast tourist arrivals or tourist revenues for a particular period. This helps them develop plans, actions and strategies for their destination.
Gamification	Refers to the process of taking approaches, techniques and technologies developed in the sphere of game design and applying them to non-game functions, typically to engage gamers in real-world applications.
Geographical information systems (GIS)	A computer-based system that can collect, store, manage, map, analyse, transform, integrate and display large amounts of geographic data.
Geo-tagging	Refers to adding geographical coordinates to photos, videos and websites.
Global positioning system (GPS)	Satellite-based navigation system that provides positioning, navigation and timing services to users in any weather conditions around the world, twenty-four hours a day.
Greenhouse gases	Gases that trap heat in the atmosphere.

Information and communication technology (ICT)	This is the umbrella term used to describe the use of computers and computer-based devices and technologies for gathering, storing, retrieving, processing, analysing, manipulating and transmitting information, and how these different applications work with each other. Some examples of ICT-based tools/applications include: geographical information systems (GIS), geographical positioning systems (GPS), location-based services (LBS) and environmental management information systems (EMIS).
Information distribution	Distributing information to stakeholders and customers in order to ensure that the right people have the right information at the right time. For example, tourists may request information about a destination and should receive relevant and correct information on this in a timely manner.
Information gathering	The collection of information from various sources and the evaluation of this information for its usefulness, accuracy and relevance in order to assist in formulating plans, strategies and actions. For example, a DMO may collect data on the tourists that visit the destination in order to build a solid customer base and use this information for marketing and promotion activities.
Information management	Managing the quantity and quality of information needed by destination managers to ensure that the best decisions are made for all stakeholders involved in the tourism development process at the destination. Destination managers are faced on a daily basis with vast amounts of information from different sources. ICT can be used to collect, store, manage, analyse and deliver the information to support them in their operational, tactical and strategic decision-making.
Intelligent Transport Systems (ITS)	An ICT-based tool/application that can manage ground transportation at a destination as well as providing useful travel information to the tourists at the destination. Different technologies can be built into an ITS but with specific reference to tourism, ITS can include route guidance systems, traveller information systems, automated vehicle locations, fleet management systems and automated traffic management systems.

	In cars, ITS can help a driver navigate and find the best routes and avoid traffic and collisions. In trains and buses, it can be used for managing operations and providing passengers with automatic ticketing and traffic information. On the roads, it can be used in coordinating traffic signals, detecting and managing incidents and displaying information for drivers, passengers and pedestrians.
Internet	A worldwide computer network that works by using a common set of communication protocols know as Internet protocols.
Internet protocol (IP)	Standards that are used to code the information that supports computer-to-computer communication over the Internet.
Interpretation	This refers to informing the tourist about the importance of a destination so that he/she has greater enjoyment of the destination, with the ultimate aim of creating a positive attitude towards conservation, preservation, history, culture and landscape. Interpretation can be achieved through such methods as education, objects, media, signage, trained guides, maps and first-hand experiences.
Intranet	An organisation's internal network that uses World Wide Web technologies to distribute information throughout the organisation.
In-trip	Refers to the stage of a tourist's trip when they are at the destination.
Involvement	This stage of tourism development at the destination is characterised by an increase in tourist arrivals, where tourists visit the destination more regularly than in the exploration stage. Facilities are beginning to be provided at the destination mainly for tourists, and marketing activities promoting the destination have begun. Pressures are also being placed on local government authority for more and/or better infrastructure and the locals are beginning to become involved in tourism activities and maintain strong interactions with the tourists.

Legislation, regulation or licensing	Used by a government authority to aid in sustainable tourism development by ensuring requirements are complied with and enforcing penalties if they are not. For example, the ruling government at the destination can create specific laws relating to sustainable tourism development.
Local satisfaction	Local communities act as hosts for tourists visiting a destination. They must be contented with tourism development and tourist activities in their community, since if the locals are not pleased, they will not encourage tourists to visit the destination.
Location-based services (LBS)	An ICT-based tool/application that can collect and deliver information to and from a mobile device depending on the automatic location of the user. The aim of an LBS is to provide targeted information to the user based on his/her geographic location. Such information includes but is not limited to places to visit, eat and stay, as well as emergency and health services.
Marketing	Marketing is a process that involves identifying customers' needs and wants and focusing on the design and delivery of products and services to satisfy these needs and wants. In sustainable tourism, marketing can assist destinations to become more sustainable by: destination market segmenting in order to attract the types of tourists they want, promoting particular forms of tourism, influencing tourists' behaviour by enlightening them about sustainability, promoting product offerings of small and medium-sized enterprises, reducing seasonality by promoting off-season opportunities, promoting alternative destinations and hence dispersing the benefits, increasing send per head and per stay and promoting the use of more sustainable forms of transport.
Mashup	The interaction between one or more digital information sources, usually with collaborative content.
mCommerce	Transactions that take place wirelessly, through which users of mobile services can make airline, hotel, car rental and restaurant bookings.
Mobile technology	Technology that is moveable/portable.

Partnerships	Collaboration between the various stakeholders in the tourism industry. For example, a partnership may be formed between accommodation providers and transport operators to provide an integrated product to the tourist.
Performance monitoring	Process used to ascertain how the organisation is performing based on its mission, vision, goals and objectives.
Photo sharing	The taking and sharing of photos and videos.
Podcasts	Multimedia digital files which can be downloaded from the Internet and played on a portable media device such as a computer, MP3 player or iPod.
Post-trip	Refers to the stage of a tourists' trip after they have left the destination.
Pre-trip	Refers to the stage of a tourist's trip before they have arrived at the destination.
Product planning	Integrated and strategic approach to planning the tourism product. In planning the tourism product, issues to be considered include but are not limited to: the type of product to offer, where accommodation should be located, how to develop the attractions, the effects on the community, access to and from the destination and obtaining the views of the stakeholders involved.
Radio frequency identification	Refers to the transfer of data through the attachment of a radio frequency identification tag or label to objects that contains an integrated circuit connected to an antenna, which can be read by special readers.
Really simple syndication (RSS)	Content which changes quickly, such as news headlines and blogs, is delivered to the user via a website in the form of a feed reader without the user having to visit individual websites for this information.
Recommender systems	Applications that can provide suggestions to customers based on their needs and constraints on products and services, and thus influence the decision-making process.
Rejuvenation	Rejuvenation of a destination can occur if the destination changes the focus of the tourist product which is currently offered in order to re-create interest in the destination.

Resource description framework (RDF)	Resource description framework is a W3C recommendation for an agreed means of describing information in a form able to be read and used by computer applications. It is the foundation of the Semantic Web, as it allows information to be broken into very small pieces with attached meaning.
Semantic Web	'Semantic Web' was a term first coined by Sir Tim Berners-Lee to describe the web in a form where information is readily retrieved and processed by both humans and machines.
Site selection	Selection of an area for tourism development. For example, a site can be selected for the development of a resort, attraction or conference centre, or for the staging of an event.
Site maintenance	Maintenance of an area after it has been developed for tourism.
Social media	Online tools/applications/networks/platforms/media which provide anyone with the ability to interact, collaborate, create and share content which they or someone else has created.
Social networking	Refers to using the web and/or mobile technologies to expand the number of social connections one has; today, in reality, this also encompasses business connections.
Solid waste management	Refers to management of the quantity and quality of garbage and hazardous substances produced, reused, recycled and scattered in public places at the destination.
Stagnation	This stage of tourism development at a destination is characterised by a peak in visitor numbers, with carrying capacity levels reached or exceeded and many social, cultural and economic problems existing at the destination as a result of tourism. The destination has a well-established image but it is no longer fashionable, with more artificial attractions than natural ones. The destination is very dependent on repeat visitors and conventions, with greater effort being placed on trying to retain visitor numbers.

Sustainable consumption The consumption of goods and services to satisfy basic needs and improve the quality of life, but minimising the use of non-renewable natural resources and by-products of toxic materials, waste and pollution.

Sustainability indicators and monitoring Indicators can be used to measure the existence of a current issue or the severity of this issue, the risk associated with an issue and the potential need for action. They can also signal upcoming situations or problems and identify, measure and monitor the results of these actions.

In sustainable tourism development, indicators can aid destinations in setting their sustainable tourism objectives by acting as a baseline assessment of a condition or issue, tracking how they are progressing, setting targets for policies, assessment of actions and evaluation and reviewing and modifying of policies. Indicators are intended to provide information in a straightforward, numerical and easy-to-understand format.

Sustainable tourism development A positive, comprehensive and integrated approach to tourism development which involves resource management and working together with stakeholders for the long-term viability and quality of social, economic and environmental resources.

There are many facets to sustainable tourism development, with some examples including reducing tourism's negative impacts, minimising tourism leakages, environmental management and protection, infrastructure development and investment, co-operation between the public and private sectors, host community's involvement in tourism development, host community's benefiting from tourism, respecting cultures and tourist education.

Tagging Tagging may have a variety of meanings. For example it may be a keyword or a term assigned to a piece of information, such as metadata, making the information generally easier to search and locate. Typically tags are assigned in an informal manner by the information item's creator, thus producing a folksonomy. Tagging has become commonplace in Web 2.0 and this has led to, for example, the

	generation of Tag Clouds. In geo-tagging the meta-data associated with the information is geographical: co-ordinates, altitude, etc.
Tax	Usually levied on a tourism business, the tourist or resources such as an effluent charge or waste to influence demand for a product or to change the behaviour of the tourist or the user of the resource. The funds raised by taxes can be used to develop sustainable activities at the destination.
Tourist education	Method of providing information to the tourists to foster a deeper appreciation of the destination, including appropriate behaviour, experiences and values. These education programmes are designed to allow the tourists to contemplate the effects of their actions on the environment and to modify their behaviour.
Tourism information system (TIS)	Data warehouses that manage business-critical information in order to provide quality information, assisting in decision making by serving as a decision support system for destination managers.
Tourist satisfaction	Refers to whether tourists' expectations matched their experiences at the destination. Satisfaction is a subjective concept and is determined by many influencing factors such as safety and security, quality of sites and attractions and hospitality at the destination. This is critical in a tourist's decision to return to a destination or encourage others to visit or not.
Tourist seasonality	Fluctuations in tourist arrivals throughout the year, with most destinations experiencing a high and a low season.
Transportation	Movement of people to and from a destination and in and around a destination.
Triple bottom line	Measurement of a business' economic, environmental and socio-cultural performance over a period of time.
Virtual tourism	An ICT-based tool/application based on the Internet, through which anyone can experience a destination's culture, history and other points of tourist interest in a visual and interactive manner without actually visiting it. Examples of this include on-line guided tours of museums and heritage sites.

Visitor management techniques	These techniques are used to monitor visitor flows and control tourist numbers, and aim to provide visitor satisfaction whilst protecting the environment. They include but are not limited to queues, reservations, lottery, pricing, timed entry, zoning, permits and set-up of protected areas.
VoIP	A collection of technologies that permit the Internet to be used as the transmission medium for telephony. Sometimes called Internet telephony.
Wastewater management	Management of sewage at destinations' tourist establishments. Inappropriate management of wastewater can lead to pollution of beaches, rivers, lakes and ground water, damage flora and fauna and contribute to the spread of diseases.
Water availability and consumption	Overall use of water in relation to its supply and the water-saving measures implemented to conserve water. Water is essential for tourism and in areas where water shortages exist, development can be constrained.
Weather, climate and ocean change forecasting software	Software used to monitor changes in the weather, climate and ocean. The Science Application International Corporation provides such software.
Web 2.0	'[T]he business revolution in the computer industry caused by the move to the internet as platform, and an attempt to understand the rules for success on that new platform' (O'Reilly 2006). This has led to development of web-based services such as social networking sites, video-sharing sites, blogs, wiks and folksonomies.
Web 3.0	The third phase of evolution of the Internet.
Web-based technologies	Technology which uses the Internet as the platform for delivery of this technology.
Wi-Fi	The wireless transfer of data over a computer network.
Wi-max	Similar to Wi-Fi, but can provide wireless exchange of data over longer distances.
Wiki	Websites which allow for the easy creation and editing of web pages by any user.

References

Adams, J. 2005. Hypermobility: A challenge to governance. In: Lyall, C. and Tait, J. (eds.). *New modes of governance: developing an integrated policy approach to science, technology, risk and the environment.* Aldershot, Ashgate. [online]. Last accessed 10 December 2011 at: http://john-adams.co.uk/wp-content/uploads/2006/hypermobility%20for%20new%20modes%20of%20governance%20in%20press.pdf.

Ali, A. 2009. *An investigation into information and communication technologies-based applications for sustainable tourism development of destinations.* PhD thesis, Queen Margaret University.

Agardy, M. T. 1993. Accommodating ecotourism in multiple use planning of coastal and marine protected areas. *Ocean and Coastal Management*, 20 (3), 219–239.

Agarwal, S. 1994. The resort cycle revisited: implications for resorts. *Progress in Tourism, Recreation and Hospitality Management*, 5, 194–208.

Ahn, B. Y., Lee, B. and Shafer, S. C. 2002. Operationalizing sustainability in regional tourism planning: an application of the limits of acceptable change framework. *Tourism Management*, 23 (1), 1–15.

Altalo, M. G., Hale, M., Orestes, A. and Alverson, H. 2002. *Requirements of the U.S. recreation and tourism industry for climate, weather and ocean information.* San Diego, Energy Solutions Group – Science Applications International Cooperation.

Altinay, M. and Hussain, K. 2005. Sustainable tourism development: a case study of North Cyprus. *International Journal of Contemporary Hospitality Management*, 17 (3), 272–280.

Andereck, K., Valentine, K., Knopf, R. and Vogt, C. 2005. Residents' perceptions of community tourism impacts. *Annals of Tourism Research*, 32 (4), 1056–1076.

Archer, B., Cooper, C. and Ruhanen, L. 2005. The positive and negative impacts of tourism. In: Theobald, F. W. (ed.). *Global tourism 3rd ed.* Burlington, Elsevier Butterworth-Heinemann, 79–102.

Avdimiotis, S., Mavrodontis, T., Dermetzopoulos, S. A. and Riavoglou, K. 2006. GIS applications as a tool for tourism planning and education: a case study of Chalkidiki. *Tourism: An International Interdisciplinary Journal*, 54 (4), 405–413.

Ayeh, J. K., Leung, D., Au, N. and Law, R. 2012. Perceptions and strategies of hospitality and tourism practitioners on social media: an exploratory study. In Fuchs. M., Ricci, R. and Cantoni, L. (eds.). *Information and communication technologies in tourism 2012.* Vienna, Springer, 1–12.

Ayuso, S. 2006. Adoption of voluntary environmental tools for sustainable tourism: analysing the experience of Spanish hotels. *Corporate Social Responsibility and Environmental Management*, 13 (4), 207–220.

Ayuso, S. 2007. Comparing voluntary policy instruments for sustainable tourism: the experience of the Spanish hotel sector. *Journal of Sustainable Tourism*, 15 (2), 144–159.

Baggio, R. 2006. Complex systems, information technologies, and tourism: a network point of view. *Information Technology & Tourism*, 8 (1), 15–29.

Bahaire, T. and Elliott-White, M. 1999. The application of geographical information systems (GIS) in sustainable tourism planning: a review. *Journal of Sustainable Tourism*, 7 (2), 159–174.

Bambrook, D. and Murphy, J. 2008. ISO 14001, the green certification. *Ehlite Magazine*, 22 (Autumn), 14–15.

Barnes, J. S. 2003. Location-based services: the state of the art. *e-Service Journal*, 2 (3), 59–70.

Barney, J. 1991. Firm resources and sustained competitive advantages. *Journal of Management*, 17 (1), 99–120.

Barrow, C. J. 2006. *Environmental management for sustainable development, 2nd ed.* London and New York: Routledge.

Batet, M., Moreno, A., Sánchez, D., Isern, D. and Valls, A. 2012. Turist@: Agent-based personalised recommendation of tourist activities. *Expert Systems and Applications*, 39 (8), 7319–7329.

Baum, T. and Szivas, E. 2008. HRD in tourism: a role for government? *Tourism Management*, 29 (4), 783–794.

Beary, K. S. 2009. *How social media and the social conscience will rescue tourism.* [online]. Last accessed 3 March 2012 at: http://www.goodtravelwiki.com/page/Opinion%3A+How+Technology+and+the+Social+Conscience+Will+Rescue+Tourism.

Bechtel, C. and Jayaram, J. 1997. Supply chain management: a strategic perspective. *The International Journal of Logistics Management*, 8 (1), 15–34.

Becken, S. 2002. Analysing international tourist flows to estimate energy use associated with air travel. *Journal of Sustainable Tourism*, 10 (2), 114–131.

Becken, S. 2007. Tourists' perception of international air travel's impact on the global climate and potential climate change policies. *Journal of Sustainable Tourism*, 15 (4), 351–368.

Becken, S. and Patterson, M. 2006. Measuring national carbon dioxide emissions from tourism as a key step towards achieving sustainable tourism. *Journal of Sustainable Tourism*, 14 (4), 323–338.

Beeton, S. and Benfield, R. 2002. Demand control: the case for demarketing as a visitor and environmental management tool. *Journal of Sustainable Tourism*, 10 (6), 497–513.

Belbaly, N., Passiante, G. and Benbya, H. 2004. Knowledge based destination management systems. In: Frew, J. A. (ed.). *Information and communication technologies in tourism 2004*. New York, Springer, 337–347.

Bellotti, F., Berta, R., De Gloria, A. and Primavera, L. 2009. Designing online virtual worlds for cultural heritage. In: Höpken, W., Gretzel, U. and Law, R. (eds.). *Information and communication technologies in tourism 2009*. New York, Springer, 199–209.

Berger, S., Lehmann, H. and Lehner, F. 2003. Location-based services in the tourist industry. *Information Technology & Tourism*, 5 (4), 243–256.

Berkhout, F. and Hertin, J. 2001. *Impacts of information and communication technologies on environmental sustainability: speculation and evidence*. Geneva, Organisation for Economic Co-operation and Development.

Berno, T. and Bricker, K. 2001. Sustainable tourism development: the long road from theory to practice. *International Journal of Economic Development*, 3 (3), 1–18.

Bernstein, H. 1973. Introduction: development and the social sciences. In: Bernstein, H. (ed.). *Underdevelopment & development: The third world today*. Middlesex, Penguin Books Ltd., 13–29.

Bhat, S. and Milne, S. 2008. Network effects on cooperation in destination website developments. *Tourism Management*, 29 (6), 1131–1140.

Bhawani, V. 2009. Education for sustainable development. *Environment: Science and Policy for Sustainable Development*, 5 (2), 8–10.

BIS, Business Innovation Services. 2010. *Britain's superfast broadband future*. [online]. Last accessed 11 May 2012 at: http://www.culture.gov.uk/publications/7829.aspx.

Boers, B. and Cottrell, S. 2006. Sustainable tourism infrastructure planning: a GIS based approach. In: Peden, J. G. and Schuster, R. M. (eds.). *Northeastern recreation research symposium*. Pennsylvania, U.S. Department of Agriculture, Forest Service, 151–160.

Boers, B. and Cottrell, S. 2007. Sustainable tourism infrastructure planning: a GIS-supported approach. *Tourism Geographies*, 9 (1), 1–21.

Bohdanowicz, P. 2005. European hoteliers' environmental attitudes: greening the business. *Cornell Hotel and Restaurant Administration Quarterly*, 46 (2), 188–204.

Bonanni, L., Hockenberry, M., Zwarg, D., Csikszentmihályi, C. and Hiroshi, I. 2010. *Small business applications of sourcemap*. Proceedings of the 28th International Conference on Human factors in Computing Systems – CHI '10. Atlanta, Georgia, USA, 2010. ACM.

Bornhorst, T., Ritchie, B. and Sheehan, L. 2010. Determinants of tourism success for DMOs & destinations: an empirical examination of stakeholders' perspectives. *Tourism Management*, 31 (5), 572–589.

Bramwell, B. and Lane, B. 1993. Sustainable tourism: an evolving global approach. *Journal of Sustainable Tourism*, 1 (1), 1–5.

Bramwell, B. and Lane, B. 2000. Collaboration and partnerships in tourism planning. In: Bramwell, B. and B. Lane (eds.). *Tourism collaboration and partnerships: politics, practice and sustainability*. Clevedon, Channel View Publications, 1–19.

Bramwell, B. and Lane, B. 2009. Economic cycles, times of change and sustainable tourism. *Journal of Sustainable Tourism*, 17 (1), 1–4.

Bramwell, B. and Sharman, A. 1999. Collaboration in local tourism policymaking. *Annals of Tourism Research*, 26 (2), 392–415.

Broads Authority. 2011. *A strategy and action plan for sustainable tourism in the Broads 2011–2015*. [online]. Last accessed 28 February 2012 at: http://www.broads-authority.gov.uk/broads/live/authority/strategy/Tourism_Strategy_for_the_Broads_2011.pdf.

Buckley, R. 2012. Sustainable tourism: research or reality. *Annals of Tourism Research*, 39 (2), 528–546.

Budeanu, A. 2009. Environmental supply chain management in tourism: the case of large tour operators. *Journal of Cleaner Production*, 17 (16), 1385–1392.

Buhalis, D. 1997. Information technology as a strategic tool for economic, social, cultural and environmental benefits enhancements of tourism at destination regions. *Progress in Hospitality and Tourism Research*, 3 (1), 71–93.

Buhalis, D. 1998. Strategic use of information technologies in the tourism industry. *Tourism Management*, 19 (5), 409–421.

Buhalis, D. 1999. Limits of tourism development in peripheral destinations: problems and challenges. *Tourism Management*, 20 (2), 183–185.

Buhalis, D. 2000. Marketing the competitive destination of the future. *Tourism Management*, 21 (1), 97–116.

Buhalis, D. 2003. *eTourism information technology for strategic tourism management*. Harlow, Financial Times Prentice Hall.

Buhalis, D. and Deimezi, O. 2004. E-tourism developments in Greece: information communication technologies adoption for the strategic management of the Greek tourism industry. *Tourism and Hospitality Research*, 5 (2), 103–130.

Buhalis, D. and Law, R. 2008. Progress in information technology and tourism management: 20 years on and 10 years after the Internet – the state of eTourism research. *Tourism Management*, 29 (4), 609–623.

Buhalis, D. and O'Connor, P. 2006. Information communication technology – revolutionizingtourism. In: Buhalis, D. and C. Costa (eds.). *Tourism management dynamics: trends, management, tools*. Oxford, Elsevier Ltd, 196–209.

Buhalis, D. and Pistidda, L. 2008. The impact of WiMAX on tourist destinations. In: O'Connor, P., Höpken, W. and Gretzel, U. (eds.). *Information and communication technologies in tourism 2008*. New York, Springer, 383–394.

Buhalis, D. and Spada, A. 2000. Destination management systems: criteria for success. *Information Technology & Tourism*, 3 (1), 41–58.

Buhalis, D. and Zoge, M. 2007. The strategic impact of the Internet on the tourism industry. In: Sigala, M., Mich, L. and Murphy, J. (eds.). *Information and communication technologies in tourism 2007*. New York, Springer, 481–492.

Butler, W. R. 1980. The concept of a tourist area cycle of evolution: implications for management of resources. *The Canadian Geographer*, 24 (1), 5–12.

Butler, W. R. 1991. Tourism, environment, and sustainable development. *Environmental Conservation*, 18 (3), 291–309.

Butler, W. R. 1999. Sustainable tourism: a state-of-the-art review. *Tourism Geographies*, 1 (1), 7–25.

Canadian Environmental Assessment Research Council. 1988. *Evaluating environmental impact assessment: an action prospectus*. Quebec, Canadian Environmental Assessment Research Council.

Carson, D. and Sharma, P. 2002. A model of Australian tourism information: implications for information systems. In: Wöber, K., Frew, J. A. and Hitz, M. (eds.). *Information and communication technologies in tourism 2002*. New York, Springer, 49–58.

Carter, R. 2005. *Making the most of ICT-based opportunities for developing tourism in destinations*. Geneva, United Nations Conference on Trade and Development Expert Group Meeting on ICT and Tourism for Development.

Ceballos-Lascuráin, H. 1996. *Tourism, ecotourism, and protected areas: the state of nature-based tourism around the world and guidelines for its development*. Gland, IUCN.

Ceron, J. P. and Dubois, G. 2003. Tourism and sustainable development indicators: the gap between theoretical demands and practical achievements. *Current Issues in Tourism*, 6 (1), 54–75.

Chalkiti, K. and Sigala, M. 2008. Information sharing and idea generation in peer-to-peer online communities: the case of 'DIALOGOI'. *Journal of Vacation Marketing*, 14 (2), 121–132.

Chancellor, C. and Cole, S. 2008. Using geographic information system to visualize travel patterns and market research data. *Journal of Travel & Tourism Marketing*, 25 (3), 341–354.

Chmura, N. 2011. *The relationship between sustainable strategic management and integrated marketing communication efforts: a case study of Florida's voluntary hotel eco-certification program*. PhD thesis, 2nd year interim report, Queen Margaret University.

Choi, H. and Sirakaya, E. 2006. Sustainability indicators for managing community tourism. *Tourism Management*, 27 (6), 1274–1289.

Christodoulopoulou, C., Garofalakis, J., Giannakoudi, T. and Koskeris, A. 2000. *Innovative ICT applications to support the tourism sector of Ionian Islands*. Geneva, European Council.

Cigolini, R., Cozzi, M. and Perona, M. 2004. A new framework for SCM. *International Journal of Operations & Production Management*, 24 (1), 7–41.

Cigolini, R., Margherita, P. and Tommaso, R. 2011. An object-oriented simulation meta-model to analyse supply chain performance. *International Journal of Production Research*, 49 (19), 5917–5941.

Clarke, J. 1997. A framework for approaches to sustainable tourism. *Journal of Sustainable Tourism*, 5 (3), 224–233.

Coccossis, H. 1996. Tourism and sustainability: perspectives and implications. In: Priestley, G. K., Edwards A. J. and Coccossis, H. (eds.). *Sustainable tourism? European experiences*. Oxon, CAB International, 1–21.

Cognizant. 2008. *Creating a green supply chain: information technology as an enabler for a green supply chain*. [online]. Last accessed 10 January 2011 at: http://www.cognizant.com/InsightsWhitepapers/Creating_a_Green%20Supply_Chain_WP.pdf.

Cole, S. 2006. Information and empowerment: the keys to achieving sustainable tourism. *Journal of Sustainable Tourism*, 14 (6), 629–644.

Cole, S. 2007. Implementing and evaluating a code of conduct for visitors. *Tourism Management*, 28 (2), 443–451.

Collins, A. 1999. Tourism development and natural capital. *Annals of Tourism Research*, 26 (1), 98–109.

Collins, C. and Buhalis, D. 2003. Destination management systems utilisation in England. In: Frew, J. A., Hitz, M. and O'Connor, P. (eds.). *Information and communication technologies in tourism 2003*. New York, Springer, 202–211.

Connell, J. and Page, S. J. 2008. Exploring the spatial patterns of car-based tourist travel in Loch Lomond and Trossachs National Park, Scotland. *Tourism Management*, 29 (3), 561–580.

Cooper, C., Fletcher, J., Fyall, A., Gilbert, D. and Wanhill, S. 2005. *Tourism: principles and practice, 3rd ed.* Harlow: Pearson Education Limited.

Cooper, C., Ruhanen, L. and Craig-Smith, S. 2004. Developing a knowledge management approach to tourism research. *The Tourism State of the Art II Conference*. Glasgow, University of Strathclyde.

Corbett, C. J. and Klassen, R. D. 2006. Extending the horizons: environmental excellence as key to improving operations. *Manufacturing and Service Operations Management*, 8 (1), 5–22.

Corigliano, M. A. and Baggio, R. 2004. Mobile technologies diffusion in tourism: modelling a critical mass of adopters in Italy. In: Frew, J. A. (ed.). *Information and communication technologies in tourism 2004*. New York, Springer, 16–26.

Cornell Hospitality. 2010. *The hotel industry seeks the elusive green bullet – Cornell Hospitality roundtable proceedings*. New York, Cornell University.

Croes, R. 2006. A paradigm shift to a new strategy for small island economies: Embracing demand side economics for value enhancement and long term economic stability. *Tourism Management*, 27 (3), 453–465.

Cronin, M. 1996. *The Internet strategy handbook*. Boston, Harvard Business School Press.

Currie, R. R., Seaton, S. and Wesley, F. 2008. Determining stakeholders for feasibility analysis. *Annals of Tourism Research*, 36 (1), 41–63.

Curtin, J., Kauffman, R. J. and Riggins, F. J. 2007. Making the 'MOST' out of RFID technology: a research agenda for the study of the adoption, usage, and impact of RFID. *Information Technology and Management*, 8 (2), 87–110.

Davis, F. D. 1989. Perceived usefulness, perceived ease of use, and user acceptance of information technology. *MIS Quarterly*, 13 (3), 319–340.

Dawkins, R. 1976. *The selfish gene*. Oxford, Oxford University Press.

de Sausmarez, N. 2007. Crisis management, tourism and sustainability: the role of indicators. *Journal of Sustainable Tourism*, 15 (6), 700–714.

Devaraj, S., Krajewski, L. and Wei, C. J. 2007. Impact of eBusiness technologies on operational performance: the role of production information integration in the supply chain. *Journal of Operations Management*, 25 (6), 1199–1216.

Dewhurst, F., Spring, M. and Arkle, N. 2000. Environmental change and supply chain management: a multi-case study exploration of the impact of Y2000. *Supply Chain Management: An International Journal*, 5 (5), 245–261.

Diagle, J. J. and Zimmerman, A. C. 2004. The convergence of transportation, information technology, and visitor experience at Acadia National Park. *Journal of Travel Research*, 43 (2), 151–160.

Din, H. K. 1996. Tourism development: still in search of a more equitable mode of local involvement. *Progress in Tourism and Hospitality Research*, 2 (3 & 4), 273–281.

Dubois, D. 2005. Indicators for an environmental assessment of tourism to national level. *Current Issues in Tourism*, 8 (2 & 3), 140–154.

Dubois, G. and Ceron, P. J. 2006. Tourism/leisure greenhouse gas emissions forecasts for 2050: Factors for Change in France. *Journal of Sustainable Tourism*, 14 (2), 172–191.

Dwyer, L., Edwards, D., Mistilis, N., Roman, C. and Scott, N. 2009. Destination and enterprise management for a tourism future. *Tourism Management*, 30 (1), 63–74.

Edgell, L. D. 2006. *Managing sustainable tourism: a legacy for the future*. New York: The Haworth Hospitality Press.

Edwards, S., Blythe, P., Scott, S. and Weihong-Guo, A. 2010. Tourist information delivered through mobile devices: findings from the image project. *Information Technology & Tourism*, 8 (1), 31–46.

El-Gayar, O. F. and Fritz, B. D. 2006. Environmental management information systems (EMIS) for sustainable development: a conceptual overview. *Communications of the Association for Information Systems*, 17 (2006), 756–784.

Elliott-White, M. and Finn, M. 1998. Growing in sophistication: the application of geographical information system in post-modern tourism marketing. *Journal of Travel & Tourism Marketing*, 7 (1), 65–84.

Erdmann, L. and Behrendt, S. 2003. *The future impact of ICT on environmental sustainability second interim report*. Geneva, European Commission.

Erdmann, L. and Goodman, J. 2004. *The future impact of ICTs on environmental sustainability*. Geneva, European Commission.

Eriksson, O. 2002. Location based destination information for the mobile tourist. In: Wöber, K., Frew, A. J. and Hitz, M. (eds.). *Information communication technologies in tourism 2002*. New York, Springer, 255–264.

Eslami, A. Foumani, S. B., Khazraei, R., Pourjafar, Z., Ghaebi, K., Dehghanzad, S., Karimi, Z. and Kheirandish, R. 2011. Implementation of GIS in natural resources. *Annals of Biological Research*, 2 (5), 533–540.

European Commission. 2006. *A pocketbook of e-business indicators: a portrait of e-business in 10 sectors of the EU economy*. Bonn: eBusiness W@tch.

Farrell, T. A. and Marion, J. L. 2002. The protected area visitor impact management (PAVIM) framework: a simplified process for making management decisions. *Journal of Sustainable Tourism*, 10 (1), 31–51.

Farrell, B. and Twining-Ward, L. 2005. Seven steps towards sustainability: tourism in the context of new knowledge. *Journal of Sustainable Tourism*, 13 (2), 109–122.

Farsari, Y., Butler, R. and Prastacos, P. 2007. Sustainable tourism policy for Mediterranean destinations: issues and interrelationships. *International Journal of Tourism Policy*, 1 (1), 58–78.

Feick, R. and Hall, G. B. 2000. The application of a spatial decision support system to tourism-based land management in small island states. *Journal of Travel Research*, 39 (2), 163–171.

Florida Department of Business and Professional Regulations. 2010. *Division of hotels and resturants annual report 2011–2012*. [online]. Last accessed 10 November 2011 at: http://www.dep.state.fl.us/greenlodging/.

Florida Green Lodging Program. 2011a. [online]. Last accessed 22 March 2012 at: http://www.dep.state.fl.us/greenlodging/files/designationapplication1.pdf.

Florida Green Lodging Program. 2011b. *Florida green lodging program designation application*. [online]. Last accessed 22 March 2012 at: http://www.dep.state.fl.us/greenlodging/files/designationapplication1.pdf.

Florida Legislature. 2008. *Florida statutes 286.29*. [online]. Last accessed 22 March 2012 at: http://www.leg.state.fl.us/Statutes/index.cfm?App_mode=Display_Statute&Search_String=&URL=0200-0299/0286/Sections/0286.29.html.

Flouri, E. and Buhalis, D. 2004. Wireless technologies for tourism destinations. In: Frew, J. A. (ed.). *Information and communication technologies in tourism 2004*. New York, Springer, 27–38.

Font, X. 2005. Sustainable tourism standards in the global economy. In: Theobald, F. W. (ed.). *Global tourism, 3rd ed.* Burlington, Elsevier Butterworth-Heinemann, 213–229.

Font, X., Sanabria, R. and Skinner, E. 2003. Sustainable tourism and ecotourism certification: raising standards and benefits. *Journal of Ecotourism*, 2 (3), 213–218.

Font, X., Tapper, R., Schwartz, K. and Kornilaki, M. 2008. Sustainable supply chain management in tourism. *Business Strategy and the Environment*, 17 (4), 260–271.

Fotis, J., Buhalis, D. and Rossides, N. 2012. Social media use and impact during the holiday travel planning process. In: Fuchs, M., Ricci, F. and Cantoni, L (eds.). *Information and communication technologies in tourism 2012*. Vienna, Springer, 13–24.

Frew, J. A. 2000. Information and communications technology research in the travel and tourism domain: perspective and direction. *Journal of Travel Research*, 39 (2), 136–145.

Fuchs, M. and Höpken, W. 2005. Towards @Destination: a DEA-based decision support framework. In: Frew, J. A. (ed.). *Information and communication technologies in tourism 2005*. New York, Springer, 57–66.

Garcia, A., Linaza, M., Arbelaitz, O. and Vansteenwegen, P. 2009. Intelligent routing system for a personalised electronic tourist guide. In: Höpken, W. Gretzel, U. and Law, R., (eds.). *Information and communciation technologies in tourism 2009*. New York, Springer, 185–197.

Garrod, B. and Fyall, A. 1998. Beyond the rhetoric of sustainable tourism? *Tourism Management*, 19 (3), 199–212.

Gezici, F. 2005. Components of sustainability: two cases from Turkey. *Annals of Tourism Research*, 33 (2), 442–455.

Ghandour, R. and Buhalis, D. 2003. Third-generation mobile services and the needs of mTravellers. In: Frew, A. J., Hitz, M. and O'Connor, P. (eds.). *Information and communication technologies in tourism 2003*. New York, Springer, 222–231.

Ghose, R. 2001. Use of information technology for community empowerment: transforming geographic information systems into community information systems. *Transactions in GIS*, 5 (2), 141–163.

Giannakis, M. 2011. Conceptualizing and managing service supply chains. *The Service Industries Journal*, 31 (11), 1809–1823.

Gilbert, A., Hoa, N. and Binh, V. 1998. A strategic model for using information technology in developing strategic tourism. *Journal of Vietnam Studies*, 1 (1), 1–17.

Go, F. and Williams, A. 1994. Competing and cooperating in the changing tourism channel system. *Journal of Travel and Tourism Marketing*, 2 (2–3), 229–248.

Gössling, S. 2000. Sustainable tourism development in developing countries: some aspects of energy use. *Journal of Sustainable Tourism*, 8 (5), 410–425.

Gössling, S. 2002. Global environmental consequences of tourism. *Global Environmental Change*, 12 (4), 283–302.

Gössling, S. 2009. Carbon neutral destinations: a conceptual analysis. *Journal of Sustainable Tourism*, 17 (1), 17–37.

Gössling, S. and Hall, M. C. 2006. An introduction to tourism and the global environmental change. In: Gössling, S. and Hall, M. C. (eds.). *Tourism and global environmental change*. London, Routledge, 1–33.

Gössling, S. and Peeters, P. 2007. 'It does not harm the environment!' an analysis of industry discourses on tourism, air travel and the environment. *Journal of Sustainable Tourism*, 15 (4), 402–417.

Gossling, S., Peeters, P., Ceronc, J., Dubois G., Pattersone, T. and Richardson, R. B. 2005. The eco-efficiency of tourism. *Ecological Economics*, 54 (15), 417–434.

Gratzer, M., Winiwarter, W. and Werthner, H. 2002. *State of the art in eTourism*. Paper presented at the 3rd South Eastern European Conference on e-Commerce 2002.

Gratzer, M., Werthner, H. and Winiwarter, W. 2004. E-business in tourism. *International Journal of Electronic Business*, 2 (5), 450–459.

Green, C. G. and Murrmann, S. K. 2005. Technology as a tool for citizen participation in community development and tourism: the rebuilding of Lower Manhattan. In: Frew, J. A. (ed.). *Information and communication technologies in tourism 2005*. New York, Springer, 102–113.

Green Hotel Association. 2008. *What 'are' green hotels?* [online]. Last accessed 20 January 2012 at: http://greenhotels.com/index.php.

Green Travel News. 2011. *The future of travel: green value*. [online]. Last accessed 20 May 2011 at: http://greentravelerguides.com/2011/01/green-travel-trend/.

Gretzel, U., Go, H., Lee, K. and Jamal, T. 2009. Role of community informatics in heritage tourism development. In: Höpken, W., Gretel, U. and Law, R. (eds.). *Information and communication technologies in tourism 2009*. New York, Springer, 1–12.

Gretzel, U., Yuan, Y. and Fesenmaier, D. 2000. Preparing for the new economy: advertising strategies and change in destination marketing organisations. *Journal of Travel Research*, 39 (2), 146–156.

Grossman, L. 2012. The beast with a billion eyes. [online]. Last accessed 30 January 2012 at: http://www.time.com/time/magazine/article/0,9171,2104815,00.html#ixzz1mlqJMhbl.

GSTC 2012. Welcome to sustainable tourism [online]. Last accessed 4 July 2012 at: http://www.gstcouncil.org/about/learn-about-gstc.html.

Gunn, C. and Var, T. 2002. *Tourism planning, 4th ed.* New York and London, Routledge.

Gurstein, M. 2000. *Community informatics: enabling communities with information and communications technologies*. Hershey, Idea Group.

Hall, M. C. 2000. *Tourism planning: policies, processes and relationships*. Essex, Pearson Education Limited.

Hall, M. C. and Lew, A. A. 1998. *Sustainable tourism: a geographical perspective*. New York, Addison-Wesley Longman Limited.

Hall, M. C. and Gössling, S. 2009. Global environmental change and tourism enterprise. In: Leslie, D. (ed.). *Tourism enterprises and sustainable development*. New York, Routledge, 17–35.

Hamill, J. and Stevenson, A. 2012. 'Creating the buzz': Merchant City (Glasgow) case study. In: Sigala, M., Christou, E. and Gretzel, U. (eds.). *Social media in travel, tourism and hospitality*. Surrey, Ashgate, 39–52.

Hardy, L. A. and Beeton, S. 2001. Sustainable tourism or maintainable tourism: managing resources for more than average outcomes. *Journal of Sustainable Tourism*, 9 (3), 168–192.

Hardy, L. A., Beeton, S. and Pearson, L. 2002. Sustainable tourism: an overview of the concept and its position in relation to conceptualisations of tourism. *Journal of Sustainable Tourism*, 10 (6), 475–496.

Harewood, S. 2008. Coordinating the tourism supply chain using bid prices. *Journal of Revenue and Pricing Management*, 7 (3), 266–280.

Harrison, A. and van Hoek, R. 2008. *Logistic management and strategy: competing through the supply chain, 3rd ed.* Essex, Pearson Education Limited.

Harrison, L. and Husbands, W. 1996. *Practising responsible tourism: international case studies in tourism planning, policy and development*. New York, John Wiley & Sons.

Harvard Business Review. 2010. Is your supply chain sustainable? *Harvard Business Review*, October 2010, pp. 74–82.

Hasse, J. 2003. Tourism and participatory geographical information systems (PAGIS). *BBS Teaching & Research Review*, 6. [online]. Last accessed 21 September 2006 at: http://www.uwe.ac.uk/bbs/trr/Issue6/Is63_1.pdf#search=%22julia%20hasse%22.

Hasse, J. and Milne, S. 2005. Participatory approaches and geographical information systems (PAGIS) in tourism planning. *Tourism Geographies*, 7 (3), 272–289.

Haywood, K. M. 1986. Can the tourist-area life cycle be made operational? *Tourism Management*, 7 (3), 154–167.

Hegmann, G., Cocklin, C., Creasey, R., Dupuis, S., Kennedy, A., Kingsley, L., Ross, W., Spaling, H. and Stalker, D. 1999. *Cumulative effects assessment practitioners guide*. Quebec, AXYS Environmental Consulting Ltd. and the CEA Working Group for the Canadian Environmental Assessment Agency.

Hetherington, A. 1991. *Tourism planning: an integrated and sustainable development approach*. New York, Van Nostrand Reinhold.

Hinze, A., Voisard, A. and Buchanan, G. 2009. TIP: Personalizing information delivery in a tourist information system. *Information Technology & Tourism*, 11 (3), 247–264.

Hjalager, A. 1996. Tourism and the environment: the innovation connection. *Journal of Sustainable Tourism*, 4 (4), 201–218.

Holloway, C. J. 2002. *The business of tourism, 6th ed.* Harlow, Prentice Hall.

Honey, M. and Rome, A. 2001. *Protecting paradise: certification programs for sustainable tourism and ecotourism*. Washington, DC, Institute of Policy Studies.

Höpken, W., Scheuringer, M., Linke, D. and Fuchs, M. 2008. Context-based adaptation of ubiquitous web applications in tourism. In: O'Connor, P., Höpken, W. and Gretzel, U. (eds.). *Information and communciation technolgies in tourism 2008*. New York, Springer, 533–544.

Horan, P. and Frew, A. J. 2007. Destination eMetrics. In Frew, J.A. (ed.). *Proceedings of the travel distribution summit, Europe Research Conference 2007*. London, Axon Imprint, 25–44.

Hovinen, G. R. 2002. Revisiting the destination lifecycle model. *Annals of Tourism Research*, 29 (1), 209–230.

Howie, F. 2003. *Managing the tourist destination*. London and New York, Continuum.

Hughes, G. 2002. Environmental indicators. *Annals of Tourism Research*, 29 (2), 457–477.

Hunter, C. 1995. On the need to re-conceptualise sustainable tourism development. *Journal of Sustainable Tourism*, 3 (3), 155–165.

Hunter, C. 1997. Sustainable tourism as an adaptive paradigm. *Annals of Tourism Research*, 24 (4), 850–867.

HVS. 2012. Current trends and opportunites in hotel sustainability. New York, HVS. [online]. Last accessed 1 May 2012 at: www.hvs.com/Content/3218.pdf.

Inskeep, E. 1991. *Tourism planning: an integrated and sustainable development approach*. New York, Van Nostrand Reinhold.

International Air Travel Association (IATA). 2007. *RFID business case for baggage tagging*. [online]. Last accessed 20 January 2012 at: http://www.iata.org/whatwedo/stb/Documents/RFID%20for%20baggage%20business%20case%202%201.pdf.

International Panel on Climate Change (IPCC). 2007. *Climate change 2007: synthesis report*. Geneva, IPCC.

International Union for Conservation of Nature and Natural Resources. 1980. *World conservation strategy: living resource conservation for sustainable development*. Switzerland, International Union for Conservation of Nature and Natural Resources.

Internet World Stats. 2011. *Internet usage statistics: the Internet big picture, world Internet users and population stats*. [online]. Last accessed 5 December 2011 at: http://www.internetworldstats.com/stats.htm.

Ioannides, D. 2001. Sustainable development and the shifting of tourism stakeholders: towards a dynamic framework. In: McCool, F. S. and Moisey, R. N. (eds.). *Tourism, recreation and sustainability*. London, CAB International, 55–76.

Ioris, A. R. A., Hunter, C. and Walker, S. 2008. The development and application of water management sustainability indicators in Brazil and Scotland. *Journal of Environmental Management*, 88 (4), 1190–1201.

Isaksson, S. 2010. *Possible applications of RFID technology in tourism services. Proceedings of Umea's 14th Student Conference in Computing Science* [online]. Last accessed 15 April 2012 at: http://www8.cs.umu.se/kurser/5DV054/Proc_USCCS10.pdf#page=57.

Johnston, R. J. and Tyrrell, T. J. 2005. A dynamic model of sustainable tourism. *Journal of Travel Research*, 44 (2), 124–134.

Kassinis, G. and Soteriou, C. A. 2003. Greening the service profit chain: the impact of environmental management practices. *Production and Operations Management*, 12 (3), 386–403.

Kastenholz, E. 2004. Management of demand as a tool in sustainable tourist destination development. *Journal of Sustainable Tourism*, 12 (5), 388–408.

Kazasis, F., Anestis, G., Moumoutzis, N. and Christodoulakis, S. 2003. Intelligent information interactions for tourism destinations. In: Frew, A. J., Hitz, M. and O'Connor, P. (eds.). *Information and communication technologies in tourism 2003*. New York, Springer, 1–9.

Kelly, J. and Williams, P. W. 2007. Modelling tourism destination energy consumption and greenhouse gas emissions: Whistler, British Columbia, Canada. *Journal of Sustainable Tourism*, 15 (1), 67–90.

Kernel, P. 2005. Creating and implementing a model for sustainable development in tourism. *Journal of Cleaner Production*, 13 (2), 151–164.

Keske, C. and Smutko, S. 2010. Consulting communities: using audience response system (ARS) technology to assess community preferences for sustainable recreation and tourism development. *Journal of Sustainable Tourism*, 18 (8), 951–970.

Kirk, D. 1998. Attitudes of environmental management held by a group of hotel managers in Edinburgh. *International Journal of Hospitality Management*, 17 (1), 33–47.

Ko, T. G. 2005. Development of a tourism sustainability assessment procedure: a conceptual approach. *Tourism Management*, 26 (3), 431–445.

Kotler, P. and Levy, J. S. 1971. Demarketing, yes, demarketing. *Harvard Business Review*, 49 (6), 74–80.

Koutsoutos, A. and Westerholt, C. 2005. Business impact of ICT. *International Journal of Technology, Policy and Management*, 5 (1), 25–47.

Kozak, M. and Nield, K. 2004. The role of quality and eco-labelling systems in destination benchmarking. *Journal of Sustainable Tourism*, 12 (2), 138–148.

Krozer, Y. and Christensen-Redzepovic, E. 2006. Sustainable innovations at tourist destinations. *Tourism Review International*, 10 (1), 113–124.

Kumar, K. 2001. Technologies for supporting supply chain management. *Communications of the ACM*, 44 (6), 58–61.

La Micela, A., Roberti, P. and Jacucci, G. 2002. From individual tourism organisation to a single virtual tourism organisation for destination management. In: Wöber, K., Frew, J. A. and Hitz, M. (eds.). *Information and communication technologies in tourism 2002*. New York, Springer, 87–96.

Laws, E. 1995. *Tourist destination management: issues, analysis and policies*. New York, Routledge.

Lawson, S. 2006. Computer simulation as a tool for planning and management of visitor use in protected natural areas. *Journal of Sustainable Tourism*, 14 (6), 600–617.

Lawson, S., Itami, B., Gimblett, R. and Manning, R. 2003. Benefits and challenges of computer simulation modeling of backcountry recreation use in the Inyo National Forest. *Journal of Leisure Research*, 38 (2), 187–207.

Lawson, S. and Manning, R. 2003. Research to inform management of wilderness camping at Isle Royale National Park: Part I – descriptive research. *Journal of Park and Recreation Administration*, 21 (3), 22–42.

Lebe, S. S. and Milfelner, B. 2006. Innovative organisation approach to sustainable tourism development in rural areas. *Kybernetes*, 35 (7/8), 1136–1146.

Lee, K. 2001. Sustainable tourism destinations: the importance of cleaner production. *Journal of Cleaner Production*, 9 (4), 313–323.

Lee, B. and Graefe, A. 2004. GIS: a tool to locate new park and recreation services. *Parks & Recreation*, pp. 34–41.

Lee, J. and Mills, J. 2007. Exploring tourist satisfaction with mobile technology. In: Sigala, M., Mich, L. and Murphy, J. (eds.). *Information and communication technologies in tourism 2007*. New York, Springer, 141–152.

Leiner, B. M., Cerf, V. G., Clark, D. D., Kahn, R. E., Kleinrock, L., Lynch, D. C., Postel, J., Robers, L. G. and Wolff, S. 2009. A brief history of the internet. *ACM SIGCOMM Computer Communication Review*, 39 (5), 22–31.

Leiner, N. and Stoll-Kleemann, S. 2009. *Supporting sustainable development with Web 2.0 applications*. Environmental Informatics and Industrial Environmental Protection: Concepts, Methods and Tools Conference, 9–11 September 2009, Berlin, Germany, 279–287.

Lew, A. and McKercher, B. 2005. Modeling tourist movements: a local destination analysis. *Annals of Tourism Research*, 33 (2), 403–423.

Li, G., Song, H. and Witt, F. W. 2005. Recent developments in econometric modeling and forecasting. *Journal of Travel Research*, 44 (1), 82–99.

Li, W. 2004. Environmental management indicators for eco-tourism in China's nature reserves: a case study in Tianmushan Nature Reserve. *Tourism Management*, 25 (5), 559–564.

Lin, T. 2010. Carbon dioxide emissions from transport in Taiwan's national parks. *Tourism Management*, 31 (2), 285–290.

Lindberg, K. 1991. *Policies for maximizing of tourism's logical and economic benefits*. Washington, DC, World Resources Institute.

Linton, D. J., Klassen, R. and Jayaraman, V. 2007. Sustainable supply chains: an introduction. *Journal of Operations Management*, 25 (6), 1075–1082.

Liu, Z. 2003. Sustainable tourism development: a critique. *Journal of Sustainable Tourism*, 11 (6), 459–475.

Liburd, L. J. 2005. Sustainable tourism and innovation on mobile tourism services. *Tourism Review International*, 9 (2), 107–118.

Litvin, S. W., Goldsmith, R. E. and Pan, B. 2007. Electronic word of mouth in hospitality and tourism management. *Tourism Management*, 29 (3), 458–468.

Lozano-Oyola, M., Blancas, F., González, M. and Caballero, R. 2012. Sustainable tourism indicators as planning tools in cultural destinations. *Ecological Indicators*, 18, 659–675.

Ma, X. J., Buhalis, D. and Song, H. 2003. ICTs & Internet adoption in China's tourism industry. *International Journal of Information Management*, 23 (6), 451–467.

Manning, E. W. and Dougherty, T. D. 2000. Planning sustainable tourism destinations. *Tourism Recreation Research*, 25 (2), 3–14.

Martin, S. B. and Uysal, M. 1990. An examination of the relationship between carrying capacity and the tourism lifecycle: Management and policy implications. *The Journal of Environmental Management*, 31 (4), 327–333.

Martinis, A., Kabassi, K., Skotti, E., Karris, K. and Charou, E. 2009. *Environmental routes setting methodology: the case of Corfy & Paxoi Ilands*. International Conference on Tourism Development and Management, 11–14 September 2009, 309–312.

Martinis, A., Halvatzaras, D. and Kabassi, K. 2011. Promotion of eco-tourism using the practice of Wikipedia: the case-study of environmental and cultural paths in Zakynthos. In: Migliorini, P., Minotou, C., Lusic, D., Hashem, Y. and Martinis, A. (eds.). *Book of abstracts. International conference on organic agriculture and agro-eco tourism*, DIO.

Mason, P. 2003. *Tourism impacts, planning and management*. Oxford, Elsevier Butterworth-Heinemann.

Mason, P. 2005. Visitor management in protected areas: from 'hard' to 'soft' approaches? *Current Issues in Tourism*, 8 (2 & 3), 181–194.

Mason, P. and Mowforth, M. 1996. Codes of conduct in tourism. *Progress in Tourism and Hospitality Research*, 2 (3), 151–167.

Matthews, H. S., Hendrickson, C. T. and Weber, C. L. 2008. The importance of carbon footprint estimation boundaries. *Environmental Science and Technology Viewpoint*, 42 (16), 5839–5842.

McAdam, D. 1999. The value and scope of geographical information systems in tourism management. *Journal of Sustainable Tourism*, 7 (1), 77–92.

McCool, S. and Lime, D. 2001. Tourism carrying capacity: tempting fantasy or useful reality? *Journal of Sustainable Tourism*, 9 (5), 372–388.

McKercher, B., Prideaux, B., Cheung, C. and Law, R. 2010. Achieving voluntary reductions in the carbon footprint of tourism and climate change. *Journal of Sustainable Tourism*, 18 (3), 297–317.

McKercher, B., Shoval, N., Ng, E. and Birenboim, A. 2012. First and repeat visitor behaviour: GPS tracking and GIS analysis in Hong Kong. *Tourism Geographies*, 14 (1), 147–161.

McLaren, T., Head, M. and Yuan, Y. 2002. Supply chain collaboration alternatives: understanding costs and benefits. *Internet Research: Electronic Networking Applications and Policy*, 12 (4), 348–364.

McWilliams, A. and Siegel, D. 2000. Corporate social responsibility and financial performance: correlation or misspecification? *Strategic Management Journal*, 21 (5), 603–609.

Medlik, S. 2003. *Dictionary of travel, tourism and hospitality*. Oxford, Butterworth-Heinemann.

Mefford, N. R. 2011. The economic value of a sustainable supply chain. *Business and Society Review*, 116 (1), 109–143.

Mertes, J. and Hall, J. 1995. *Park, recreation, open space and greenway guidelines*. Washington, DC, National Recreation and Park Association.

Michael, E. 2007. *Micro-clusters and networks: the growth of tourism. Advances in tourism research series*. Oxford, Elsevier.

Middleton, V. and Clarke, J. 2001. *Marketing in travel and tourism, 3rd ed*. Oxford, Butterworth-Heinemann.

Mihalic, T. 1998. Ecological labelling in tourism. *UK CEED Bulletin Special Focus: Environmental Valuation*. Spring, 33–35.

Mihalic, T. 2000. Environmental management of a tourist destination: a factor of tourism competitiveness. *Tourism Management*, 21 (1), 65–78.

Millar, R. D., Morrice, G. J., Horne, L. P. and Aspinall, J. R. 1994. The use of geographic information systems for analysis of scenery in the Cairngorm mountains, Scotland. In: Price, F. M. and Heywood, I. D. (eds.). *Mountain environments and GIS*. London, Taylor & Francis, 119–132.

Miller, G. 2001. The development of indicators for sustainable tourism: results of a Delphi survey of tourism researchers. *Tourism Management*, 22 (4), 351–362.

Miller, G., Rathouse, K., Scarles, C., Holmes, K. and Tribe, J. 2010. Public understanding of sustainable tourism. *Annals of Tourism Research*, 37 (3), 627–645.

Miller, G. and Twining-Ward, L. 2005. *Monitoring for a sustainable tourism transition: the challenge of developing and using indicators*. Wallingford, CABI Publishing.

Miller, G. and Twining-Ward, L. 2006. Monitoring as an approach to sustainable tourism. In: Buhalis, D. and Costa, C. (eds.). *Tourism management dynamics: trends, management and tools*. Oxford, Elsevier, 51–57.

Milne, S. 1987. The Cook Islands tourist industry: ownership and planning. *Pacific Viewpoint*, 28 (2), 119–38.

Milne, S. and Ateljevic, I. 2001. Tourism, economic development and the global-local nexus: theory embracing complexity. *Tourism Geographies*, 3 (4), 369–393.

Milne, S., Speidel, U., Goodman, T. and Clark, V. 2005. ICT and regional economic development: the case of Kiwitrails. In: Frew, J. A. (ed.) *Information and communication technologies in tourism 2005*. New York, Springer, 114–124.

Mintel. 2011. *Green innovations in tourism-international, February 2011*. London, Mintel.

Mistilis, N. and Buhalis, D. 2012. Challenges and potential of the Semantic Web for tourism. *e-Review of Tourism Research (eRTR)*, 10(2), 51–55.

Moore, M. and Bordeleau, D. 2001. *The environmental management information system (EMIS) of the intelligent environmental management system.* [online]. Last accessed 3 May 2005 at: http://www.eco-web.com/editorial/00044.html.

Moscardo, G. 2000. Understanding wildlife tourism market segments: an Australian marine study. *Human Dimensions of Wildlife*, 5 (2), 36–53.

Moscardo, G. 2007. There's no such thing as sustainable tourism: innovation through challenging assumptions. In: Liburd, L. J. and Hergesell, A. (eds.). *BEST education network think tank.* Sydney, University of Technology, 138–147.

Moscardo, G. and Walker, K. 2006. The impact of interpretation on passengers of expedition cruises. In: Dowling, K. R. (ed.). *Cruise ship tourism.* London, CABI Publishing, 105–114.

Moskvitch, K. 2011. *Internet of things blurs line between bits and atoms* [online]. Last accessed 12 May 2012 at: http://www.bbc.co.uk/news/business-13632206.

Mowforth, M. and Munt, I. 1998. *Tourism and sustainability: new tourism in the third world.* London, Routledge.

Müller, H. 1994. The thorny path to sustainable tourism development. *Journal of Sustainable Tourism*, 2 (3), 131–136.

Murphy, E. P. 1985. *Tourism: a community approach.* New York and London, Methuen.

Murphy, E. P. and Murphy, E. A. 2004. *Strategic management for tourism communities: bridging the gap.* Clevedon, Channel View Publications.

Murphy, P. E. and Price, G. G. 2005. Tourism and sustainable development. In: Theobald, F. W. (ed.). *Global tourism, 3rd ed.* Burlington, Elsevier Butterworth-Heinemann, 167–193.

Murphy, P. R. and Poist, R. F. 2003. Green perspectives and practices: a comparative logistics study. *Supply Chain Management: An International Journal*, 8 (2), 122–131.

Mycoo, M. 2006. Sustainable tourism using regulations, market mechanisms and green certification: a case study of Barbados. *Journal of Sustainable Tourism*, 14 (5), 489–511.

Nagel, M. H. 2000. Environmental supply-chain management versus green procurement in the scope of a business and leadership the scope of a business and leadership perspective. *IEEE Proceedings of the 2000 IEEE International Symposium*, 8–10 May 2000, 219–224.

Nair, V., Daud, M., Bardaie, M. Z. and Mohd, A. 2003. *An ICT approach towards ecotourism rating.* Paper presented at the WTO Asia-Pacific Seminar on the Development of a National Certification System for Sustainable Tourism, Malaysia, December 11–12 2003.

Nath, B., Reynolds, F. and Want, R. 2006. RFID technology and applications. *IEEE Pervasive Computing*, 5 (1), 22–24.

National Business Travel Association. 2009. *Business travel holds firm despite economic conditions.* [online]. Last accessed 20 May 2011 at: http://www.gbta.org/usa/pressreleases/Pages/rls052109.aspx.

National Geographic Intelligent Travel Blog. 2012. *About intelligent travel.* [online] Last accessed 4 July 2012 at: http://www.gstcouncil.org/about/learn-about-gstc.html.

Ndou, V. and Petti, C. 2007. DMS business models design and destination configurations: choice and implementation issues. *Information Technology & Tourism*, 9 (1), 3–14.

Nielsen, N. C. and Liburd, J. L. 2008. Communication in the age of Web 2.0. The case of the Salt River Bay National Park in St. Croix of the U.S. Virgin Islands. *Journal of Travel and Tourism Marketing*, 25 (3), 282–298.

Nodder, C., Mason, D., Ateljevic, J. and Milne, S. 2003. ICT adoption and use in New Zealand's small and medium tourism enterprises: a cross sectoral perspective. In: Frew, J. A., Hitz, M. and O'Connor, P. (eds.). *Information and communication technologies in tourism 2003.* New York, Springer, 355–363.

O'Connor, P. 2000. *Electronic information distribution in tourism and hospitality.* London, CABI.

O'Connor, P. and Frew, J. A. 2002. The future of hotel electronic distribution: expert and industry perspectives. *Cornell Hotel and Restaurant Administration Quarterly*, 43 (3), 33–45.

O'Connor, P. and Frew, J. A. 2004. An evaluation methodology for hotel electronic channels of distribution. *International Journal of Hospitality Management*, 23 (2), 179–199.

Odinma, A. C., Oborkhale, L. I. and Kah, M. M. O. 2007. The trends in broadband wireless network technologies. *The Pacific Journal of Science and Technology*, 8 (1), 118–125.

Oh, S., Lehto, X. Y. and Park, J. 2009. Travelers' intent to use mobile technologies as a function of effort and performance expectancy. *Journal of Hospitality Marketing & Management*, 18 (8), 765–781.

Oertel, B., Steinmüller, K. and Kuom, M. 2002. Mobile multimedia services for tourism. In: Wöber, K., Frew, J. A. and Hitz, M. (eds.). *Information and communication technologies in tourism 2002*. New York, Springer, 265–284.

OFCOM 2010. *Facts and figures*. [online]. Last accessed 2 March 2011 at: http://media.ofcom.org.uk.

Organisation of American States. 1997. *Sustaining tourism by managing its natural and heritage resources*. Washington, Organisation of American States.

Organisation for Economic Co-operation and Development. 2002. *Technology policy and the environment*. Paris, Organisation for Economic Co-operation and Development.

O'Reilly, T. 2005. *What is Web 2.0: design patterns and business models for the next generation of software* [online]. Last accessed 12 March 2012 at: http://oreilly.com/web2/archive/what-is-web-20.html.

O'Reilly, T. 2006. *O'Reilly's new compact definition of Web 2.0*. [online]. Last accessed 5 February 2007 at: http://fastwonderblog.com/2006/12/10/oreillys-new-compact-definition-of-web-20/.

O'Reilly, T. 2006. *O'Reilly radar*. [online]. Last accessed 3 March 2012 at: http://radar.oreilly.com/2006/12/web-20-compact-definition-tryi.html.

Oztaysi, B., Baysan, S. and Akpinar, F. 2009. Radio frequency identification (RFID) in hospitality. *Technovation*, 29 (9), 618–624.

Page, J. S. 2003. *Tourism management: managing for change*. Oxford: Butterworth-Heinemann.

Page, J. S. 2005. Tourism planning and management: why do we need tourism planning and management? In: Ryan, C., Page, J. S. and Aicken, M. (eds.). *Taking tourism to the limits: issues, concepts and managerial perspectives*. Oxford, Elsevier, 9–14.

Page, J. S. 2011. *Tourism management: an introduction, 4th ed*. Oxford, Elsevier.

Page, J. S. and Connell, J. 2006. *Tourism: a modern synthesis*. London, Thomson Learning.

Pagell, M. and Wu, Z. 2009. Building a more complete theory of sustainable supply chain management using case studies of 10 exemplars. *Journal of Supply Chain Management*, 45 (2), 37–56.

Palmer-Tous, T., Riera-Font, A. and Rosselló-Nadal, J. 2007. Taxing tourism: the case of rental cars in Mallorca. *Tourism Management*, 28 (1), 271–279.

Park, D. and Yoon, Y. 2011. Developing sustainable rural tourism evaluation indicators. *International Journal of Tourism Research*, 13 (5), 401–415.

Park, J. and Oh, I. 2012. A case study of social media marketing by travel agency: the salience of social media marketing in the tourism industry. *International Journal of Tourism Sciences*, 12 (1), 93–106.

Peeters, P., van Egmond, T. and Visser, N. 2004. European tourism, transport and environment. *TTRA European Chapter Conference 2004*, Rotterdam, Breda.

Petti, C. and Ndou, V. 2004. Virtual networks in the tourism industry. In: Frew, J. A. (ed.). *Information and communication technologies in tourism 2004*. New York, Springer, 446–457.

Pew Internet and American Life Project. 2008. *The future of the Internet III*. [online]. Last accessed 3 January 2009 at: http://www.pewinternet.org/PPF/r/270/report_display.asp.

Pezzey, J. 1992. *Sustainable development concepts: an economic analysis*. Washington, World Bank.

Pforr, C. 2001. Concepts of sustainable development, sustainable tourism, and ecotourism: definitions, principles, and linkages. *Scandinavian Journal of Hospitality and Tourism*, 1 (1), 68–70.

PhoCusWright. 2009. *Going green: the business impact of environmental awareness on travel*. New York, PhoCusWright. [online]. Last accessed 5 April 2010 at: http://travelgreen.org/files/PhocusWright.pdf.

PhoCusWright. 2012. *Mobile hits the mainstream: leisure and business traveller trends*. New York, PhoCusWright.

Pigram, J. J. 1990. Sustainable tourism-policy considerations. *The Journal of Tourism Studies*, 1 (2), 2–9.

Poon, A. 1993. *Tourism, technology and competitive strategies*. Oxon, CAB International.

Portio Research. 2012. *Mobile factbook – April 2012*. UK, Portio Research Limited.

Presenza, A., Sheehan, L. and Ritchie, J. R. B. 2005. *Towards a model of the roles and activities of destination management organizations*. [online]. Last accessed 13 February 2007 at: http://hotel.unlv.edu/res_journalPubsArticle.html.

Prosser, R. 1994. Societal change and growth in alternative tourism. In: Cater, E. and Lowman, G. (eds.). *Eco-tourism: a sustainable option?* West Sussex, Wiley, 19–37.

QSR. 2010. *What to do about waste. A look at how some restaurants are cutting down. Special report November 2010*. [online]. Last accessed 10 December 2011 at: http://www.qsrmagazine.com/reports/what-do-about-waste.

Raghuvanshi, T. K., Belwal, R. and Solomon, N. 2007. An approach to develop tourism potential in Ethiopia through geographic information system. *The Consortium Journal of Hospitality & Tourism*, 11 (1), 35–44.

Rai, A., Patnayakuni, R. and Seth, N. 2006. Firm performance impacts of digitally enable supply chain integration capabilities. *MIS Quarterly*, 30 (2), 225–246.

Ranganathan, C., Dhaliwal, S. J. and Thompson S. H. T. 2004. Assimilation and diffusion of web technologies in supply-chain management: an examination of key drivers and performance impacts. *International Journal of Electronic Commerce*, 9 (1), 127–161.

Rasinger, J., Fuchs, M. and Höpken, W. 2007. Information search with mobile tourist guides: a survey of usage intention. *Information Technology & Tourism* 9 (3), 177–194.

Rebollo, V. F. J. and Baidal, I. A. J. 2003. Measuring sustainability in a mass tourist destination: pressures, perceptions and policy responses in Torrevieja, Spain. *International Journal of Sustainability in Higher Education*, 11 (2 & 3), 181–203.

Rheingold, H. 1993. *The virtual community: homesteading on the electronic frontier reading*. Reading, MA, Addison-Wesley University Press.

Ricci, F. 2002. Travel recommender systems. *IEE Intelligent Systems*, November/December 2002, 55–57.

Ritchie, J. R. B. and Crouch, G. 2003. *The competitive destination: a sustainable tourism perspective*. Wallingford, CABI Publishing.

Ritchie, B. R. J. and Ritchie, J. R. B. 2002. A framework for an industry supported destination marketing information system. *Tourism Management*, 23 (5), 439–454.

Ruhanen, L. 2008. Progressing the sustainability debate: a knowledge management approach to sustainable tourism planning. *Current Issues in Tourism*, 11 (5), 429–455.

Rusko, T. R., Kylänen, M. and Saari, R. 2009. Supply chain in tourism destinations: the case of Levi Resort in Finnish Lapland. *International Journal of Tourism Research*, 11 (1), 71–87.

Russell. R. and Faulkner, B. 1999. Movers and shakers: chaos makers in tourism development. *Tourism Management*, 20 (4), 411–423.

Ryan, C. and Cave, J. 2005. Structuring destination image: a qualitative approach. *Journal of Travel Research*, 44 (2), 43–150.

Saarinen, J. 2006. Traditions of sustainability in tourism studies. *Annals of Tourism Research*, 33 (4), 1121–1140.

Sainaghi, R. 2006. From contents to processes: versus a dynamic destination management model (DDMM). *Tourism Management*, 27 (5), 1053–1063.

Sasidharana, V., Sirakaya, E. and Kerstetter, D. 2002. Developing countries and tourism ecolabels. *Tourism Management*, 23 (2), 161–174.

Sausen, R., Isaksen, I., Grewe, V., Hauglustaine, D., Lee, D. S., Myhre, G., Köhler, M. O., Pitari, G., Schumann, U., Stordal, F. and Zerefos, C. 2005. Aviation radiative forcing in 2000: an update of IPCC (1999). *Meteorologische Zeitschrift*, 114, 555–561.

Saveriades, A. 2000. Establishing the social tourism carrying capacity for the tourist resorts of the east coast of the Republic of Cyprus. *Tourism Management*, 21 (2), 147–156.

Savitsky, B., Allen, J. and Backman, K. F. 2000. The role of geographic information systems (GIS) in tourism planning and rural economic development. *Tourism Analysis*, 4 (3/4), 187–199.

Schein, E. 1993. *Career anchors: discovering your real values*. San Diego, CA: Pfeiffer & Company.

Schianetz, K., Kavanagh, L. and Lockington, D. 2007. Concepts and tools for comprehensive sustainability assessments for tourism destinations: a comparative review. *Journal of Sustainable Tourism*, 15 (4), 369–389.

Schmallegger, D. and Carson, D. 2007. *Reaching the independent traveller: product distribution issues for Aboriginal tourism enterprises in remote Australia*. Paper presented at the 3rd International Conference on Tourism, Athens, Greece, July 2007.

Scott, M. 2011. *The role of information and communication technology (ICT) in supporting sustainable tourism: an in-trip tourist perspective*. PhD thesis, 2nd year interim report, Queen Margaret University.

Senge, P. 2010. The sustainable supply chain. An interview with Peter Senge by Steven Prokesch. *Harvard Business Review*, October 2010.

Sharda, N., Georgievski, M., Ahmed, I., Armstrong, L., Brogan, M., Woodward, A., Gurpreet, K. and Clark, M. 2006. *Leading-edge developments in tourism ICT and related underlying technologies*. Queensland, Sustainable Tourism Cooperative Research Centre.

Sharda, N. and Ponnada, M. 2008. Tourism blog visualizer for better tour planning. *Journal of Vacation Marketing*, 14 (2), 157–167.

Sharma P., Wilson, D. and Kelly, S. 2009. *Tourist information voice system (TIVS): a location aware and feature triggered commentary system for tour groups*. Queensland, Sustainable Tourism Cooperative Research Centre.

Sharpley, R. and Sharpley, J. 1997. *Rural tourism: an introduction*. London, Routledge.

Sharpley, R. 2000. Tourism and sustainable development: exploring the theoretical divide. *Journal of Sustainable Tourism*, 8 (1), 1–19.

Shaw, G. and Williams, M. A. 2004. *Tourism and tourism spaces*. London, Sage.

Sheehan, L. and Ritchie, B. R. J. 2005. Destination stakeholders: exploring identity and salience. *Annals of Tourism Research*, 32 (3), 711–734.

Sheldon, P. 1997. *Tourism information technology*. New York, CAB International.

Sheldon, P., Knox, J. M. and Lowry, K. 2005. Sustainability in a mature mass tourism destination: the case of Hawaii. *Tourism Review International*, 9 (1), 47–59.

Shephard, K. 2007. Higher education for sustainability: seeking affective learning outcomes. *Higher Education for Sustainability*, 9 (1), 87–98.

Shoval, N. and Isaacson, M. 2006. Tracking tourist in the digital age. *Annals of Tourism Research*, 34 (1), 141–159.

Sigala, M. 2008. WEB 2.0, social marketing strategies and distribution channels for city destinations: enhancing the participatory role of travellers and exploiting their collective intelligence. In: Gascó-Hernández. M. and Torres-Coronas. T. (eds.). *Information communication technologies and city marketing: digital opportunities for cities around the world*. Romania, IDEA Publishing, 220–244.

Sigala, M. 2008. A supply chain management approach for investigating the role of tour operators on sustainable tourism: the case of TUI. *Journal of Cleaner Production*, 16 (15), 1589–1599.

Sigala, M. 2010. Measuring customer value in online collaborative trip planning processes. *Marketing Intelligence and Planning*, 28 (4), 418–443.

Sigala, M., Christou, E. and Gretzel, U. 2012. *Social media in travel, tourism and hospitality*. Surrey, Ashgate.

Simchi-Levi, D., Kaminsky, P. and Simchi-Levi, E. 2000. *Designing and managing the supply chain*. Boston, MA, Irwin McGraw-Hill.

Simón, G. J. F., Narangajavana, Y. and Marqués, P. D. 2004. Carrying capacity in the tourism industry: a case study of Hengistbury Head. *Tourism Management*, 25 (2), 275–283.

Simpson, P. and Wall, G. 1999. Environmental impact assessment for tourism. In: Pearce, G. D. and Butler, W. R. (eds.). *Contemporary issues in tourism development*. London and New York, Routledge, 232–238.

Sirakaya, E. 1997. Attitudinal compliance with ecotourism guidelines, *Annals of Tourism Research*, 24 (4), 919–950.

Solis, B. and JESS3. 2008. *The conversation prism: the art of listening, learning and sharing*. [online]. Last accessed 4 February 2012 at: http://www.theconversationprism.com/.

Staab, S., Werthner, H., Ricci, F., Zipf, A., Gretzel, U., Fesenmaier, D., Paris, C. and Knoblock, C. 2002. Intelligent systems for tourism. *IEE Intelligent Systems*, 17 (6), 53–64.

Staab, S. and Werthner, H. 2002. Intelligent systems for tourism. *IEE Intelligent Systems*, 53–65.

Stamboulis, Y. and Skayannis, P. 2003. Innovation strategies and technology for experience-based tourism. *Tourism Management*, 24 (1), 35–43.

Stankey G. H., Cole, D. N., Lucas, C. R., Petersen, E. M. and Frissell, S. S. 1985. *The limits of acceptable change (LAC) system for wilderness planning*. Ogden, USDA.

Steuer, J. 1992. Defining virtual reality: dimensions determining telepresence. *Journal of Communication*, 42 (4), 73–93.

Stevels, A. 2002. Green supply chain management much more than questionnaires and ISO 14.001. *2002 IEEE International Symposium on Electronics and the Environment*, 96–100.

Stockholm Environment Institute. 2008. *Environmental accounting for people and places*. [online]. Last accessed 10 January 2011 at: http://www.resource-accounting.org.uk/.

Sustainable Tourism Cooperative Research Centre. 2004. *Benchmarking location based systems*. Queensland, Sustainable Tourism Cooperative Research Centre.

Sustainable Tourism Cooperative Research Centre. 2009. *Earthcheck*. [online]. Last accessed 10 January 2009 at: http://www.ec3global.com.au/productsprograms/earthcheck/Default.aspx.

Swarbrooke, J. 1999. *Sustainable tourism management*. Oxon, CAB International.

Tan, G., Shaw, J. M. and Fulkerson, B. 2000. Web-based supply chain management. *Information Systems Frontiers*, 2 (1), 41–55.

Tapper, R. and Font, X. 2004. Tourism supply chains. *Report of a Desk Research Project for The Travel Foundation*, Final report on January 31 2004.

Tapscott, D. and William, A. 2006. *Wikinomics: how mass collaboration changes everything*. New York, Penguin.

Taylor, W. 2004. Community informatics in perspective. In: Marshall, S., Taylor, W. and Yu, X. (eds.). *Using community informatics to transform regions*. Philadelphia, Idea Group Inc., 1–17.

Teo, P. 2002. Striking a balance for sustainable tourism: implications of the discourse on globalisation. *Journal of Sustainable Tourism*, 10 (6), 459–474.

The BTI Consulting Group. 2001. *Market opportunities in the environmental management information systems market*. Boston, The BTI Consulting Group.

The Travel Foundation. 2012. [online]. Last accessed 3 July 2012 at: http://www.thetravelfoundation.org.uk/about_us/about_the_travel_foundation.

Theobald, W. F. 2005. *Global tourism, 3rd ed.* Burlington, Elsevier Butterworth-Heinemann.

Tilden, F. 1957. *Interpreting our heritage*. Chapel Hill, NC, University of North Carolina Press.

Tomlin D. C. 1991. Cartographic modelling. In: Maguire, J. D., Goodchild, F. M. and Rhind, W. D. (eds.). *Geographical information systems: principles and applications*. London, Longman, 361–374.

Tourism Sustainability Group. 2007. *Action for more sustainable European tourism: report of the Tourism Sustainability Group*. Geneva: European Commission.

Trousdale, J. W. 1999. Governance in context: Boracay Island, Philippines. *Annals of Tourism Research*, 26 (4), 840–867.

Truong, T. and Foster, D. 2006. Using HOLSAT to evaluate tourist satisfaction at destinations: The case of Australian holidaymakers in Vietnam. *Tourism Management*, 27 (5), 842–855.

Tsaur, S., Lin, Y. and Linc, J. 2006. Evaluating ecotourism sustainability from the integrated perspective of resource, community and tourism. *Tourism Management*, 27 (4), 640–653.

TUI. 2010. *Thomson announces sustainable tourism commitments at The Economist Sustainable Business Summit*. [online] Last accessed 5 March 2012 at: http://www.prnewswire.com/news-releases/thomson-announces-sustainable-tourism-commitments-at-the-economist-sustainable-business-summit-119235549.html.

Tumas, G. and Ricci, F. 2009. Personalized mobile city transport advisory system. In: Höpken, W. Gretzel, U. and Law, R., (eds.). *Information and communication technolgies in tourism 2009*. New York, Springer, 173–183.

Turner, J. A. 2006. *Introduction to neogeography (O'Reilly Short Cuts Series)*. [online]. Last accessed 5 January 2007 at: http://oreilly.com/catalog/9780596529956/.

Tyrrell, T. J. and Johnston, R. J. 2006. The economic impacts of tourism: a special issue. *Journal of Travel Research*, 45 (1), 3–7.

Umeda, S. and Zhang, F. 2006. Supply chain simulation: generic models and application examples. *Production Planning and Control*, 17 (2), 155–166.

United Nations. 2000. *United Nations millennium declaration 2000*. [online]. Last accessed 10 March 2012 at: http://www.un.org/millennium/.

United Nations. 2010. *The millennium development goals report*. [online]. Last accessed March 1 2012 at: http://www.un.org/millenniumgoals/reports.shtml.

United Nations Conference on Environment and Development. 1992. *The earth summit*. Rio de Janeiro, Brazil, June 13–14. Canada, United Nations Conference on Environment and Development.

United Nations Conference on Trade and Development. 2004. *Partnership for development: information and knowledge for development*. Paris, United Nations Conference on Trade and Development.

United Nations Environment Programme. 2000. *Building an environmental management information system (EMIS)*. Geneva, United Nations Environment Programme.

United Nations Environment Programme. 2003. *Tourism and local agenda 21: the role of local authorities in sustainable tourism*. Paris, United Nations Environment Programme.

United Nations World Tourism Organisation. 1996. *Agenda 21 for the travel and tourism industry: towards environmentally sustainable development*. Madrid, United Nations World Tourism Organisation.

United Nations World Tourism Organisation. 2001. *Global code of ethics for tourism*. Madrid, United Nations World Tourism Organisation.

United Nations World Tourism Organisation. 2004a. *Indicators of sustainable development for tourism destinations: a guidebook*. Madrid, United Nations World Tourism Organisation.

United Nations World Tourism Organisation. 2004b. *World Tourism Organisation survey of destination management organisations*. Madrid, United Nations World Tourism Organisation.

United Nations World Tourism Organisation. 2005. *Making tourism more sustainable – a guide for policy makers*. Madrid, United Nations World Tourism Organisation.

United Nations Environment Programme/United Nations World Tourism Organisation. 2005. *Making tourism more sustainable: a guide for policy makers*. Madrid, World Tourism Organisation.

United Nations World Tourism Organisation. 2012. *International tourism to reach one billion in 2012*. [online]. Last accessed 16 January 2012 at: http://media.unwto.org/en/press-release/2012-01-16/international-tourism-reach-one-billion-2012.

Usoro, A., Sharratt, W. M., Tsui, E. and Shekhar, S. 2007. Trust as an antecedent to knowledge sharing in virtual communities of practice. *Knowledge Management Research & Practice*, 5 (3), 199–212.

van der Duim, R. and van Marwijk, R. 2006. The implementation of an environmental management system for Dutch tour operators: an actor-network perspective. *Journal of Sustainable Tourism*, 14 (5), 449–472.

Veronneau, S. and Roy, J. 2009. RFID benefits, costs, and possibilities: the economical analysis of RFID deployment in a cruise corporation global service supply chain. *International Journal of Production Economics*, 122 (2), 692–702.

Virgin Atlantic. 2011. *Sustainability report Winter 2011/2012*. London, Virgin Atlantic. [online]. Last accessed 4 May 2012 at: www.virgin-atlantic.com/corporate/ . . . /newsustainabilityreport.pdf.

VisitFlorida. 2006. *2006 Florida visitor study*. [online]. Last accessed 4 July 2011 at: ftp://ftp.whoi.edu/pub/users/phoagland/Florida%20Tourism%20Studies/2006_Visitors_study.pdf.

Vogelsong, H. and Graefe, A. 2001. Economic impact analysis: a look at useful methods. *P&R*, 28–36.

Vukonic, B. 1997. Selective growth and targeted destinations. In: Wahab, S. and Pigram, J. J (eds.). *Tourism development and growth: the challenges to sustainability*. New York and London, Routledge, 95–108.

Wall, G. and Mathieson, A. 2006. *Tourism: change, impacts and opportunities*. Essex, Pearson Education Limited.

Wang, B. and Manning, R. 1999. Computer simulation modeling for recreating management: a study on carriage road use in Acadia National Park, Maine, USA. *Environmental Management*, 23 (2), 193–203.

Wang, Y., Yu, Q. and Fesenmaier, D. 2002. Defining the virtual tourist community: implications for tourism marketing. *Tourism Management*, 23 (4), 407–417.

Weaver, D. 2006. *Sustainable tourism*. Amsterdam, Elsevier.

Wei, J. and Ozok, A. 2005. Development of a web-based mobile airline ticketing model with usability features. *Industrial Management and Data System*, 105 (9), 1261–1277.

Werthner, H. and Klein, S. 1999. *Information technology and tourism – a challenging relationship*. New York, Springer.

Werthner, H. and Ricci, F. 2003. *Electronic commerce and tourism*. [online]. Last accessed 21 December 2006 at: http://dietorecs.itc.it/Papers/werthnercacmvers2.pdf.

Wheeller, B. 1994. Egotourism, sustainable tourism and the environment – a symbiotic, symbolic or shambolic relationship. In: Seaton, A. V., Jenkins, C. L., Wood, R. C., Dieke, P. U. C., Bennett, M. M., MacLellan, L. R. and Smith, R. (eds.). *Tourism: the state of the art*. West Sussex, John Wiley & Sons Ltd., 647–654.

Williamson, J. T. 2010. Predicting building performance: the ethics of computer simulation. *Building Research & Information*, 38 (4), 401–410.

Wilson, S., Fesenmaier, D., Fesenmaier, J. and Van Es, J. 2001. Factors for success in rural tourism development. *Journal of Travel Research*, 40 (2), 132–138.

Wöber, W. K. 2003. Information supply in tourism management by marketing decision support systems. *Tourism Management*, 24 (3), 241–255.

World Bank. 2006. *Communication and sustainable tourism*. Global e-conference and summer speaker series on the role of development communication in sustainable tourism, May 29 2006. Washington. World Bank Development Communication Division.

World Commission on Environment and Development. 1987. *Our common future*. Oxford, Oxford University Press.

World Travel and Tourism Council. 2003. *Corporate social leadership in travel and tourism*. London, World Travel and Tourism Council.

Wright, P. 1998. Tools for sustainability analysis in planning and managing tourism recreations in the destination. In: Hall, M. C. and Lew, A. A. (eds.). *Sustainable tourism: a geographical perspective*. Essex, Addison Wesley Longman Limited, 75–91.

Xiang, Z. and Gretzel, U. 2009. Role of social media in online travel information search. *Tourism Management*, 31 (2), 179–188.

Xiao, H. 2006. Towards a research agenda for knowledge management in tourism. *Tourism and Hospitality Planning & Development*, 3 (2), 143–157.

Yang, K. and Jolly, L. D. 2008. Age cohort analysis in adoption of mobile data services: gen Xers versus baby boomers. *Journal of Consumer Marketing*, 25 (5), 272–280.

Yeoman, I. 2005. *Tomorrow's world – consumer and tourist*. VisitScotland, 1 (2), 1–31.

Yon, M. 2005. *Partnership agreement between Florida Department of Environmental Protection and ProTeam Incorporated.* Tallahassee, FL, Florida Department of Environmental Protection, Division of Waste Management. [online]. Last accessed 22 March 2011 at: http://www.dep.state.fl.us/greenlodging/partners/files/pro_team.pdf.

Yoon, S. W. and Lee, K. D. 2003. The development of the evaluation model of climate changes and air pollution for sustainability of cities in Korea. *Landscape and Urban Planning*, 63 (3), 145–160.

Youell, R. 1998. *Tourism: an introduction*. Harlow: Longman.

Yuan, Y., Gretzel, U. and Fesenmaier, D. 2006. The role of information technology use in American convention and visitors bureaus. *Tourism Management*, 27 (2), 326–341.

Zehrer, A. and Hobbhahn, T. 2007. A speech dialog system (SDS) as an additional communication channel in tourism – a vision for the destination of Innsbruck. In: Sigala, M., Mich, L. and Murphy, J. (eds.). *Information and communication technologies in tourism 2007*. New York, Springer, 1–10.

Zhang, X., Song, H. and Huang, Q. G. 2009. Tourism supply chain management: a new research agenda. *Tourism Management*, 30 (3), 345–358.

Zhu, K., Kraemer, L. K., Xu, S. and Dedrick, J. 2004. Information technology payoff in e-business environments: an international perspective on value creation of e-business in the financial services industry. *Journal of Management Information Systems*, 21 (1), 17–54.

Zhu, Q. and Cote, P. R. 2004. Integrating green supply chain management into an embryonic eco-industrial development: a case study of the Guitang Group. *Journal of Cleaner Production*, 12 (8–10), 1025–1035.

Zins, A. H., Bauernfeind, U., Del Missier, F., Venturini, A. and Rumetshofer, H. 2004. An experimental usability test for different destination recommender systems. In: Frew, J. A. (ed.), *Information and communication technologies in tourism 2004*. New York, Springer, 249–258.

Zipf, A. and Malaka, R. 2001. Developing location based services for tourism: the service providers' view. In: Sheldon, P., Wöber, K. and Fesenmaier, D. (eds.). *Information and communication technologies in tourism 2001*. New York, Springer, 83–92.

Index